W9-BZE-922

A Theory of Rights

A THEORY OF RIGHTS
*Persons Under Laws, Institutions,
and Morals*

Carl Wellman

*Professor of Philosophy
Washington University
St. Louis*

89-937

ROWMAN & ALLANHELD
PUBLISHERS

ROWMAN & ALLANHELD

Published in the United States of America in 1985
by Rowman & Allanheld, Publishers
(a division of Littlefield, Adams & Company)
81 Adams Drive, Totowa, New Jersey 07512

Library of Congress Cataloging in Publication Data
Wellman, Carl.
  A theory of rights.
  Bibliography: p.
  Includes index.
  1. Law—Philosophy. 2. Civil rights. 3. Natural
law. I. Title.
K230.W44T45 1985   340'.1   84-22299
ISBN 0-8476-7397-9

85 86 87 / 10 9 8 7 6 5 4 3 2 1

Printed in the United States of America

TABLE OF CONTENTS

ACKNOWLEDGMENTS

I have read widely and reread often in the philosophical and legal literature dealing with the nature of rights and the conceptual analysis of the language in which we talk about legal and moral rights. For almost fifteen years now, I have discussed problems in the theory of rights with innumerable colleagues. It is now impossible, alas, to identify those from whom I have learned the most, for my memory is unreliable and the origins of my ways of thinking obscure to me. What I can do, and here do gladly, is to recognize publicly my many intellectual debts and repay with thanks my now unknown philosophical benefactors.

Bernard Gert, Lars Lindahl, Rex Martin and Joseph Raz kindly provided sympathetic but incisive comments on portions of a preliminary draft of this book. James Nickel read that entire draft with care and wrote out detailed criticisms and general advice for revision. Here, at least, my memory is clear and my gratitude lively.

Thomas Hill, Jr., Barbara Levenbook, Neil MacCormick, and Lance Stell scrutinized one or more chapters of the revised manuscript and each has saved me from unclear expression or erroneous thesis. The written comments of L. Wayne Sumner on the entire manuscript have encouraged me to complete my ambitious project at the same time that they have forced me to rethink my arguments and revise my conclusions.

Stanley Paulson is in a class by himself. He has read and reread every version from rough draft to polished manuscript with meticulous attention to philosophical argument, legal example, and felicitous language. His voluminous written criticisms, often expanded in conversation, have been invaluable to me at every stage of my thinking and in every aspect of my writing.

The National Humanities Center has also made a very special contribution to this book. By awarding me a fellowship for the academic year of 1982-83, it released me from the distractions of my usual teaching and administrative duties. The facilities of the Center, the moral support of the staff, and the conversations with the other fellows made my year at the Center as philosophically productive as it was personally pleasant.

Chapter 1

INTRODUCTION

The rhetoric of rights, long familiar in the courtroom, has come to dominate the arenas of practical politics and moral reform. The Reagan administration is often and loudly charged with violating the welfare rights of the American citizen because of its economic policies, while debate continues as to whether United States military and economic aid to foreign countries ought to be contingent upon their respect for the human rights of their own citizens. In the last dozen years, the civil rights movement has given birth to the welfare rights movement, the women's rights movement and the students' rights movement. A rising tide of medical malpractice suits and increasing governmental regulation of medical experimentation testify to a growing concern with the rights of patients and human subjects. The personal relationships within the institution of the family are changing rapidly, and probably radically, in the name of women's and children's rights. Our traditional practices of slaughtering cattle and swine and our modern techniques of raising poultry are currently under attack as violations of the moral rights of animals.

As an enemy of injustice, I rejoice in this increasing appeal to and recognition of legal and moral rights, but as a philosopher, I find myself perplexed and deeply disturbed by the contemporary rhetoric of rights. Listening to debates of legal, political and moral issues conducted in terms of allegations about rights, I see some fundamental philosophical problems. (1) What is a right? It is far from clear precisely what it means to assert or deny that someone has a right, such as the right to life or to social security. Explaining what it is to have such a right seems to include, but to go beyond, defining the meaning of expressions like "the right to life," or "the human right to social security." In addition, one wants to explain the main features of rights—that a right is possessed by someone, that it holds against others, that it can usually be exercised, waived, forfeited or renounced. (2) How can one know whether some alleged right is genuine? It is easy enough, perhaps too easy, to assert the existence of a legal right to preferential hiring or a human right to an adequate standard of living, but any such assertion is open to doubt or outright denial. That people disagree about alleged rights is only to be expected; what is disturbing is that there does not seem to be any rational method for resolving such disputes. What is needed is the identification of the grounds of rights, of the reasons that would justify the assertion or denial of any specified right. (3) Even if the existence of some specified right can be established, what follows for human conduct? The human right to life might, if genuine, have a variety of practical implications. It might imply that capital punishment is always morally wrong, or that it is not morally wrong for a person to kill in self-defence, or that a murderer has forfeited his or her right not to be executed, or that the state owes each of its citizens the means of sustaining his or her life, or that a terminally ill patient can make a doctor's act of euthanasia morally permissible by waiving his or her right to life. Only if one can distinguish between practical implications that do and those that do not follow from any right, can the appeal to rights illuminate moral choice and social reform. (4) What kinds of beings can have a right? Environmentalists sometimes advocate a ban on hunting whales on the grounds that each natural species has a right to continuing existence or that future generations have a right to inherit a world as rich in natural resources as our world. Some moral reformers rest their case for vegetarianism on the rights to life, liberty and freedom from suffering of the animals we raise and kill for food. Personal and judicial decisions concerning abortion or the termination of intensive care depend for their rational justification upon whether or not a human fetus or an irreversibly comotose person are capable of having any legal or human right to life. (5) What, if anything, is so important about a right? It might appear that the permissibility of abortion or euthanasia hinges in some simple and conclusive manner upon the possession of the right to life by a fetus or a terminally ill patient, but this is surely not so. The human fetus might have a human right to life, but it might be overriden by the pregnant woman's right to privacy; the irreversibly comotose patient might lack any human right to life, but it might still be morally wrong to terminate intensive care on other grounds. In part, the problem is a theoretical one. Can the expression "a right" be defined in more basic terms, such as that of a duty or a value, or does the concept of a right enrich the language of the law or of ethics in some distinctive and irreducible way? In part, the problem concerns human practice and the quality of human life. How, if at all, does the possession of a right constitute a practical advantage for the right-holder and enrich his or her life?

I am not the first philosopher to have thought of these questions. Indeed, during the past decade there has been a proliferation of journal articles, and more recently books, dealing with legal, human and special moral rights. Although much of this literature simply appeals to rights in arguing for some legal or ethical conclusion, ignoring the philosophical problems I have listed or simply taking for granted some solution to them, philosophers and jurists have given increasing attention to the conceptual analysis and normative theory required to enable us to understand and to reason about assertions of rights. Many of the recent books and articles concerning the theory of rights have been of very high quality, and together they have considerably increased our philosophical understanding of rights. Nevertheless, the existing philosophical literature fails to provide an adequate philosophical theory of rights in at least two respects. First, most of it focuses upon a single species of right. Jurists typically develop their theories of legal rights with little or no attention to moral rights, and moral philosophers debate the nature of human rights in ignorance of the alternative theories so well defined and argued in traditional or contemporary jurisprudence. Even when two species of rights are compared or contrasted, most often legal with moral rights, other species of rights have been ignored. Seldom have jurists explored the parallels, or divergences, between legal rights and other sorts of institutional rights, such as the rights conferred upon a student by the rules and regulations of a private university or the rights defined by the positive morality of a society. Philosophers defending the existence and importance of noninstitutional ethical rights have discussed human rights with too little attention to those human rights constituting a species of legal rights by virtue of their institutionalization in the European Convention. The time is ripe, I believe, for philosophers to turn to the articulation of a general theory of rights, a theory broad enough to deal with the many and various species of rights in a way that will reveal both similarities and differences. A second inadequacy in the existing literature is the way in which most articles, and even most books, address only one, or at best two, of the problems I have listed above. For example, debates about the rights of children typically discuss the grounds of children's rights or the lack of them without asking whether they, especially infants, are the kinds of beings of whom it makes sense to ascribe rights. Although philosophical discussions of animal rights do sometimes address the question of whether nonhuman animals are capable of possessing rights in any meaningful sense, they too often do so without any careful consideration of the nature of rights or the meaning of the expression "a right." Yet, whether it makes sense to ascribe rights to animals surely depends on just what it means to assert or deny the existence of a right. No doubt exposition is more precise and treatment more thorough when a philosopher focuses his or her attention on one problem at a time; the attempt to discuss everything at once is inevitably superficial and confusing. At the same time, philosophical theory provides no perspective on rights as long as the treatment of each problem is isolated from the solution of other philosophical problems concerning rights. Eventually, what is needed is a systematic theory of rights, one that will deal with each of the central problems in relation to and in the light of the others.

The purpose of this book, therefore, is to provide a general and systematic theory of rights. A general theory must reveal what it is that the various species of rights share that makes them rights, without denying or obscuring the differences between very different species of rights. The theory should be adequate to deal with the full range of rights: human rights as well as legal rights, the rights of positive morality as well as noninstitutional moral rights. It must provide solutions to a set of important philosophical problems concerning rights. And the several solutions cannot be advanced in isolation from one another; at the very least, they must not be inconsistent. Ideally, they should cohere in such a way that accepting one solution provides some support for the others.

A complete theory of rights would, I suppose, explain every feature of rights and of our language of rights in full detail. My ambition is much more limited. Although my goal is a general and systematic theory of rights, I shall attempt only a partial theory in the present work. Specifically, I shall focus upon the philosophical analysis of the language of rights and the explanation of the nature of rights. The problems I shall address are primarily conceptual problems, and my solutions will provide a new and coherent way of thinking about rights, rights of every sort. Although this book will omit any consideration of many important issues, especially the specification of the grounds of rights, it will enable philosophers and jurists to think more clearly about such issues in the future. To attempt more at this stage would be to accomplish less.

Overall Strategy

My goal, then, is to formulate, explain and defend a general and systematic theory of rights. How can I hope to achieve this ambitious, perhaps overly ambitious, goal? My strategy is simple enough to explain, although it will prove difficult indeed to execute. I shall begin with Hohfeld's fundamental legal conceptions, especially his conceptions of a legal claim, a legal liberty, a legal power and a legal immunity. Although I agree with him that these conceptions are essential to any adequate understanding of legal rights, I must go on to provide philosophical analyses of these concepts he refused to define. Second, I shall construct a model of a legal right out of Hohfeldian legal elements. Since legislation and judicial reasoning are not uniformly and unambiguously written in terms of Hohfeld's legal conceptions, the expression "a right" as used in or referring to the law typically cannot be defined in Hohfeldian terms. Still, a model of a legal right can be defined in terms of Hohfeld's fundamental legal conceptions, and such a model can illuminate many features of the language of legal rights and of the ways in which legal rights function in any modern legal system. Third, I hope to identify and define nonlegal analogues of Hohfeld's legal conceptions. For example, the student's academic liberty under the rules and regulations of Washington University to dress as he or she pleases in class within the bounds of decency is analogous to my legal liberty of dressing as I like in public within the bounds of decency. Again the ethical claim of the promisee against the promiser to do as promised is very like the creditor's legal claim against the debtor to be repaid the amount borrowed, probably with interest. Fourth, I intend to construct models of the various species of institutional and ethical rights out of the institutional and ethical elements defined in this way. In effect, I will be using my model of a legal right as a point of departure for my models of all the other species of rights. Finally, I expect to use these models in my solution of the most important, and recalcitrant, philosophical problems concerning rights. Their application to questions about the meaning of the expression "a right" and about the nature of the various species of rights is fairly obvious and direct. But indirectly, they should provide helpful clues to the solution of other problems. For example, if a right is construed as a complex of claims, liberties, powers and immunities, the problem of what kinds of beings can meaningfully be said to possess rights boils down to the question of what kinds of beings are capable of possessing elements such as claims, liberties, powers and immunities. Again, my Hohfeldian models of a right suggest that any complete justification of the assertion that some specified right exists must have a complexity comparable to the complex structure of the right justified and that the grounds of rights can only be the sorts of reasons that would establish the existence of claims, liberties, powers and immunities. Whether my strategy is a good one, or even a viable one, cannot be determined in advance. The only real test is whether it succeeds or fails to lead to an adequate, or at least interesting and illuminating, theory of rights. Still, it may be useful to address here two questions that may occur to the thoughtful reader.

If one's goal is to construct a *general* theory of rights, one that applies equally to various species of nonlegal rights, why should one begin with Hohfeld's *specifically legal* conceptions? As a moral philosopher without formal training in the law, I have only gradually and rather reluctantly come to recognize several reasons for approaching the theory of ethical rights via a consideration of legal rights. (1) Philosophical theories tend to become intolerably abstract and even arbitrary when constructed and defended without a continuing reference to and testing against examples of the phenomena to be explained. It is far easier to identify paradigm cases or clear instances of rights in the law than in other spheres of life. There can be no doubt that under normal circumstances the creditor has a legal right to repayment, the owner has the legal right to consume food purchased from the grocer, and that a depositor has a legal right to close out his account with his banker. But there is considerable doubt and continuing debate about which of the human rights affirmed in the United Nations *Universal Declaration* are genuine, and alleged moral rights of other sorts are almost equally open to challenge. (2) The content of legal rights is typically defined with much more precision than the content of alleged nonlegal rights. Even granting the existence of such traditional human rights as the rights to life, liberty and property, what is the content of these rights? Moral philosophers and political theorists interpret these rights very differently, and there seems to be no way to decide which philosopher's or political theorist's conception is the correct one. To be sure, lawyers also disagree about the content of this or that legal right; such is the stuff of lawsuits. But the legal processes of adjudication, and sometimes legislation, gradually define the content of any legal right in ever greater detail and with increasing precision. Only when paradigm instances of rights are characterized in determinate language can they serve to distinguish between accurate and misleading general conceptions of rights. Nothing like this exists in the case of ethical rights, or even with the conventional rights of positive morality. (3) The language of rights belongs to our practical discourse, and much of the importance of rights lies in their relevance to human conduct. The practical relevance of legal rights is made evident in the courts, where they are applied to particular cases arising from the actual, alleged or contemplated actions of a defendant. The practical relevance of other species of rights is not exhibited in the same way, certainly not in any analogous way, that might show as clearly just how rights bear on human conduct. (4) Just as moral rights have been the subject of considerable philosophical writing, so there is a large body of juristic writing about legal rights. At the very least, the moral philosopher cannot ignore this parallel literature. But the literature of jurisprudence promises a more fruitful starting place than its counterpart in moral philosophy, because it contains a number of alternative theories of legal rights articulated with a precision and in a detail unmatched by books and articles in ethics. For all these reasons, it seems best to begin a general theory of rights with a close examination of specifically legal rights.

A second general question arises. Even granted the wisdom of taking legal rights as one's paradigms of rights in general, why should one construct one's model of a legal right in terms of Hohfeld's fundamental conceptions? After all, there are other giants of analytic jurisprudence, most notably Austin, Bentham, Kelsen and Hart. I am not, of course, proposing to ignore the work of these and other philosophers of law. In fact, my considered opinion is that H. L. A. Hart has come closer than any other philosopher or jurist to formulating an adequate general theory of rights. Why, then, do I suggest that one should begin with Hohfeld's conceptual scheme? The short answer is that Hohfeld's conceptual analysis is more directly and obviously relevant to legal rights than are those of the others. The focus of Austin's attention was upon the concept of a law, and Kelsen focused upon the concept of a legal norm. Bentham's analyses of the various sorts of rights are buried in his more general work and incidental to his treatment of the completeness of a law and the unity of a legal system. Hart's primary concern has been the analysis of a legal rule and the concept of law itself. But what Hohfeld did, especially in the first of his two famous articles, was to classify the fundamental positions of some party, given the facts, under the law. Since to possess a legal right is surely to have a special legal position, Hohfeld's conceptual classification bears immediately upon any theory of rights. The long answer is that an examination of Hohfeld's *Fundamental Legal Conceptions* will yield invaluable insights into the nature of legal rights and the language in which we speak of them. This longer answer is the substance of the rest of this book.

Hohfeld's Contributions

I propose to begin with Hohfeld's fundamental legal conceptions, not because I imagine that his conceptual analysis constitutes an adequate theory of rights, but because no adequate theory can afford to ignore his perceptive and systematic interpretation of the language of rights. His conceptions provide excellent stepping-stones. Without them, we can find no firm footing in the conceptual swampland of the rhetoric of rights; with them, we can stride ahead to reach theoretical heights beyond his vision. In particular, his conceptions encapsulate five important contributions to the theory of rights.

(1) Hohfeld's fundamental legal conceptions remove several persistent ambiguities in the language of rights. Through a detailed and meticulous examination of legal language, both as found in court decisions and

as revealed in the literature of jurisprudence, Hohfeld shows that "the word 'right' is used generically and indiscriminately to denote any sort of legal advantage, whether claim, privilege, power, or immunity" (Hohfeld, 1919, 71). In order to avoid such conceptual confusion, he distinguishes sharply between these four fundamental legal conceptions.

> X has a legal *claim* against Y with respect to some action if and only if Y has a legal duty to X to perform that action.

For example, a creditor has a legal claim against the debtor to repayment if and only if the debtor has a legal duty to the creditor to repay the debt, and to say that the owner of a piece of property has a legal claim against the neighbor that the neighbor not enter on his land is to say that the neighbor has a legal duty to the owner not to trespass on his private property. Notice that negative legal claims require that the duty-bearer forbear or refrain from some specific sort of conduct.

> X has a legal *privilege* in face of Y to perform some action if and only if X has no legal duty to Y to refrain from doing that action.

Thus, the owner of a piece of property has a legal privilege in face of his neighbor of entering his own land, no matter how insistently his neighbor demands that he stay away, simply because he has no legal duty to his neighbor to abide by his neighbor's wishes in this matter. The neighbor, on the other hand, has a legal privilege to enter on his land only if the owner has given him leave and license to do so. Again, if Able attacks Baker so as to endanger his life or limb, then Baker has the privilege of striking Able in self-defence, although under normal circumstances Baker has no legal privilege of striking Able at all.

> X has a legal *power* over Y with respect to some legal relation if and only if X is able to perform some action that changes this legal relation of Y in some way.

For example, the owner of a book has the legal power of giving the book to a friend so that the friend's legal relation of nonownership changes to that of ownership. Other paradigm cases of legal powers are the power of any sane adult to make a legally valid will and the legal power of a creditor to extinguish the debtor's legal duty of repayment by cancelling the debt.

> X has a legal *immunity* from Y with respect to some legal relation if and only if Y is unable to perform any action that would change this legal relation of X.

Thus, a property owner is legally immune from his neighbor's selling or giving away his property; no act of his neighbor would have the legal effect of thus alienating his legal ownership of this piece of real estate. A classic example is the constitutional immunity of every individual subject to the jurisdiction of the United States from Congressional legislation prohibiting or denying free speech.

It is essential to distinguish between legal claims, privileges, powers and immunities in order to avoid pernicious ambiguities. Imagine that having become the proud owner of a second car, I rent my neighbor's garage for twenty dollars a month, payable in advance, in order to protect my vehicle from the elements. When I go to put my car in his garage, I find his truck blocking my entrance. When I demand that he move his truck from the garage or return my rent, he refuses on both counts, on the ground that my legal right to park in his garage is merely a legal privilege and not a legal claim against him; that is, in return for my payment he has merely extinguished my legal duty to him not to park my car in his garage but has not created any legal duty of his to provide a parking space for me inside his garage.

Again, does a thief have the legal right to purchase merchandise with stolen cash? Clearly, a thief has no legal privilege of doing so because he has a legal duty to return the stolen property to its rightful owner, a duty inconsistent with using it to make a purchase. But a thief does have a legal power of making a purchase with stolen money because the law recognizes such a transaction as legally valid. Were the thief to try to sell a stolen television set, however, the law would not recognize his legal power to do so. The conception of a legal power must not be confused with that of a legal privilege, for the absence of a legal privilege to perform some act-in-the-law does not imply the absence of a legal power to do so. Hohfeld's fundamental legal conceptions enable one to distinguish clearly between claim-rights, privilege-rights, power-rights and immunity-rights.

(2) Hohfeld's fundamental legal conceptions take account of the adversarial context of assertions or denials of rights. On his view, each of these conceptions refers to a legal relation between two persons (or parties). Thus, a legal liberty is always a liberty of X in face of Y, and a legal power is a power of X over Y. Who are X and Y? What values may be substituted for these variables? Hohfeld takes them to be the parties to a possible or potential lawsuit. As an American Legal Realist, he believed that the law should be understood primarily in terms of its application in courts of law. Notice the full title of his two papers: "Fundamental Legal Conceptions as Applied to Judicial Reasoning." The practical significance of the language of the law lies in its application to some confrontation between plaintiff and defendant in the courtroom. Since legal proceedings are adversarial in nature, the language of legal rights is meaningful only in the context of some possible

legal confrontation between the two parties of the legal relation at issue. Thus, to say that I have a legal liberty in face of my neighbor of barbecuing in my back yard is to say that my legal position is such that if my neighbor were to go to court and attempt to obtain a court order that I cease and desist from thus producing noxious smoke and odors that invade his property, he would probably lose his case. In the absence of any possible application to some such courtroom confrontation between legal adversaries, the language of legal rights—the very conceptions of legal claims, liberties, powers and immunities—would lose its meaning, or so Hohfeld presupposes.

What is true of Hohfeld's legal conceptions is, I believe, equally true of the concept of a moral right. Hart correctly observed that the expression "I have a right to . . ." is typically used in two contexts: "(A) when the claimant has some special justification for interference with another's freedom which other persons do not have. . . . (B) when the claimant is concerned to resist or object to some interference by another person as having no justification" (Hart, 1955, 183). It is no accident that rights are asserted or denied only when two parties are, or at least could be imagined to be, in conflict, for the language of rights is essentially adversarial. What is at issue in any debate over some alleged moral right is whose will ought to prevail in the event of a confrontation between the right-holder and some party against whom the right, if genuine, would hold.

In this respect, the concept of a right is more complex than many other fundamental normative concepts. The language of *value* is concerned with possible objects of desire and potential goals of human action. It presupposes the context of purposive action and distinguishes between desirable and undesirable, justified and unjustified ends of conduct. The language of *obligation* presupposes a moral agent trying to decide between alternative acts or courses of conduct. It distinguishes between right and wrong choices, between what ought and ought not to be done by a moral agent in a given situation. Even in the absence of any man Friday, Robinson Crusoe could use the languages of value and obligation with full significance. But the language of *rights* would lose all meaning without the presence, at least in imagination, of a second moral agent whose will might, under some conceivable circumstances, conflict with Crusoe's. Hohfeld's fundamental legal conceptions are peculiarly suited for the analysis of rights because they recognize the adversarial context presupposed by any meaningful assertion or denial of a right.

(3) Hohfeld's fundamental legal conceptions provide a useful vocabulary for the analysis of complex legal positions. He was convinced that the solution of legal problems was made much more difficult by the tendency of our legal language to treat as simple what is in fact highly

complex. We say, for example, that I own my watch. Philosophers then imagine that ownership consists in some legal relation between me and my watch and speculate about the nature of this peculiar relationship. How can I still be legally in possession of my property when it is physically in the possession of some thief? More practically minded lawyers debate the implications of my ownership for the success of my suit to recover my watch or the legal validity of the thief's sale of my property to some innocent third party. Both philosophical and legal problems would be far easier to solve if we thought of legal property rights in terms of Hohfeld's fundamental legal conceptions.

Hohfeld provides a sample of what such an analysis might be:

> Suppose, for example, that A is fee-simple owner of Blackacre. His "legal interest" or "property" relating to the tangible object that we call *land* consists of a complex aggregate of rights (or claims), privileges, powers, and immunities. First, A has multiple legal rights, or claims, that *others*, respectively, shall *not* enter on the land, that they shall not cause physical harm to the land, etc., such others being under respective correlative legal duties. Second, A has an indefinite number of legal privileges of entering on the land, using the land, harming the land, etc.; that is, within limits fixed by law on grounds of social and economic policy, he has the privileges of doing on or to the land what he pleases; and correlative to all such legal privileges are the respective legal no-rights of other persons. Third, A has the legal power to alienate his legal interest to another, i.e., to extinguish his complex aggregate of jural relations and create a new and similar aggregate in the other person; also the legal power to create a privilege of entrance in any other person by giving "leave and license"; and so on indefinitely. Correlative to all such legal powers are the legal liabilities in other persons—this meaning that the latter are subject *nolens volens* to the changes of jural relations involved in the exercise of A's powers. Fourth, A has an indefinite number of legal immunities, using the term immunity in the very specific sense of non-liability or non-subjection to a power on the part of another person. Thus A has the immunity that no ordinary person can alienate A's legal interest or aggregate of jural relations to another person; the immunity that no ordinary person can extinguish A's own privileges of using the land; the immunity that no ordinary person can extinguish A's right that another person X shall not enter on the land or, in other words, create in X a privilege of entering on the land. Correlative to all these immunities are the respective legal disabilities of other persons in general. [Hohfeld, 1919, 96-97]

What is gained by the interpretation of a complex legal position in terms of Hohfeld's simpler legal conceptions? First and foremost, explicitness. The legal consequences of ownership are many and various, but they are merely implicit in our ordinary language of the law. The expression "A is fee-simple owner of Blackacre" is remarkably inarticulate. Only a trained lawyer could begin to interpret it correctly. Hohfeld's terminology spells out the legal meaning of the apparently simple but actually very complex assertion so that others can read its significance. A considerable practical advantage is the way in which a Hohfeldian interpretation is directly applicable to actual or potential court cases. Since the fundamental jural relations are defined in terms of potential adversaries in legal proceedings, a Hohfeldian analysis of any complex legal position is immediately useful for the practicing lawyer. On a more theoretical level, the translation of legal language into legal claims, privileges, powers, and so on, facilitates generalization about legal positions. Since similar fundamental legal relations enter into a wide variety of complex legal positions, these serve as "lowest common denominators" by which comparison is possible. Conversely, differences between superficially similar legal positions can be identified in Hohfeldian terms. When the legal positions of the owner and the lessee of a home are spelled out in terms of fundamental legal conceptions, both the similarities and differences are made evident. The understanding of legal language is improved, for both practicing lawyers and philosophers of law, by its interpretation in terms of fundamental legal conceptions.

(4) Hohfeld's fundamental legal conceptions lay the foundation for a powerful logic of rights. The very process of analyzing a complex legal position into Hohfeldian elements is more a matter of making explicit what is implied by ordinary legal language than of translating it into precisely synonymous terms. Thus, to say that A is fee-simple owner of Blackacre is to imply that A possesses the various kinds of legal claims, privileges, powers and immunities specified by Hohfeld. But the meaning of the original expression and the Hohfeldian analysis are not quite the same, for new legislation or court decisions could modify in this or that respect the precise nature of ownership. In this respect, interpreting the ordinary language of the law in terms of fundamental legal conceptions is like translating ordinary language into the vocabulary of symbolic logic. Because the notation of modern logic has a precision lacking in our everyday vocabulary, the original expression and its symbolic formulation are not exact synonyms. Although some of the original meaning may be lost or misrepresented, the new formulation has the great advantages of revealing more clearly and precisely the core of the original meaning, of suggesting alternative readings of an originally ambiguous expression, and of enabling one to subject the assertion to logical manipulation in order to reach new conclusions.

Many logical inferences can be shown to be valid simply by applying rules of truth-functional logic. The atomic propositions can be taken as units and manipulated using the propositional calculus, a set of rules that depend upon the meanings of connectives such as "and," "not," or "if . . . then." But many other logical inferences hinge on the inner structure of these atomic propositions. Only when the p's and q's are analyzed into the logical notation of quantification can one draw out the full implications of a set of premises. The shift from a merely truth-functional logic to one containing special rules of quantification exposes the internal structure of the propositions and enables one to manipulate them in accordance with a more powerful logic. The Hohfeldian analysis of complex legal positions into fundamental legal conceptions is very similar. It exposes to view the internal logical structure of propositions about, say, ownership or trusteeship, and enables one to draw new and more subtle inferences from them.

These new inferences are possible because of the logical properties of the fundamental legal conceptions. Recall that each of the four legal advantages Hohfeld distinguishes stands for a legal relation, a relation of one party to some second party under the law. Since every legal relation has two ends, as it were, it can be looked at and spoken of from the very different perspectives of two distinct parties. Accordingly, for each legal advantage there is, and logically must be, a correlative legal disadvantage or burden. Thus, X has a legal claim against Y that Y perform some action if and only if Y has a legal duty to X to perform that action. X has a legal privilege in face of Y to do some action if and only if Y has no legal claim against X that X not do the action. X has a legal power over Y of changing some legal relation of Y if and only if Y has a legal liability of having this legal relation of Y changed by some voluntary action of X. X has a legal immunity from Y with respect to some legal relation of X if and only if Y has a legal disability of changing this legal relation of X by any action of Y. Hohfeld sums up these logical relations in his table of jural correlatives:

claim	privilege	power	immunity
duty	no-claim	liability	disability

[Hohfeld, 1919, 36]

(I have replaced the word "right" in Hohfeld's tables with the word "claim," a synonym he suggests himself, in order to reserve judgment on his theory of legal rights.)

That these logical relations must hold true can be seen by reflecting upon the meanings Hohfeld has assigned to his chosen terminology. In effect, he defines the conceptions of a claim, a privilege and a no-claim in terms of a legal duty, and the conceptions of a liability, a disability and an immunity in terms of a legal power. Although this undermines his insistence that he has identified eight *fundamental* legal conceptions, conceptions incapable of definition, it undergirds his assertions that these conceptions contain four pairs of logical correlatives. Although his definitions are stipulative, they are not arbitrary. *If* one grants him his assumption that legal duties and legal powers are jural relations between two parties under the law, then any asserted legal position of one party logically implies a correlative legal position of the other party. When inferring a correlative legal position from some given legal position, one must always switch the parties, often change from the active to the passive verb form (or vice versa), and sometimes insert a negative. Thus, the logical correlative of X's claim to be repaid is Y's duty to repay, and the logical correlative of X's privilege of entering on Y's land is Y's no-claim that X *not* enter on his land.

Reflection upon the meanings Hohfeld assigns to his terms reveals four pairs of logical opposites. While the existence of one jural correlative logically implies the existence of its correlative legal position, the existence of one jural opposite logically implies the non-existence of its opposed legal position. Notice that while jural correlatives are pairs of legal positions possessed by different parties to a legal relation, jural opposites are legal positions each of which might be possessed by one and the same party to a legal relation. Hohfeld's pairs of jural opposites (1919, 36) are as follows:

claim	privilege	power	immunity
no-claim	duty	disability	liability

These pairs of legal positions are such that any given person subject to the law must logically have one of each pair but logically cannot have both. For example, it is logically necessary that the reader of this book have the legal privilege in face of its author of burning his copy of the book *or* that the reader have a legal duty to the author not to burn his copy of the book, but it is logically impossible for the reader to have both the legal privilege in face of the author of burning the book and a legal duty to the author to refrain from doing so.

Hohfeld's tables of jural correlatives and jural opposites have been subjected to extensive criticism. I willingly concede that, taken by themselves, they are misleading. Isolated pairs of terms do nothing to indicate when one must shift from one party to the other, from an active to a passive verb, or from a positive to a negative action. But read in the light of the text from which they are extracted, they are entirely accurate and reveal logically valid inferences. Although Hohfeld did not himself develop the logic of legal positions very far, he did lay the foundations for the impressive work of such logicians as Stig Kanger, Ingmar Pörn and Lars Lindahl. The analysis of legal positions into his fundamental legal conceptions makes it far easier to know what does, and what does not, follow from the assertion of any legal position.

(5) Hohfeld's fundamental legal conceptions make explicit the practical relevance of legal rights. Although Hohfeld was consciously engaged in the clarification of legal language, he was determined that his conceptual analysis should not be so abstract as to be of merely philosophical interest. Because his aim was the practical solution of legal problems, his

subject was the interpretation of legal conceptions "as applied in judicial reasoning"; that is to say, as they bear on court cases. Since purely natural events are not subject to legal regulation, every case that comes to court concerns some actual, alleged or contemplated human action of one of the parties. Accordingly, the content of any fundamental legal conception is some specific act or omission. For example, an owner has the legal power of *selling* his or her property to a willing buyer, a creditor has a legal claim *to be repaid,* and a defendant has a legal privilege of *not testifying* against himself or herself. When legal rights are interpreted in terms of these legal conceptions, their practical relevance, their bearing upon practice, is made explicit and specific.

Although everyone agrees that the concept of a right is essentially and importantly practical, there is an unfortunate tendency to use nouns rather than verbs in speaking or thinking about rights. Although there is no doubt that each and every citizen of the United States has a constitutional right to life, there is uncertainty and debate about exactly what this implies in respect of the legality of suicide or euthanasia. Is the right to life a legal claim not to be killed holding against all others, or does it also contain a legal duty not to take one's own life? And does the possessor of the legal right to life have the legal power to waive his or her right, so that an act of euthanasia need not constitute a violation of the patient's right to life? Only when the content of this right is thought of in terms of legal claims, privileges, powers and immunities, rather than the state or condition of life or being alive, can one know just how this important right bears on human conduct.

I do not pretend that the only way to reveal the practical relevance of rights is to interpret them in Hohfeldian terms. The vocabulary of practical discourse is large and varied. But at the very least, the formulation of a model of legal rights in terms of fundamental legal conceptions will ensure the applicability of one's philosophical theory to practice. And if one wants to ensure the other advantages I have described in this section, Hohfeld's conceptions may be more than one possible alternative among many; they may well provide the ideal conceptual framework for the development of a general and systematic theory of rights. I propose, therefore, to begin with Hohfeld. One cannot, however, end with his two journal articles as they stand. One must develop some of his ideas more fully than he did in order to make explicit insights that he saw only dimly, if at all; and in several crucial respects, one must correct errors in his ways of thinking about legal rights. Starting with and thinking critically about his *Fundamental Legal Conceptions,* let us now go beyond Hohfeld to a more adequate Hohfeldian analysis of the language of legal rights.

Chapter 2

BEYOND HOHFELD

Wesley Hohfeld's great contribution to jurisprudence was to identify eight "fundamental" legal conceptions. He did not invent these conceptions, for they are implicit in the law and in our thinking about the law. Nor was he the first to have noted their fundamental importance for any adequate understanding of the law, for jurists such as John Salmond and Henry T. Terry had previously made many of the same distinctions he drew. Hohfeld went beyond his predecessors, however, in the rigor with which he distinguished between these quite different conceptions and, above all, in framing them in a logically complete conceptual scheme.

I am convinced that these legal conceptions are fundamental in the sense of being essential for any adequate theoretical understanding of the law, but Hohfeld took them to be fundamental in another sense. Because each conception is logically distinct from all the others, Hohfeld assumed that each is simple and irreducible. Therefore, he eschewed any formal or verbal definitions of his terminology. Instead, he provided a sort of ostensive definition of each concept by giving illustrations from various legal cases. On this basis, he exhibited the logical relations between these conceptions in his tables of jural opposites and jural correlatives. Unfortunately, Hohfeld's conceptual analysis leaves many traditional philosophical problems unresolved and even raises some new questions. Just what is a legal duty? Are legal duties logically independent of moral duties? When one has a duty to some second party, how does one identify the party to whom the duty is owed? Is there any logical connection between having a legal claim against someone and having a legal power over that party? Precisely how, if at all, does a legal power confer some sort of control upon its possessor? Any philosophically adequate analysis of Hohfeld's fundamental legal conceptions must enable one to answer questions such as these. Accordingly, it is necessary to go beyond Hohfeld to provide a much fuller interpretation of the conceptions he identified but refused to define. This is the primary purpose of this chapter. In the process, we will challenge some of the presuppositions that underlie his discussion and argue for a very different way of thinking about legal duties and legal powers.

Legal Positions

First, I want to consider Hohfeld's universe of discourse. The short title of his two articles assures us that he is writing about fundamental legal conceptions, but this is slightly misleading. While fundamental legal conceptions are, of course, the focus of his attention, his subject is considerably more broad than this. Most of his second paper goes on to show how nonfundamental legal concepts can be analyzed in terms of the more fundamental ones he has distinguished. Thus, he reduces a variety of rights *in rem* and rights *in personam* to multital and paucital rights or aggregates of legal claims. He also sketches an even more complex analysis of fee-simple ownership into legal claims, liberties, powers and immunities. Clearly, his universe of discourse includes complex legal conceptions as well as simple or fundamental ones.

In some broad sense, Hohfeld is obviously doing conceptual analysis of our legal language. His subject may be taken to be legal terminology or the meanings of expressions in our legal language or the referents of these terms. But let us try to be more precise about the status of this legal terminology. Is Hohfeld writing about the language used *in* the law (for example, the concepts embedded in statutes) or the language used to speak *of* the law (for example, the concepts used by the lawyer or social scientist describing the content of a given legal system)? The full title of his two articles is "Some Fundamental Legal Conceptions as Applied in Judicial Reasoning." Such reasoning is both in and of the law. The judge must reason *about* the law in describing his or her legal sources and in interpreting the legal rules and principles to which he or she appeals. At the same time, the judge's conclusion *is* the law applicable to this case, at least until his or her holding is reversed by some court of appeal; and the judge's decision may be a legally valid precedent to be applied to future cases as well. Accordingly, legal conceptions such as those of a legal claim or trusteeship are both concepts used in the law and concepts used in speaking of the law.

What is the law? Hohfeld seems to have thought of the practical significance of legal terminology exclusively in terms of its application to court cases. Since every court case arises from some alleged or contemplated action and concerns a dispute between two adversaries, each of Hohfeld's fundamental legal conceptions refers to a legal relation between two parties regarding some specific action. If his way of looking at the law is too narrow, it may not reveal the full significance of the language of the law. At the very least, we should recognize that judges are not the only ones who apply legal conceptions. Within the legal system itself, police officers, bailiffs, wardens in penal institutions, parole officers, and administrators in various governmental agencies apply the law in carrying out their legally assigned duties and exercising their legally conferred powers. On a much wider scale, private citizens apply legal conceptions to themselves and others whenever they do such things as make out income tax returns or demand repayment of a loan. Even for a Legal Realist who wishes to conceive of the law in terms of its actual functioning or operations in a society, the law cannot be identified solely with its judicial application. It *might* be true, however, that every application of the law outside the courtroom is mirrored in a possible court case. If so, the judicial application of legal conceptions could provide a fully adequate model for the meaning of legal terminology. Whether this is so will depend, among other things, upon whether imperfect or unenforceable duties are taken to be real. For the moment, let us take note of Hohfeld's perspective on the law and reserve judgment on its adequacy.

At least we know that his universe of discourse is legal conceptions as applied in judicial reasoning, that is, as applied in and of the law. If we look again and more closely at the title of his two articles, we will notice that he is writing of "Some Fundamental Legal Conceptions." His proper subject is not all legal language or every legal conception, but only a portion of this universe of discourse. With which legal conceptions is he concerned?

There is another way of characterizing Hohfeld's universe of discourse that promises to be more illuminating. He often speaks of fundamental legal conceptions as "legal relations" or, more often, "jural relations"; and he asserts that complex legal interests can and should be analyzed into simple jural relations. Thus, another way of defining his universe of discourse is in terms of jural relations, both simple and complex. Although he is not writing a treatise on the nature of a jural relation, he does make it clear that ultimately every jural relation is a legal relation between two natural persons regarding some specific human action. So far, so good.

But if we try to push this idiom any farther, we will surely run into trouble. To speak of legal conceptions as referring to jural relations suggests that linguistic expressions such as "a claim" or "a power" denote legal entities, much as expressions like "a chair" or "a pleasure" denote physical or psychological objects. The best way to avoid a host of insoluble metaphysical problems is flatly to deny the existence of any non-natural realm of legal objects.

In order to avoid being misled, we must distinguish more carefully than Hohfeld does between legal terminology, the conceptions that give meaning to our legal language, and the objects (if any) to which legal terms and the conceptions they express refer. It is not jural relations that take their significance from the law; it is linguistic expressions such as "a legal claim" or "a legal duty" that derive their meaning from the law. And it is legal terms, not whatever legal reality they might denote, that must be clear and direct in their meaning. So let us begin with words, not legal relations.

Hohfeld correctly observes that expressions such as "a right of owner-ship" or "a liberty of entering on the land" both take significance from the law and must be predicated of human beings. The reason he gives is that the essential purpose of the law is to regulate the conduct of human beings. To what, then, does one refer when one speaks of rights, duties, liberties, and so forth? One is speaking of the relevance of the law for the conduct of the human beings subject to it. Hohfeld's tables of "jural relations" are really classifications of the different ways in which the law can bear on the action of any person under the law. This interpretation is confirmed by the last five words in the full title of Hohfeld's articles, ". . . as Applied in Judicial Reasoning." The essence of judicial reasoning is the application of the law to the parties before the court. Hohfeld's universe of discourse is the distinct applications of the law to the persons subject to it.

He is not, however, talking simply about the law. He is writing of the applications of the law *to* human subjects. Recall his observation that the meaning of expressions like "a right" or "a duty" will be clear and direct only if we keep in mind that they are predicated of human beings. Thus, to predicate legal claims, privileges, etc. of persons is to characterize these persons as subject to the law and, hence, as potential parties to a law suit. It is, in short, to describe persons in terms of their positions under the law. In the end, Hohfeld shows us that the law bears on or applies to human action in two radically different ways: by constraining our choices and by enabling us to change our legal positions. This is why his fundamental legal conceptions divide neatly into two subsets, four definable in terms of the concept of a legal duty and four definable in terms of the concept of a legal power.

There are at least three reasons why it is much better to think of Hohfeld's universe of discourse as legal positions than as jural relations. The expression "legal position" is obviously figurative, a spatial meta-phor. This makes it harder to imagine that our legal terminology literally refers to some realm of nonnatural objects called "claims," "privileges," "powers," and so on. Better yet, the expression "a legal position" suggests the nonfigurative significance of the sorts of legal expressions about which Hohfeld was writing. To speak of one's position under the law is at least to suggest the relevance of the law to the person or the way in which the law bears on one's conduct. Finally, it is better not to assume without argument and insinuate with one's terminology that every legal position involves two parties. If a person can apply the law to himself or herself, then it might be possible for some legal positions to be nonrelational.

One of the great advantages that Hohfeld claims for the analysis of complex legal positions in terms of his fundamental legal conception is that this will enable us to make accurate and illuminating generalizations about the law. But how broadly can we thus generalize?

Are all legal positions necessarily relations between two parties? Hohfeld assumes without argument or explanation that every simple legal position is a jural relation between two and only two natural persons under the law. Accordingly, each of his fundamental legal conceptions has an internal relational structure. Every duty is a duty *to* some second party, every liberty is a liberty *in face of* one and only one other person, and every legal power is a power *over* another person. Is this assumption correct? Is every elementary legal position by very definition a relation between two parties? Since Hohfeld nowhere explicitly defends this thesis, we must try to find arguments implicit in his articles or invent arguments to insert into his mouth.

Hohfeld tells us that he is writing of legal conceptions "as applied in judicial reasoning." He defines his subject in this way in order that his conceptual analysis may have practical, not merely philosophical, import. It would be quite natural for an American Legal Realist to assume that the practical significance and real meaning of legal conceptions is shown most clearly in, and even exhausted by, their application to court cases. And since every legal action involves a confrontation between two legal adversaries, a plaintiff and a defendant, the legal position of any person subject to the law *must* consist in that party's legal position vis-à-vis some potential legal adversary.

Now it seems to me that Hohfeld is on the right track. If one wishes to understand what it means to speak of a person's position under the law or the way in which the law is relevant to the conduct of any individual subject to the legal system, one must focus upon the application of the law to that person in legal reasoning. But I would deny that the law is applied to those subject to it only in judicial reasoning. Although court cases may well provide paradigm examples of the application of the law, by far the largest number of applications of law occur outside the courtroom. A policeman who tickets a parked car or apprehends a fleeing thief is applying the law to one subject to it. A welfare administrator who grants or denies an application for AFDC benefits, or a customs official who refuses to allow a returning citizen to bring a second bottle of scotch into the country without paying the prescribed duty on it, is also applying legal concepts to the individual. And each spring when the conscientious, or prudent, citizen fills out his or her income tax form, the person subject to the law applies the law to himself or herself. Since not every application of fundamental legal concepts is an application within an adversarial legal process, this general argument for holding that all legal positions are necessarily relational is unsound.

But Hohfeld might well be able to advance more specific arguments to support his view regarding each of his species of simple legal positions. Since his eight fundamental legal conceptions divide into two subsets— four definable in terms of the concept of a legal duty, and four definable in terms of a legal power, we need consider only these two. How are we to interpret the legal position of the duty-bearer under the law? Presumably, to be bound by a legal duty (notice the metaphor of a legal tie, rope or chain) is (literally) to be constrained by the law. Now it is impossible for anyone to be constrained unless there is someone else who is actually, or at least potentially, doing the constraining. Thus, implicit in the simplest concept of a legal duty are the two legal positions of the party constrained and the constraining party.

Let us grant for the moment that no person can be constrained unless there is someone else actually or potentially imposing constraint upon that duty-bearer. Must the constrainer ultimately be a single individual? Recall that Hohfeld maintains that a simple legal duty is a legal relation between two and only two natural persons, one duty-bearer and one second party. He seems to identify the duty-bearer with the defendant in a potential legal action and the legal constrainer with the plaintiff who could initiate that legal action. No doubt the potential plaintiff has the legal power to set the process of legal enforcement in motion, but can the plaintiff be said to impose any legal constraint all by himself or herself? The plaintiff is in the position of legal constrainer only because of his or her power to take legal action in a court of law. Any constraint he or she can impose is obviously *via* a judicial holding against the defendant. Nor does any decision of the court enforce itself. In the end, force is applied to the individual subject to the law by police officers, officers of the court, or officials in our penal institutions. Hohfeld's Legal Realism is not realistic enough. To identify the actual operations of a legal system with what takes place in the courtroom is to omit most of what makes constraint by a legal system real.

Even the broader perspective I have just suggested is not, however, sufficient. To understand fully one's legal position under the law one must recognize that an individual can, and often does, apply the law to himself or herself. Motorists often stop at a red light when there is no policeman waiting to arrest them; most of us send in our monthly payments on our mortgages before the bank threatens to foreclose; and many taxpayers fill out their income tax returns in strict accordance with the law. Typically people comply with the law in large measure because they feel duty-bound to do so. Does their being constrained by the law consist simply and solely in the threat of enforcement through the courts? Surely not. Most citizens recognize an obligation of fidelity to law and feel morally bound to obey the law, at least laws they do not find unjust, inhumane or pointless. The person subject to the law can be, and often is, morally constrained by the law. Moral constraint is not imposed by some second party, some other person; it is an impersonal constraint imposed by moral reasons. Not only is Hohfeld mistaken in presupposing that all legal constraint is ultimately imposed by one second party; he is mistaken in assuming that legal constraint is necessarily imposed by other persons.

A Hohfeldian might object, however, to my appeal to the constraint of the obligation of fidelity to law as irrelevant. This constraint, real and important as it may be, is a moral constraint. The concept of a *legal* duty must be analyzed in terms of purely legal, not moral constraint. And in the end all purely legal constraint lies in actual or threatened enforcement through the legal system. But why imagine that the threat of legal enforcement is a purely legal constraint? Surely it is a prudential constraint. Merely threatened or possible enforcement by legal officials constrains those subject to it only because the fact of such enforcement is a prudential reason to obey the law. Prudential reasons are surely no more "purely legal" than moral reasons. They may, to be sure, be of more practical importance because they provide more effective or more universal motives to obey the law. But moral reasons are as genuine as prudential reasons, and in the end, almost all legal constraint is imposed by reasons, prudential or moral, and only indirectly by persons. Therefore, the very concept of a legal duty need not be explicated in terms of a legal relation between two persons, the party constrained and the second party imposing the legal constraint.

Let us turn, then, to the concept of a simple legal power. A legal power might be defined as a power conferred by the law to change some legal position. Hohfeld is correct, I believe, in holding that ultimately the law confers such powers only upon natural persons. Thus, the legal powers of a corporation are to be understood as the powers of persons acting in their capacities as agents of that artificial person. Moreover, a legal position, as I have defined that concept, is always the position of some person subject to or under the law. Since the metaphor of a legal position literally refers to the way in which the law bears on human conduct, every legal position is necessarily a position of some person. It follows that the concept of a legal power is relational by its very nature.

Every legal power is a power of someone to change the legal position of someone. So far, Hohfeld is entirely correct.

But is every legal power necessarily a legal power of one person to change the legal position of *one other* person? Let us begin by reflecting upon Hohfeld's own paradigm, that of a legal action of one plaintiff against one defendant. Suppose that Judge Jones decides a medical malpractice suit in favor of the plaintiff and against the defendant, ordering the doctor to pay $50,000 to the patient. Assuming that the court had jurisdiction, in rendering his decision the judge is exercising his legal power to change the legal positions of both parties to the suit. The judge brings into existence a legal claim of the patient to be paid $50,000 by the doctor and imposes upon the doctor a legal duty to pay the patient $50,000. Nor, by Hohfeld's own logic, can the judge's legal power be analyzed into two separate and independent legal powers, the legal power to create a claim of the plaintiff and the power to impose a duty upon the defendant, for the concepts of a legal claim and a correlative legal duty refer to one and the same legal relation seen from the different perspectives of the parties between whom it holds. Moreover, the judicial decision may well serve as a legal precedent for other court cases in the future. Thus, the judge in effect has a legal power to make new law and in doing so to change the legal position of *all* those subject to the legal system.

Another illuminating example is that of contracts that confer a legal right upon some third party. Although not all contracts intended to benefit some third party create a legal claim of the beneficiary to the intended benefit, some do precisely that. Let us imagine that the party who will become legally bound to perform some action beneficial to the third party has made the relevant offer. The first party now has the legal power to create, by accepting the offer and tendering the specified consideration, both a legal duty binding upon the second party and a legal claim of the third party. Once more it is impossible to analyze this legal power into two separate legal powers because it is the power to make precisely the sort of contract that has both second and third parties. I conclude that although every legal power is necessarily a legal power over someone, it need not be a power over some*one,* some one individual whose position would be changed by its exercise.

Hohfeld is also mistaken in holding that the party whose position would be changed by the exercise of the power is necessarily someone other than the person who possesses the legal power. One can, and often does, have a legal power over oneself. The patient who has the legal power of consenting to surgery has the legal power of extinguishing his legal claim against the doctor that the doctor not cut into his body with a knife. The owner of a piece of property has the legal power of extinguishing his or her own legal position as owner by selling the property to a willing buyer or giving it to a willing donee. To be sure, there is a conceptual distinction between being the possessor of a legal power and being affected by it. It does not follow, however, that these two logically different positions must be occupied by different natural persons.

Our conclusion must be that a simple legal position need not be a legal relation between two parties. Since the concept of legal constraint implies neither the existence of a single person imposing the constraint nor indeed that the constraint is imposed by one or more persons, the concept of a legal duty is not essentially relational. Although the concept of a legal power is relational, necessarily relating the possessor of the power to the party whose legal position would be changed by its exercise, this relationship can exist between a person and himself/herself or between one person and several others.

Not only does Hohfeld conceive of every legal position as relating one person to some second party; he also imagines that standing at one end of each legal relation is advantageous and occupying the position at the other end disadvantageous. He often seems to equate the notion of a legal advantage with that of a benefit conferred by the law. Accordingly, it might be thought that legal claims, privileges, powers and immunities are legal advantages simply because those who hold any of these legal positions necessarily benefit from actions in conformity to them.

But this need not be so. If I deposit my entire life savings of $15,000 with my stock broker on the understanding that he purchase as many shares of Arabian Oilwell as he can in my name, then he has a duty to me to invest my money in this manner. Unfortunately, his performance of this duty to me may cause me to lose my entire savings. Similarly, my surgeon may have a contractual duty to me to perform a very delicate operation upon me and, in fulfilling his legal obligation to me, may unexpectedly cause my death. Given my weak will, it may not be in my best interests to possess the legal power to gamble away my salary month after month. Although legal claims, privileges, powers and immunities are typically beneficial to their possessor, they are not invariably and necessarily so.

Perhaps, however, we have been reading the text in too naive a fashion. Perhaps Hohfeld held, or should have held, a qualified beneficiary analysis of legal advantages. It is not that the possessor of a legal advantage always does in fact benefit from his or her legal position, but that the possessor is *intended* by the law to benefit *directly* from the position. Even this, however, does not seem to be generally true. Legal powers are typically conferred upon public officials, not in order that they might benefit from their legal positions, but for the public benefit. Indeed, the private citizen's legal power of arrest is probably not intended by the law so much to benefit the possessor directly as to benefit the community indirectly. And if the individual has a legal liberty to engage in homosexual acts with a consenting adult or to ride a motorcycle without wearing a crash helmet, the intention of the law may well be to respect the moral autonomy of the possessor of the legal privilege rather than directly to benefit him or her.

Turning from a legal advantage to its logical correlative, it is clear that not every legal liability is a burden or disadvantage in any sense contrasted with being a beneficial position. The job applicant's liability to being hired for a desirable position is, and is probably intended by the law to be, a beneficial legal position. Hohfeld himself recognized this fact when he wrote:

> We are apt to think of liability as exclusively an onerous relation of one party to another. But, in its broad technical significance, this is not necessarily so. Thus X, the owner of a watch, has the power to abandon his property . . . and correlatively to X's power of abandonment there is a liability in every other person. But such a liability instead of being onerous or unwelcome, is quite the opposite. As regards another person, M, for example, it is a *liability to have created in his favor (though against his will) a privilege and a power* relating to the watch,—that is, the privilege of taking possession and the power, by doing so, to vest title in himself. [Hohfeld, 1919, 60. Hohfeld's italics.]

Those words in parentheses, "though against his will," suggest a very different sense in which some legal positions might be legal advantages and others legal disadvantages. To say that a position is a legal advantage might be to say that the law is on the side of its possessor in any confrontation with the second party, that the law favors the will of one who holds that position in any conflict with the opposed will of the holder of the logically correlative position.

On this interpretation, legal claims and privileges, powers and immunities are supposed to be legal advantages in the sense that having a faster horse or longer arms are advantages to a jockey or a prizefighter respectively; they help one to win in one's contest with one's adversary. Legal claims and powers are much like swords; one can use them to take legal action against one's enemies. Legal privileges and immunities are more like shields; they are legal defences against any action by one's opponent in the law. Thus, a legal advantage helps one's will to prevail over one's opponent outside the courtroom because it would enable one to win one's case against one's legal adversary in court.

Are legal claims, privileges, powers and immunities necessarily legal advantages in this sense? At best, this could be true of relational legal positions; where there is no second party to one's legal position, holding the position cannot enable one to prevail against that missing party. More disturbing is the fact that such legal positions will in fact help the holder's will prevail only if the law is recognized and respected. One may lack the financial resources to take one's case to court, the court may decide the case incorrectly, or the court order may not be effectively enforced. Finally, there seem to be exceptions to Hohfeld's generalization. Having a legal power, for example, becomes a legal *dis*advantage upon occasion. Suppose that I sue my surgeon for medical malpractice and allege that at the time I gave my consent to the operation I was legally incompetent to give free informed consent. I may lose my case and my legal adversary may have his way if the court decides that I had the legal power at issue.

Hohfeld went too far when he imagined that legal claims, privileges, powers and immunities were by very definition or by their very conception legal advantages. Still, there is wisdom to be gleaned from pondering his generalization. Much, although not all, of their practical significance lies in their relevance to confrontations between opposed wills, and in such adversarial confrontations, they typically, although not necessarily, do favor the will of the party who holds one of these positions vis-à-vis the will of the adversary. This is why the conceptions of a claim, a privilege, a power and an immunity are especially appropriate for the analysis of rights.

Legal Duties

Hohfeld's conception of a legal duty is essentially relational; to have a duty under the law is necessarily to be duty-bound *to* some other party who has a correlative legal claim holding against the duty-bearer. But how can one identify the party to whom one owes any specified legal duty? Hohfeld does not tell us. More fundamentally, what is it about Hohfeld's very conception of a legal duty that implies that every legal duty is a duty to some second party? After all, John Austin and H. L. A. Hart hold that in addition to relative duties, there are absolute legal duties, duties that are not owed to any determinate second party. Surely Hohfeld was aware of Austin's analytical jurisprudence. Why, then, does he reject it without comment?

We have already seen how Hohfeld's preoccupation with concrete cases in private law—that is, with confrontations between a plaintiff and a defendant—led him to conceive of every legal position as a position at one end of a legal relation. His paradigm of a legal relation seems to be the relation between claimant and duty-bearer. Although he never defines this relation or even describes its nature, there is one hint in his papers as to how he thinks about it. "The entire legal relation—the *vinculum juris*— resulting from the agreement may be called a primary, contractual obligation" (1919, 202). This brief sentence should be compared with a longer passage in Henry T. Terry's *Some Leading Principles of Anglo-American Law*, a work to which Hohfeld often refers with respect.

> When two persons made a contract the law created between them a tie or *obligatio*, the word obligation being applied to denote indifferently either element of the relation, the right or the duty. The metaphorical idea of a tie or connection was constantly kept in mind. In the Institutes the definition of an obligation is, *Juris vinculum quo necessitate astringimur alicujus solvendae rei*. One kind of obligation was called *nexum*, and a release or discharge of the obligation was designated as *solutio*, or unloosing. [Terry, 1884, 104]

The language of Roman jurisprudence was permeated with this metaphor of a legal obligation as a rope or chain that binds the duty-bearer. The linguistic roots of this metaphor are the infinitives *ligare*, meaning "to tie," *vincire* and *nectere*, "to bind," and *solvere*, "to loosen" or even "to untie." Hohfeld inherited this root metaphor embedded in the language he uses to characterize the legal relation of duty-bearer to right-holder. He conceives of a legal duty as the position of a person bound or constrained by the law.

How, then, does he imagine that the law imposes a constraint upon the action of the duty-bearer? What binds one is the threat of legal sanctions imposed by the court. The position of the duty-bearer is, therefore, the position of a potential defendant in a lawsuit brought by the plaintiff with the correlative claim. Given the assumptions that to have a legal duty is to be bound or constrained by the law and that the law constrains one by the threat of being sued, the very concept of a legal duty implies a necessary relation to some second party with the power of taking legal action against the duty-bearer.

But are the legal positions of duty-bearer and right-holder, as conceived by Hohfeld, really logical correlatives? The duty-bearer is taken to be the person bound or constrained by the law because he or she is liable to societal compulsion in the form of legal sanctions imposed by a court for disobedience to the command of law. The right-holder is taken to be the person with the legal power to impose societal compulsion by taking legal action against the duty-bearer in the courts. According to Hohfeld's own logic, however, the correlative of a legal power is, *not* a legal duty, but a legal liability. What went wrong here?

Because Hohfeld refused to give any philosophical analysis of his conception of a legal duty, he failed to see that his conception of a duty of B to A is not a fundamental legal conception at all. It is really a complex concept presupposing the two simpler concepts of legal constraint and of the legal power to take legal action. He imagined that these two are necessarily connected because he assumed that legal constraint consists in the threat of legal sanctions imposed by a court on the initiative of some plaintiff. Even if this assumption is correct, there is a hidden complexity in his conception of a relative duty; but should we grant his presupposition?

How does the law constrain the conduct of a person subject to it? Admittedly, the duty-bearer is legally bound by his or her liability to suffer sanctions imposed by a court of law. The first and most obvious thing to notice, however, is that the threat of legal sanctions does not always originate from some potential claimant. The duties of criminal law are enforced at the initiative of the public prosecutor, much as the duties of civil law are on the action of a private plaintiff. Less obviously, but more importantly, the judge is not the only one to apply the law to one subject to it. A policeman on patrol may arrest a suspect or order a loiterer to move on; a policewoman may collect a fine for parking too long or deduct points against one's driving license for a moving violation of the traffic laws. Similarly, a case worker in a welfare agency may terminate one's benefits because of one's failure to abide by some regulation. Thus, a variety of officials in the legal system constrain one's conduct in accordance with the law.

Many of the sanctions that constrain the duty-bearer to obey the law are informal ones imposed by private persons. A teacher or government worker may lose his or her job if illegal conduct is discovered; even the allegation of such conduct may keep an applicant from obtaining such a position. Disapproval of the violation of one's legal duties is general, although not universal, so that a concern for one's reputation and public image constrain the duty-bearer to obedience to law. For many respectable persons, the threat of shame and humiliation is more of a constraint than the liability to some penalty imposed by a court of law.

Finally, each individual continually applies the law to himself or herself. Even Justice Holmes' "bad man" does so when he cynically calculates his chances of violating the law with impunity, but most of those subject to the law have more mixed motives. One may be constrained to obey the law of the land out of a loyalty, often rather chauvinistic, to one's country. One may see oneself morally bound to obey the law by a conscientious regard for moral considerations.

But, it may be objected, such moral constraint is too soft to count as genuine constraint; it cannot be compared to the hard constraint imposed upon the subject by court-imposed sanctions. Notice, however, that what constrains the duty-bearer is not the sanction itself, but the liability to or prospect of the sanction. Prison walls may prevent a murderer from killing again, but what is supposed to constrain the legal subject is the threat of imprisonment were he or she to kill. And precisely how does the liability to court-imposed sanctions constrain a person's choice? By constituting a prudential reason not to disobey the law. Thus ultimately it is reasons, and not persons, that constrain the duty-bearer. Moreover, not all constraining reasons are prudential, and not all prudential reasons to obey the law consist in one's liability to a civil suit. A legal duty is not legal, as opposed to moral, because it is imposed by a purely legal constraint; it is a legal duty because the constraining reason, be it prudential or moral or whatever, is a reason provided by the law. The adjective "legal" refers to the source, and not the nature, of the constraint.

We may conclude that Hohfeld correctly conceives of the legal posi-tion of the duty-bearer as that of a person whose choices are constrained by law. But his conception of legal constraint is far too narrow and does not get to the bottom of constraint itself. To be sure, court-imposed sanctions are central to and crucially important in legal constraint. But since not all legal constraint arises from one's liability to sanctions, the conception of a legal duty is not in and of itself relational; a legal duty need not, conceptually or logically, be a duty to some second party with the power to take legal action against the duty-bearer. A legal duty is simply a legally constrained action, however the law may constrain the duty-bearer's conduct.

Still, many—probably most—legal duties are quite properly spoken of as duties to some second party. How shall we conceive of such relative duties in the law? Let us return to the metaphor of legal obligation as a tie that binds the subject to obedience.

> In this figure, which haunts much legal thought, the social pressure appears as a chain binding those who have obligations so that they are not free to do what they want. The other end of the chain is sometimes held by the group or their official representatives, who insist on performance or exact the penalty: sometimes it is entrusted by the group to a private individual who may choose whether or not to insist on performance or its equivalent in value to him. The first situation typifies the duties or obligations of criminal law and the second those of the civil law where we think of private individuals having rights correlative to the obligations. [Hart, 1961, 85]

In this figure of speech, a duty-imposing law is pictured as a chain. One end of the chain binds the duty-bearer and the other end is held by another party who controls the constraining chain.

What literal meaning can we give to "holding the chain of the law"? First, who holds the chain in Hart's analysis of the metaphor? It is the public prosecutor in criminal law and the individual claimant in civil law. They control the chain of the law in the sense that they, and they alone, have the legal power to go to court and initiate legal proceedings to enforce the law. We speak of a legal duty as a duty *to* some second party because we recognize that the public prosecutor or private plaintiff, as the case may be, is given special standing by the law concerning the imposition of the legal sanction that in large measure, although not entirely, imposes the constraint upon the duty-bearer. Notice that this way of conceiving the legal relation between duty-bearer and the party to whom the duty is owed necessarily makes them potential adversaries in a courtroom confrontation, just the sort of relation Hohfeld has in mind. I suggest, then, that we analyze the concept of a relative duty in the law into the two more fundamental concepts of constraint by the law and the legal power to initiate the imposition of legal sanctions by the courts.

I offer this analysis of the concept of a relative duty in the law as a stipulative definition. In ordinary language, I suspect that the expression "a legal duty to" is ambiguous. Sometimes to speak of a duty to some second party is to point out that this second party has a special legal standing in the enforcement of the duty-imposing law. At other times it is to suggest that this second party is the possessor of a legal right correlative with the duty. Since the possessor of a correlative right typically possesses the legal power to enforce his or her right, these two conceptions of a relative duty typically coincide in application. For our theoretical purposes, however, we would do well to restrict our conception of a relative duty to the first, and simpler, meaning. In this way, we can eliminate the confusing ambiguity in our everyday legal language. This simpler meaning is also more useful for the Hohfeldian purpose of analyzing complex legal phenomena into more elementary constituents. It seems more natural to define the concept of a duty to someone by an extension of the analysis of the concept of a legal duty *tout court*,—that is, by developing further the notion of legal constraint rather than by introducing a new and different notion of a legal right. Finally, this definition leaves open the highly controversial question whether there is a legal right corresponding to every relative duty in the law. One would prefer not to prejudice such a philosophical issue by a stipulative definition of one's terms.

John Austin and H. L. A. Hart distinguish between relative and absolute legal duties, between duties to some second party and duties not owed to anyone at all. For them, the very real duties imposed by criminal law are absolute in this way. Now it may be true, as Austin assumes and Hart argues (Hart, 1973, 190-195), that the criminal law does not confer any corresponding legal rights upon the individuals whose interests are served by the performance of the duties of criminal law. But, even if true, this would not make such duties nonrelative in the sense that I, following an earlier suggestion of Hart, have explained. On my analysis, duties of the criminal law are duties *to* the state, because the state, acting through its agent the public prosecutor, has the power of enforcing such duties in the courts. Given my conception of a relative duty, an absolute duty would have to be an unenforceable or imperfect duty.

Let us examine a few examples of so-called imperfect duties to see whether they are genuine, that is, whether they really do impose a legal constraint upon those subject to them. First, consider the alleged duty to mitigate damages. Each of the parties to a bilateral contract has a legal obligation not to cause injury to the other by any failure to perform as contracted; and in the event of nonperformance, the injured party can sue for and recover damages. But damages will be denied for any harm suffered as a consequence of a violation of a contract to the extent that the injured party could have prevented them by taking reasonable precautions. Hence, it is said that each party to a contract has a legal duty to mitigate any damages that might arise from the violation of the contract of the other party.

This alleged duty is, however, unenforceable. A contractor who fails to mitigate damages cannot be prosecuted for any crime, nor can he or she be sued by any private plaintiff. The only "penalty" incurred by one who fails to fulfill this alleged legal duty is the failure of any suit to recover full damages from the other party to the contract. In strictly Hohfeldian terms, the injured party has a legal disability, that is, lacks a legal power to sue, rather than a legal duty. This is recognized in the 1932 Restatement of the Law of Contracts in a note (American Law Institute, 1932, 537) that rejects the term "duty" in this situation. I suspect that this sort of rejection is often appropriate. Many of the so-called imperfect duties are really other sorts of Hohfeldian legal positions, usually disabilities or no-claims.

One might, however, object that I have oversimplified the legal position of the contractor. When the law denies to a party of a valid contract the power to recover damages he or she could and should have mitigated, it both burdens him or her with a legal disability and imposes upon him or her a legal duty; for by the very denial of the power to sue for damages, the law constrains the individual to take measures to avoid those injuries he or she would suffer without available remedy. No doubt the law does provide a motive to mitigate damages that would not be present were the injured party able to recover full damages. Nevertheless, it is a mistake to say that this is a constraint imposed upon the individual *by the law*. The constraint is imposed by the threat of suffering injury for which no remedy is provided, not by the law. To see this, simply imagine that there is no law of contract at all. The threat of suffering injury from the violation of an agreement would remain and would constrain any prudent party to the agreement to mitigate any damages that might arise from nonperformance of the unenforceable

contract. Contrast this with the duty to drive on the right side of the
·road. If there were no legal rules of the road, this particular constraint
would be removed from the motorist, although the prudential constraint
to drive defensively would be considerable. Only when the law adds a
constraint that would not be present in the absence of the law can it
accurately be said that the subject is under a *legal* constraint or has a legal
duty.

It may even be that the law denies the power to recover full damages
because it presupposes that any contractor has a moral duty to mitigate
damages. It is often the case that the law recognizes a duty it does not
enforce. But not all forms of legal recognition impose a legal duty;
sometimes they impose a legal disability or no-claim instead. One begins
to wonder whether any of the so-called imperfect duties are really duties
in the strict sense.

I shall argue, however, that there are some real legal duties that are
not duties to any second party because they are not enforceable through
the courts. Let us grant that almost all legal duties are owed to some
second party, either an individual claimant or the state, because court-
imposed sanctions are central to legal constraint. Presumably these are
legal sanctions, however, only if they are imposed by the court in
accordance with the law. Does the judge, then, have any legal duty to
decide cases according to valid law rather than on the basis of whim or
personal preference or self-interest? Article VI, section 2 of the United
States Constitution seems to assert a special form of this duty.

> This Constitution, and the laws of the United States which shall be made in
> pursuance thereof, and all treaties made, or which shall be made, under the
> authority of the United States, shall be the supreme law of the land; and the
> judges in every State shall be bound thereby, any thing in the Constitution or
> laws of any State to the contrary notwithstanding.

How should we interpret this language? Are state judges really "bound"
or legally constrained by federal law under our Constitution?

Can this duty of state judges to accord supremacy to federal law be
enforced through the courts on the initiative of some public prosecutor?
If a judge were to accept a bribe to decide a case contrary to federal law,
the judge could be indicted and tried for the crime of accepting a bribe.
But the failure or refusal to judge in accordance with federal law is not,
per se, a crime at all. Again, an individual injured by a judicial decision
contrary to federal law might conceivably sue for the removal of the
state judge by appealing to the common law writ of *quo warranto.* But this
writ is not available in every state, and even where available, its applicability is put in doubt by the established doctrine of absolute judicial
immunity. How, then, is a state judge constrained by the Constitution to

recognize the supremacy of federal law in his or her judgments? There may be the threat of being removed from office by recall or some other political process for any flagrant violation of the law in this way. Since respect for the law is general and deep in the legal profession, concern for one's reputation among the bar serves as a powerful constraint to respect federal law in one's judicial decisions. The informal sanction of public disapproval for any known violation of "our sacred Constitution" can be a powerful constraint upon the judge. Finally, there is the moral constraint of being bound by one's oath of office in which one has sworn to uphold the Constitution of the United States. Since the law can and does constrain those subject to it in many ways other than through the liability to court-imposed sanctions, the state judge has an absolute or nonrelative duty to render judgment in accordance with federal law.

Another unenforceable legal duty that is not a duty to any other party is the duty of the executor of a will to repay a debt to himself out of the estate before apportioning the estate among the heirs. The law of inheritance requires that an executor settle all outstanding claims against the deceased before dividing the estate among the heirs. If the executor happens also to be an unpaid creditor, however, he cannot take legal action against himself in order to enforce his legal duty to himself. Nor is it a crime to fail to repay oneself out of the estate. Clearly, here is an example of a duty that is not a duty to anyone at all.

But is it really a legal duty? That is, is the executor really bound or constrained by the law to repay the debt of the deceased to himself? After all, if the executor does not want to repay the debt, can he simply waive repayment and thus cancel this alleged duty? In principle, yes. But the executor may not always be in a position to waive repayment. He may lie under a strong moral obligation not to deprive his child of the opportunity to attend a private college by thus reducing his income or he may himself have debts to others he cannot repay without collecting from the estate of his friend. Thus, he cannot so easily escape the constraint of the law of inheritance. Moreover, this constraint is imposed by the law. Were he not required by law to settle all outstanding claims against the estate, he might feel free, even under an obligation, to maximize the inheritances of the wife and children of his close friend, whose will he is executing. But how does the law of inheritance bind or constrain the executor of the will? He may be exposed to informal social pressures to fulfill the institutional expectations of his legally defined social role as executor of the will. He has moral reasons to execute the will faithfully to the friend who has entrusted him with this charge and in justice to all claims against the estate. There are, then, a few absolute legal duties. Still, most legal duties are, as Hohfeld thought, duties to some second party.

Legal Claims

Although Hohfeld used the expression "a right" as the logical correlative of "a duty," I prefer his suggested alternative "a claim."

> In other words, if X has a right against Y that he shall stay off the former's land, the correlative (and equivalent) is that Y is under a duty toward X to stay off the place. If, as seems desirable, we should seek a synonym for the term "right" in this limited and proper meaning, perhaps the word "claim" would prove the best. [Hohfeld, 1919, 38]

Hohfeld's language reflects his conclusion that a legal right is a single legal claim. Since I shall argue that a legal right is a complex structure, I need language that will distinguish between the complex right and the elements out of which it is constructed. Even if my own theory of rights is mistaken, there are a number of very different ways in which Hohfeld's fundamental legal conceptions can and have been used in theories of legal rights. If we use the expression "a claim" to refer to the Hohfeldian conception, we can leave open the controversial issue of just how, if at all, legal claims are related to legal rights.

Hohfeld hints at his conception of a legal claim in two footnotes (1919, 38 and 71-72) in which he cites Mr. Justice Stayton. The fuller citation, with Hohfeld's italics, is as follows:

> "*A right* has been well defined to be a well-founded claim, and *a well-founded claim* means nothing more nor less than *a claim recognized or secured by law.*
>
> "Rights which pertain to persons, other than such as are termed natural rights, are essentially the creatures of municipal law, written or unwritten, and it must necessarily be held that a right, in a legal sense, exists, when in consequence of given facts the law declares that one person is entitled to enforce against another a claim . . ."

Presumably a legal claim is logically correlative with a legal duty because what the claimant is entitled to enforce is a corresponding legal duty, and the claimant is presumed to be entitled to enforce this duty by bringing suit against the duty-bearer in the courts.

Unfortunately, this conception of a legal claim does not fully establish the logical correlativity of claims against and duties to, at least not if one holds, as I do, that the criminal law imposes duties to the state. This correlativity would hold good between claims against and duties to, under private or civil law, for the claimant's power to sue for performance or remedy is the power to initiate court action to constrain the duty-bearer in the specified manner. But although the subject has duties to the state under the criminal law, it is unidiomatic to say that the state has any legal claim against the subject or that it has the power to take legal action against any subject alleged to have committed a crime. Nor is this limitation on the proper usage of expressions such as "a claim" or "taking legal action" merely a matter of the idiom of ordinary legal language. It reflects the very important differences between suing for performance or remedy and prosecuting for an offence. Nevertheless, I propose to extend the meaning of "a claim" so that it will apply to criminal as well as civil law. In this way, the logical correlativity of duties to and claims against can be preserved completely. Whether this deviation from ordinary language is illuminating or misleading depends upon just what is at stake in our established usage.

The meaning of the noun "a claim" was originally derived from, and hence remains tied to, the meaning of the verb "to claim." To have a claim is to be in a position to claim. According to both *Black's Law Dictionary* and the *Oxford English Dictionary* (hereafter, OED), the primary meaning of "to claim" is "to demand as one's own." Paradigms of claiming would be reclaiming a coat one has checked, demanding the return of a stolen car, insisting on receiving one's rightful inheritance and demanding possession of a house to which one holds title. In such paradigm cases, what one is demanding is possession of one's property and one's demand is grounded in, or allegedly grounded in, one's title to that thing. To claim legally is to petition a court of law to adjudicate between one's own demand for something and competing demands for the possession of the same thing. For example, Jones sues a disreputable television dealer for possession of an expensive color TV allegedly stolen from his home a few weeks ago, while the defendant insists that the television set at issue is rightfully his, not Jones', because he purchased it directly from the RCA wholesaler.

Although the paradigm of legal claiming is suing for possession grounded in the plaintiff's alleged title, it is a natural extension of this concept to make it apply to every sort of law suit. After all, the plaintiff is always demanding something in taking legal action, whether it be the performance of a legal duty or remedy for nonperformance or merely a declaratory judgment. And the plaintiff necessarily alleges that he or she is entitled to have the court intervene and enforce his or her demand in face of the competing demand of the defendant. Since civil proceedings are by their very nature adversarial, in deciding any law suit the court is adjudicating between competing demands, not necessarily for the possession of the same object, but concerning the same thing. The established usage of "a claim" in our legal language reflects this broader conception of claiming defined by the OED as "to seek or ask for on ground of right." The plaintiff is petitioning the court for something or other on the grounds of his or her alleged legal entitlement. According to established usage, therefore, to have a legal claim is simply to have the law on one's side in the event that one sues for performance or remedy.

Our legal language refuses, however, to extend the language of claiming to the criminal law. The state does not sue in the courts for punishment or take legal action against the alleged criminal; it indicts the defendant and prosecutes for an alleged criminal offence. There is nothing wrong with this established usage. It is quite appropriate that private law should have its special terminology. Nevertheless, I propose to extend the meaning of the technical term "a claim" so that it is applicable to criminal as well as private law. Whether this proposed extension will be helpful in formulating a theory of legal rights will depend upon whether it illuminates essential similarities or obscures fundamental differences. Since Hohfeld's conceptions refer to legal positions, the crucial question is whether the legal position of a public prosecutor acting for the state is strictly analogous to the legal position of a private claimant.

There are, I believe, very fundamental similarities between the legal positions of the public prosecutor and the private claimant. (1) Both possess a special standing conferred upon them by law. Not everyone can sue for the possession of some item of property; only the party with a plausible title to own it is in this position. Not everyone can prosecute an alleged criminal. Typically, although not always, even the victim can do little more than complain to the district attorney. The state almost always reserves to itself alone, acting through its public prosecutor, the standing to demand punishment in the criminal courts. (2) This special standing of both consists in having a very special sort of legal power, the power to initiate and carry forward proceedings in a court of law. Although it is unidiomatic to say that the public prosecutor has the power to initiate an action, the nature of the prosecutor's legal power is very like that of the private claimant's. (3) In both instances, the court proceedings are taken against some alleged duty-bearer. The defendant in a criminal prosecution, like the defendant in a suit for remedy, is alleged to have failed to act as the law requires. (4) Both prosecutor and claimant are petitioning the court for roughly the same sort of judgment, a judgment that will lend the weight of the law to one's demand against the defendant by enforcing the legal duty at issue in the case. Finally, (5) both public prosecutor and private claimant are in a position to succeed in court only if their demands have some legally recognized ground. A suit for the possession of property must be grounded in some legal title. Other sorts of suits prevail in court only if the plaintiff can establish some sort of individual entitlement to performance or remedy under the law. The prosecutor does not, of course, allege either title to ownership or individual entitlement, but he does allege that in demanding punishment for an offence he is exercising the sovereign's prerogative. Whether the state may properly be said to have a right to punishment of the criminal is a more complicated question that should be left open for the moment, but at least the prosecutor is like the claimant in needing and having a legally recognized ground for his or her demand. I propose that we mark these very important similarities by saying that the state has a legal claim to obedience or punishment under the criminal law.

At the same time, we must be careful not to ignore some important differences between the public prosecutor and the private claimant. (1) While the prosecutor usually has a legal duty to indict whenever he or she comes into possession of sufficient evidence of a criminal offence, a claimant seldom if ever has any duty to sue for performance or remedy. The party who has a legally valid claim remains at liberty to take court action or refrain from doing so as he or she wishes. Indeed, a claimant can usually, although not always, waive his or her claim and thus extinguish the correlative legal duty. Since the prosecutor holds public office and it is presumed that it is in the public interest to enforce the criminal law, the prosecutor is taken to have a legal duty to prosecute whenever he can do so with a reasonable prospect of success. Still, there remains considerable discretion because of the difficulty of assessing the strength of the evidence in hand and the prospects of prevailing in court. The fact that the power to prosecute is grounded in the sovereign's prerogative, at least in Anglo-American law, also attenuates the official duty to prosecute. And although no prosecutor can waive performance of any criminal duty, the state can always extinguish a criminal duty by repealing the statute that makes that act an offence and can extend reprieve, parole or even pardon to any convicted criminal. (2) The prosecutor is not one of several competing claimants for the same object. The paradigm of a private suit is petitioning a court to adjudicate between competing demands for the same property. Asking a court to impose punishment for an alleged offence is a very different thing. True enough. But not every private proceeding involves the adjudication of competing demands for possession. The established extension of the language of claiming beyond demands for possession already applies it to other sorts of private suits. Like legal actions demanding performance or remedy, criminal prosecutions are adversarial proceedings in which the court is asked to side with one party, the state, vis-à-vis the defendant. (3) While the claimant paradigmatically is demanding possession of his or her property, the prosecutor surely does not want to possess or experience the punishment he or she is demanding. Once more, however, the concept of a legal claim has already been extended to apply to civil suits in which the claimant is demanding performance or remedy rather than the possession of something as his or her own. And perhaps it may properly be said that the state is demanding to have something, satisfaction from the criminal. Historically the institution of criminal punishment can probably be traced back to the injured party's demand for revenge or retaliation. In the interest of public order and justice, the state now reserves to itself the prerogative of punishing, at least by the use of serious force, offences against the law. With this change, it may not be a figure of speech to say that the state now seeks to have the retaliation or satisfaction that private individuals used to demand for themselves. I do not wish to deny these important differences between private suits and criminal prosecutions. I do suggest that they are not so radical as to render illegitimate the extension of the language of claiming from private to criminal law.

I propose, therefore, the following definition of a legal claim: X has a legal claim against Y that Y do or forbear from doing some act A if and only if Y has a legal duty to do or forbear from doing A and X has a legal power to sue for performance or remedy in the event of threatened or actual nonperformance by Y or a legal power to prosecute Y for nonperformance. Thus defined, a legal claim is logically correlative with a corresponding relative duty to the claimant. We can, and doubtless should, remind ourselves of the differences between private and criminal law by using modifiers to distinguish between a private claim and a criminal claim under the law.

Legal Liberties

Just as a claim is the logical correlative of a duty in Hohfeld's conceptual scheme, so a privilege is the logical opposite of a legal duty.

> In the example last put, whereas X [the landowner] has a *right* or *claim* that Y, the other man, should stay off the land, he himself has the *privilege* of entering on the land; or, in equivalent words, X does not have a duty to stay off. As indicated by this case, some caution is necessary at this point; for, always, when it is said that a given privilege is the mere negation of a *duty*, what is meant, of course, is a duty having a content or tenor precisely *opposite* to that of the privilege in question. [Hohfeld, 1919, 39]

Let me begin by parting company from Hohfeld in a merely terminological way. From this point on, I shall use the expression "a liberty" where he uses "a privilege." This linguistic change does not signal any conceptual departure and can even claim Hohfeld's blessing, for he recognized the synonymy of the two terms. I prefer the label "a liberty" for several reasons. The expression "a privilege" is standardly used in the literature in several ways that are radically different from that intended by Hohfeld. Since it has proven exceedingly difficult to free the expression from these unintended meanings, clarity of expression suggests that we use a different expression to mark the conception Hohfeld had in mind. Also, since some of these other meanings are of considerable theoretical importance, it will be useful to reserve the expression "a privilege" to refer to them. Finally, the term "a liberty" will be more readily and accurately understood by contemporary philosophers and jurists, because it has almost everywhere replaced "a privilege" even in the writings of those who utilize Hohfeld's conceptual scheme.

Now on to more substantive differences. Hohfeld's conception of a legal liberty is essentially relational; every liberty under the law is a liberty of one party *against* some second party. This follows immediately from his conception of a legal liberty as the logical opposite of a contrary legal duty and his presupposition that every legal duty is necessarily a duty *to* some second party. I have argued, however, that the conception of a legal duty is not essentially relational and that in fact a few absolute legal duties do exist. Accordingly, I must distinguish between relative and absolute liberties under the law.

Following Hohfeld, one can best define a relative legal liberty as the absence of a contrary relative legal duty. Thus, X has a legal liberty in face of Y to do some kind of act A if and only if X does not have a legal duty to Y not to do A. To be general enough to cover all relative liberties this definition must be interpreted so as to apply to forbearances as well as performances; that is, one can be said to have a legal liberty to remain silent (not speak out) in precisely the same sense one can be said to have a legal liberty to speak out on some controversial issue. One can, of course, have a legal liberty in face of one party that one lacks in face of another. Typically, one has a legal liberty in face of Jones, but not in face of Smith, to enter on Smith's land because it is only to the owner of the land that one usually owes a duty not to trespass.

Just as it is sometimes useful to speak of claims holding against the world, so it will be useful to introduce the conception of a liberty against the world. X has a legal liberty against the world to do some kind of act A if and only if there is no second party to whom X has a legal duty not to do A. Assuming that I have not contracted with my employer, or anyone else, to maintain a particular kind of appearance, I have a legal liberty against the world of shaving my head bald as a billiard ball. This is to say that I lie under no legal duty to the state, any other individual or any private organization not to do so.

One may have a legal liberty against the world, however, without having an absolute legal liberty to do something. For example, a state judge has a legal liberty against the world to decide cases that come before him or her contrary to federal law simply because the judge does not have a legal duty *to* any second party to decide in accordance with federal law. But since the state judge is legally bound by article VI, section 2, of the United States *Constitution,* it would not be correct to say that the judge is absolutely or completely at liberty under the law to decide contrary to federal law. Presumably the state judge does, however, have an absolute legal liberty of discreetly scratching an itching ear during a trial. X has a legal liberty *(tout court)* to do some kind of act A if and only if X has no legal duty (either relative or absolute) not to do A. Since the concept of a legal duty is not *per se* relative, the concept of a legal liberty in and of itself is that of an absolute liberty rather than that of a liberty in face of one or more second parties.

Hohfeld conceives of a legal liberty as the mere absence of a contrary legal duty. It is sometimes objected that a legal liberty, thus conceived, is not a legal position. If the silence of the law, the mere absence of a legal prohibition, can leave one at liberty to do something, this shows that liberty is something prelegal and, indeed, extralegal. A legal liberty is not a *legal* position, a position under the law, at all; it is a position outside of or unregulated by the law. To this objection, Hohfeld responds:

> Perhaps the habit of recognizing exclusively the latter [the right-duty relation] as a jural relation springs more or less from the traditional tendency to think of the law as consisting of "commands" or imperative rules. This, however, seems fallacious. A rule of law that *permits* is just as real as a rule of law that *forbids;* and, similarly, saying that the law *permits* a given act to X as between himself and Y predicates just as genuine a legal relation as saying that the law *forbids* a certain act to X as between himself and Y. That this is so seems, in some measure, to be confirmed by the fact that the first sort of act would ordinarily be pronounced "lawful," and the second "unlawful." [Hohfeld, 1919, 48]

As far as it goes, this response is quite correct. The tendency to deny that a legal liberty is a position under the law does spring in part from an overly narrow conception of the law. And to be in a position to do something "lawfully" is to be in a position to do that act "within the limits of the law." Disregarding the spacial metaphor, which may be misleading, let us return to literal language for a moment. To speak of one's legal position under the law is to speak of the way in which the law applies to the conduct of someone subject to the law. Now to judge that the law does not forbid X to do A is to apply the law to X and to judge that the law in fact permits X to do A.

But there is more to be said, as Glanville Williams points out.

> When a person has a substantive defense in law to an action or prosecution, that is to say a legal defense on the merits, he has a liberty, *i.e.,* the conduct of which complaint is made is not a breach of duty. This is not necessarily true of a merely procedural or adjectival defense. The defense under statutes of limitation, for example, generally does not deny the duty, but alleges that the duty has become unenforceable through lapse of time. [Williams, 1956, 1129]

In other words, to have a legal liberty is not merely to be in a position to which the law does not apply; it is to have a position that is legally recognized in the law as a defense.

Legal Powers

Although Hohfeld's conceptions of a legal claim, a legal no-claim and a legal liberty can be defined in terms of legal duties, the other four fundamental legal conceptions seem to be logically independent of any of these. However, a legal liability, a legal immunity and a legal disability can be easily defined in terms of a legal power. How, then, shall we define a legal power? Hohfeld, of course, refuses to define this conception, but he does offer "an approximate explanation" of it. Read in the light of his entire discussion of legal powers, it can be summarized as follows: A legal power of X over Y is an ability, legal not mental or physical, of X to change some legal relation of Y by some voluntary act of bringing into existence one or more operative facts. Let us examine this explanation in detail to see whether it is sufficient, not just for all practical purposes, but also for our theoretical purposes.

(1) Every legal power, as conceived by Hohfeld, is necessarily a power of X over Y. He makes it clear that the conception of a power falls within his scheme of jural relations and that every fundamental jural relation holds between two and only two distinct natural persons under the law. Having decided that his conceptions really refer to legal positions and that a legal position need not be relational, we are free to question his way of conceiving a legal power.

To begin with, X and Y need not be distinct persons; any X has many legal powers over X. Indeed, Hohfeld virtually recognized this in his very first example of a legal power:

> Many examples of legal powers may readily be given. Thus X, the owner of ordinary personal property "in a tangible object" has the power to extinguish his own legal interest (rights, powers, immunities, etc.) through the totality of operative facts known as abandonment . . . [Hohfeld, 1919, 51]

That the exercise of this legal power simultaneously confers upon others a legal power to acquire title by taking possession does nothing to show that this is not a legal power of the owner over himself or herself.

Not only was Hohfeld mistaken in assuming that a legal power necessarily relates two distinct persons; he was also in error in holding that every fundamental legal power relates only two persons. He was well aware, of course, that one may have legal powers over several other persons. For example, the owner of Blackacre has the legal power of giving the couple next door door permission to walk across his land at will. This is a legal power of X, the owner, over Y and Z, the husband and wife who live next to his land. But Hohfeld denies that any such complex legal power is a fundamental one, for all can be analyzed into simpler legal powers of one party over one and only one other party. In this example, the owner's legal power really consists in his power to give the husband permission to enter on his land together with his legal power to give the wife permission to enter on his land. No doubt many, probably most, complex legal powers can be analyzed in this manner, but there are others that are not mere aggregates of logically distinguishable powers of one person over one and only one other person. For example, X, who is Y's banker, typically has the legal power of paying Y's debt to Z by transferring, upon receipt of the written order of Y (Y's check properly made out and endorsed by Z), funds from Y's bank account to Z's bank account. This cannot, even on Hohfeld's own terms, be analyzed into two logically distinct legal powers of extinguishing Y's legal duty to repay Z and of extinguishing Z's legal claim to repayment against Y because these two are logically correlative; they are one and the same jural relation viewed from the legal positions at the two ends of the duty-claim relation. Similarly, X has the legal power to discharge Y's debt to Z provided that Z accepts payment from X as a satisfactory settlement of his or her legal claim against Y. Once more, this legal power of X over both Y and Z cannot be broken down into two logically distinct and legally separable legal powers, one of X over Y and the other of X over Z.

A special case of a legal power of one party over two parties is a legal power of X over X and Y. An excellent example is provided by Hohfeld.

> Passing now to the field of contracts, suppose A mails a letter to B offering to sell the former's land, Whiteacre, to the latter for ten thousand dollars, such letter being duly received. The operative facts thus far mentioned have created a power as regards B and a correlative liability as regards A. [Hohfeld, 1919, 55]

As before, this legal power of A cannot be broken down into two separate powers, the power of creating a power of B to accept the offer, and thereby a contractual claim against A, and the power of creating a liability of A to acquire a contractual obligation to sell to B, for these two descriptions of the situation are logically equivalent. Notice also how such irreducibly complex legal powers must be parsed. In this instance, the owner's legal power is not a power to create one and the same legal position for A and B; it is a legal power of creating one legal position, a liability, for A and another legal position, a power, for B. But since these legal positions are logically correlative, the legal power cannot be analyzed into two distinct legal powers. We must conclude, then, that a legal power does not necessarily relate two and only two persons under the law. In addition to fundamental legal powers of X over Y, there are legal powers of X over X, of X over X and Y, and of X over Y and Z.

(2) Hohfeld conceives of a legal power as an ability conferred by law. He writes "The nearest synonym for any ordinary case seems to be (legal) 'ability,' " and cites *Remington V. Parkins:* "A power is an ability to do" (1919, 51). Thus, to have a legal power is to be able to do something under the law, and that something is to effect legal consequences of some sort. Just as physical proximity may put one person in a position where he or she is able to touch another, so the law of property puts an owner in a legal position where he or she is able to sell an item of personal property to a willing buyer. Exercising this legal power has the legal consequence of transferring legal title from the seller to the buyer.

Hohfeld is entirely correct in insisting that a legal power is fundamentally distinct from a legal duty or a legal liberty. One who has a legal duty is constrained by the law; one who has a legal power is enabled by the law. One who is constrained by the law is bound, figuratively speaking, to act in one manner rather than in another when choosing among available options. One who is enabled by the law is given a new option by the law; the law puts that person in a position to do something he or she could not do without the law. Without any property law, no one, no matter how powerful in the nonlegal sense, would be able to convey *legal* title from seller to buyer.

A legal liberty is like a legal power in that it can be exercised by acting in some specified manner. And neither consists, like a legal duty, in being legally constrained so to act. But a legal liberty can be defined in terms of a legal duty; to have a legal liberty is to be free from a contrary legal duty. But to have a legal power is not simply to be unconstrained by the law; it is to be enabled by the law. While the concept of a legal liberty is essentially negative, so that one can be at liberty to do something simply because no legislation applies to one, the concept of a legal power is positive, so that one can have a legal power only when some law confers a legal ability upon one.

One has a legal power, according to Hohfeld, whenever one is legally in a position to bring about some legal consequence by one's voluntary action. To practicing lawyers and most philosophers of law, however, this conception unduly stretches the meaning of the expression "a legal power." They find strange and misleading Corbin's assertion that "A has the legal power, by assaulting B, of creating a secondary right to damages in B" (Corbin, 1919, 169). MacCormick gives us an equally illuminating example from criminal law.

W. H. Davies's "Super-Tramp" always committed offences in early winter in a town with a tolerably comfortable jail. The point of doing so was to get convicted and imprisoned. The end which this served was his survival and reasonable comfort during the harsh North American winter. This illustrates well the truth that not every way of acting in knowledge of the law and with a view to making the law's provisions serve one's ends can be viewed as an exercise of legal power. [MacCormick, 1981, 75]

In this passage, MacCormick recognizes, but overstates, an important truth.

One *can* view the Super-Tramp's act of committing a crime as an exercise of a legal power, for the criminal law *does* confer upon him the ability thereby to render himself liable to prosecution and conviction. Thus, to conceive of legal powers as Hohfeld does is to conceptualize a genuine legal position of both theoretical and practical importance. Nevertheless, it is more illuminating to restrict the concept of a legal power to a narrower range of legal abilities. Why? Because to conceive of the Super-Tramp's legal ability to render himself liable to prosecution as essentially similar to the district attorney's legal power to prosecute is to overlook a fundamental difference between their positions under the law.

Any adequate legal theory must distinguish between an ability to do an act that *does bring* about specific legal consequences and an ability to do an act *of bringing* about these legal consequences. Not every act that has legal effects is an act of effecting legal consequences. In the exercise of a legal power, some specific legal consequences are internal to one's action, essential to its very nature; in the exercise of other sorts of legal abilities, the legal consequences are external to one's action, accidental to its intrinsic nature. The OED defines "power" as "ability to do or effect something or anything." Since the concept of a voluntary action is an intentional concept, the concept of a power to effect legal consequences by one's action is, strictly speaking, an intentional one also. Accordingly, any legal theory adequate to formulate both Hohfeld's insights and those of his critics will need two distinct, but related, concepts: that of a legal ability in the most general sense and that of a legal power in the strict sense. Whenever the law attaches legal consequences to some specified act, it confers upon anyone in a position to do that act a legal ability to effect those legal consequences. But only when the law attaches legal consequences to an act intending those consequences does the law confer upon anyone in a position to do that act with that intention a legal power to effect such consequences. In short, it is essential to the concept of a legal power in the strict sense that the legal efficacy of its exercise depends upon the intention of effecting specific legal consequences.

This tentative formulation of my conclusion is, however, not quite accurate. It requires qualification in two ways. For one thing, the efficacy of an exercise of a legal power is not contingent upon the actual intention of the power-holder. Suppose that I purchase a new car and sign, without reading the fine print, a loan agreement giving the automobile dealer the right to repossess my car in the event that I am more than ten days late in making any monthly payment on the loan. What matters, legally speaking, is not whether I intended to confer this right upon the dealer but whether this is the reasonable and probable interpretation of my intention. Thus, the efficacy of the exercise of a legal power is dependent, not upon the actual intention of the exerciser, but upon the legally imputed intention. For another thing, the imputed intention need not be specific in every detail. Typically the law attaches a variety of precisely defined legal consequences to the exercise of a legal power. Given the complexity of ownership in the law and of the legal precedents refining the definition of property rights, the law cannot reasonably impute to any seller, buyer, leaser or giver the intention of bringing about each and every legal consequence of an act of selling, buying, leasing or giving. The imputed intention is accordingly the intention of effecting some such consequences. What is required for the efficacy of a legal power is the imputation of some rough knowledge of the legal consequences attached to one's action and the intention of effecting something like those consequences.

Why does my distinction between a legal ability and a legal power matter? Why is it important to restrict the concept of a legal power in the way I propose? It is not simply a matter of remaining faithful to the established usage of the expression in ordinary legal language. The conception I propose makes the term "a legal power" applicable in contexts to which established usage does not, and it is entirely legitimate for a philosopher of law to depart from ordinary language in defining a term for theoretical purposes. What is important is that one have available a conceptual distinction, that between a legal power in the strict sense and a legal ability in the more general sense, to mark a difference *in* the law: the difference between making the legal consequences of an act conditional upon the imputed intention of effecting them and attaching legal consequences to an act without requiring any such condition. Accordingly, the conceptual distinction also marks a difference between the legal positions of those acting under the law, the distinction between being able to effect specific legal consequences only if one acts in such a way that one's act will have the required imputed intention and being able to effect specific legal consequences without having any such intention imputed to one's action. Finally, the conceptual distinction marks the difference between those acts where the issue of legal validity can arise and those where it cannot. Super-Tramp might try but fail to commit a crime or commit a crime but fail to get convicted and imprisoned, but no judge could possibly declare his act null and void. Why not? Since the issue of legal validity is the issue of whether the law gives legal effect to the act in the sense of recognizing its intended legal consequences, this issue can arise only in the case of acts-in-the-law, acts defined in terms of an intention of effecting some such legal consequences.

(3) Hohfeld insists that a legal power must not be confused with any sort of mental or physical ability. Thus, the connotation of the word "power" is fundamentally different when one says that an invalid still has the physical power of signing his or her will and when one says that the invalid retains his or her "legal power" to make a will. What, then, is the connotation of this latter term? Hohfeld's "approximate explanation" fails to make it clear precisely how it refers to a purely legal ability.

> A change in a given legal relation may result (1) from some superadded fact or group of facts not under the volitional control of a human being (or human beings); or (2) from some superadded fact or group of facts which are under the volitional control of one or more human beings. As regards the second class of cases, the person (or persons) whose volitional control is paramount may be said to have the (legal) power to effect the particular change of legal relations that is involved in the problem. [Hohfeld, 1919, 50-51]

What *kind* of superadded facts does Hohfeld have in mind in his explanation of a legal power? He has told us that "The facts important in relation to a given jural transaction may be either *operative* facts or *evidential* facts" (1919, 32). Presumably we should conceive of a purely legal power in terms of operative facts, for evidential facts are legally relevant only insofar as they establish or help to establish the operative facts of the case. What kind of operative facts, then, are at issue in any exercise of a legal power? Always, and necessarily, the performance of a specified act by a party with the required competence in a specified situation. The notion of volition enters into the conception of a legal power because the concept of acting is a volitional one and acting is essential to the exercise of any legal power. Hohfeld hardly makes this clear by speaking of "some superadded fact or group of facts which are under the volitional control of one or more human beings." Let us replace his notion of control over operative facts with the notion that among the operative facts is a human act.

This way of conceiving of a legal power makes it far more clear just how a legal power is distinguished from a mental or physical power. Consider the act of executing a legally valid will. Robinson Crusoe might lack the physical ability to execute a will because he has nothing on which to write or no implement with which to record his last testament or because he has fallen and become paralyzed. Someone who has suffered a sharp blow on the head might lack the psychological ability to execute a will because he or she has forgotten how to sign his or her name or become too confused to articulate clearly. But all of this is irrelevant to the legal ability to execute a will. To say that someone has a legal ability to execute a will is to say that *if* that person *were* to perform a specified act in a specified situation (and with the necessary imputed intention), then that act *would* bring into existence a legally valid will. A legal power is a legal position, a position of someone under the law. Thus, the concept of a legal power refers to the way in which the law applies to some conceivable human action. Whether the party has the mental or physical ability to act in the legally specified manner is a different matter.

(4) According to Hohfeld's explanation, a legal power is taken to be an ability to change one or more legal relations. And to change legal relations is "either to create a new relation, or to extinguish an old one, or to perform both functions simultaneously" (1919, 32). For example, when X makes an offer to Y, X thereby creates in Y a power of imposing a contractual obligation upon X by acceptance and simultaneously extinguishes Y's disability of so doing. When and if Y accepts X's offer, Y creates a contractual duty of X and simultaneously extinguishes X's previous liberty not to perform the action he now has a legal duty to perform. If, however, X withdraws or revokes the offer before it is accepted, X thereby extinguishes the liability of X previously created by the offer and replaces it with an immunity against Y's imposing upon him the contractual obligation involved in this case. As Hohfeld conceives of a legal power, its exercise always changes a legal relation in the sense of replacing a preexisting legal relation with its jural opposite.

Indeed, it seems logically necessary that this should be so. To effect some legal relation must be to bring into existence a legal relation that did not exist before. For if the exercise of a legal power did not effect some new relation, it would not have any legal consequences at all. And since every legal relation has its logical opposite, one but only one of which must apply to any given person under the law, to create a new legal relation must logically, it would seem, be simultaneously to extinguish an old relation of the opposite sort.

I believe, however, that a legal power need not involve the ability to change legal relations in this way. When a miner or homesteader stakes his or her claim, he or she creates a legal claim to a parcel of land he or she did not have before and simultaneously extinguishes his or her preexisting no-claim to acquire ownership of this land. But when he or she works the land in order not to lose that claim, he or she is not creating a new legal relation, but exercising a legal ability to sustain a preexisting claim. Again, when I periodically exercise my legal power of renewing my driver's license, I am effecting the continuation of my legal liberty of operating a motor vehicle upon the public roads and highways, not replacing my old legal liberty with some new and opposite legal relation. Finally, when the statute of limitations runs out, the debtor's legal duty of repayment to the creditor and the creditor's legal claim against the debtor to repayment terminate. But the debtor has the legal power to extend these preexisting legal relations by acknowledging his debt to the creditor. An act preventing a legal relation from lapsing or terminating is as much the exercise of a legal power as creating a new legal relation or extinguishing an old one.

There may be some sense in which exercising a legal power is necessarily to effect a legal change. The exercise must make some difference in or under the law; the act of exercising the legal power must have some legal consequence that would not have existed had that act not been performed. But this need not be to effect a change in the sense of exchanging one legal relation with its opposite. One need not introduce the notion of legal change into one's conception of a legal power at all. Hohfeld's "power to effect the particular change of legal relations" can and should be simplified to read simply "power to effect the particular legal relations."

(5) Hohfeld assumes that the only results one can effect by the exercise of a legal power are legal relations. This may be simply because he has chosen as his universe of discourse, the subject of his two articles, conceptions of legal positions. We have seen, however, that not every legal position is a legal relation. There are, for example, absolute legal duties that are not owed to any second party under the law. At the very least, then, we must generalize Hohfeld's legal relations to legal positions.

Are there any legal consequences of human action that do not consist in a position of some person subject to the law? Joseph Raz suggests that a legal change may consist in the creation or liquidation of a legal person (1972, 81). The obvious example is the legal power of a group of individuals to form a corporation. Although the exercise of this power no doubt changes the legal positions of those who make up the corporation, it also brings into existence a new person under the law. Again, when I enter a foreign country on a tourist visa, I do not so much change my legal position under its law as add one more person to those who are subject to the law of the land. And if I decide to extinguish my overly burdensome duties by committing suicide, I do not simply terminate the many ways in which the law applies to me; I also liquidate a legal person.

There can also be changes in the law that applies to those who have positions under it. When Congress exercises its legal powers of enacting or repealing a federal statute, its act has legal consequences. Although its legislative action indirectly changes the legal positions of those subject to United States law, what is directly and essentially effected is a change within the law itself. Other legal powers that do not quite fit Hohfeld's conception are the power of an individual to execute a legally valid will and the power of a notary public to certify to the authenticity of a legal document. Accordingly, we must move from Hohfeld's limited conception of power to effect legal relations to the more general conception of a power to effect legal consequences. Fortunately, we can postpone to another occasion the question of exactly how many kinds of legal consequences there can conceivably be.

(6) Hohfeld explains a legal power as a purely legal ability to change someone's legal relation by one's voluntary act. He is entirely correct to conceive of a legal power in terms of human action, for to possess a legal power is to be in a position to do something, to effect legal consequences. Thus, the concept of a legal power and the concept of its exercise are logically connected.

Hohfeld does not, however, see clearly just how the act of exercise enters into the concept of a legal power. He explains that "a change in a given legal relation may result . . . from some superadded fact or group of facts which are under the volitional control of one or more human beings" (1919, 51-51). This suggests that the act of exercise is an acting on or manipulation of the operative facts. Presumably he has in mind something like signing a formal contract or executing a valid will. Such acts of creating legally valid documents, however, are a very special case of exercising legal powers; and even here the document is legally relevant as evidence of a legally specified form of an act of contracting or bequeathing. It is not so much that one acts on the operative facts, but that one's act is among the operative facts when one exercises a legal power.

Thus, the concept of human volition enters into the concept of a legal power by being implicit in the concept of an act of exercising that power. To have a legal power is to be enabled by the law to do something that will effect legal consequences, to act with legal effect. Coming of age, becoming senile or dying brings about legal consequences. But these are not exercises of legal powers, or even abilities, for these are not human actions. These are things that happen to one, not things one does. Only a volitional act is an action in the full legal, as in the full moral, sense.

(7) How does the act of exercising a legal power bring about a legal consequence? The act of abandoning a tangible object, for example, effects legal consequences by being among the totality of operative facts known as abandonment. How, then, do operative facts operate in the law?

> Operative, constitutive, causal, or dispositive facts are those which, under the general legal rules that are applicable, suffice to change legal relations, that is, either to create a new relation, or to extinguish an old one, or to perform both of these functions simultaneously. [Hohfeld, 1919, 32]

This account is both obscure and misleading. It leaves obscure just how the application of general legal rules can render operative facts sufficient to change legal relations. It misleads by suggesting that some mysterious sort of legal causation is operating here.

Actually, operative facts are constitutive rather than causal. They constitute the conditions for the application of a legal norm. They have legal consequences in the logical rather than the causal sense of the ambiguous word "consequences." The statement that the possessor of a legal power has acted in the legally specified way implies some legal consequence. Not all by itself, of course; additional premises are required. There must be factual statements about the possessor of the legal power to establish his or her legal competence. Additional facts about the circumstances in which the act was performed are essential to the inference. And the applicable legal norms must be presupposed. For example, "Jones gave Smith permission to enter upon Blackacre at will" implies "Smith has a legal liberty of entering upon Blackacre at will," given *something like* the following additional premises: "Jones is of age, of sound mind, and the owner of Blackacre"; "Jones had not been coerced or deceived into giving permission to Smith"; and (the applicable legal norm) "if the owner of land, being of age and sound mind, gives legal permission for some second party to enter on the land under circumstances where no duress or fraud are present, then the legal duty of that second party not to trespass is extinguished and that party has a legal liberty to enter upon the land." No doubt the complexity of the law complicates actual legal reasoning far more than my example suggests. But it remains true that an operative fact, including the fact of exercising a legal power, effects legal consequences by implying them logically. This explains why operative facts "suffice to change legal relations" only "under the general legal rules that are applicable." Operative facts imply legal consequences together with the applicable law and the relevant facts about the preexisting situation to which the law is applied.

We have now examined critically all seven aspects of Hohfeld's approximate explanation of his conception of a legal power. Let me now sum up my conclusions. Any adequate theory must distinguish between a legal ability in the general sense recognized by Hohfeld and a legal power in a stricter sense he failed to note. X has a legal *ability* to effect some specific legal consequence C if and only if some specified act of X implies C, given the background facts about X and the circumstances of the act together with the applicable law. X has a legal *power* to effect some specified legal consequence C if and only if X has a legal ability to do so and this legal ability is contingent upon X's legally imputed intention of effecting some such legal consequences. It will also be theoretically useful to note that many legal powers are relative and that complex relative powers must be parsed in a certain manner. Thus, a legal power of X over Y is a legal ability of X to effect one or more specific legal positions of Y by performing a specified act that implies these legal consequences, provided it is done with the legally imputed intention of effecting some such consequences. Finally, a legal power of X over Y and Z is a legal ability of X to effect one or more specific legal positions of Y and one or more specific legal positions of Z by performing a specified act that implies these legal consequences, provided it is done with the legally imputed intention of effecting some such consequences.

Legal Immunities

Hohfeld explains his conception of a legal immunity in a single passage.

> Perhaps it will also be plain, from the preliminary outline and from the discussion down to this point, that a power bears the same general contrast to an immunity that a right does to a privilege. A right is one's affirmative claim against another, and a privilege is one's freedom from the right or claim of another. Similarly, a power is one's affirmative "control" over a given legal relation as against another; whereas an immunity is one's freedom from the legal power or "control" of another as regards some legal relation. [Hohfeld, 1919, 60)]

Thus, Hohfeld implicitly defines a legal immunity of X in terms of the absence of a legal power of Y.

Having argued for a distinction between legal powers in the strict sense and legal abilities in a more general sense, I can capture Hohfeld's meaning only by defining a legal immunity as some second party's lack of a legal ability. On my view, one party X has a legal immunity against some second party Y from some specific legal consequence C if and only if Y lacks the legal ability to do any action whatsoever that would imply the consequence C for X. While this conception defines a legal immunity in terms of the lack of a legal ability in the most general sense, it restricts the relevant legal consequences to those which are consequences for the possessor of the immunity, that is to say, it restricts them to legal positions.

One could, if one wished, introduce a narrower conception of the same sort defined as the absence of a legal power of some second party. I shall not bother to do so, however, for I doubt that very much would be gained thereby. The practical importance of possessing an immunity is the safety it confers upon one's legal position. As Corbin remarks, "A, knowing that he has a certain immunity, can answer this question, 'Which one of my existing legal relations is safe from alteration by B?' " (1919, 170). The fact that B lacks a legal power in the strict sense to effect some legal position of A would not ensure safety from that position if B did possess a legal ability in the more general sense to effect this legal consequence for A. Also, the crux of the distinction between a legal power and a legal ability is the difference between the acts of exercising them. Although this difference is of the essence for the legal position of the party whose action constitutes that exercise, it does not seem essential to the legal position of the patient of any such action.

Revised Logic

Although Hohfeld claims to have identified eight fundamental (simple and irreducible) legal conceptions, his tables of jural opposites and jural correlatives belie this claim. Using his own logic, one can readily reduce his eight legal conceptions to two primitives—a legal duty and a legal power. I have complicated his conceptual scheme by distinguishing between a duty *per se* and a duty to some second party and, again, between a power in the strict sense and a legal ability. The logic of my conceptual scheme is, accordingly, more complex than that of his.

Hohfeld's table of legal opposites survives my analysis, although the terminology changes somewhat. The pairs of opposites in my scheme are as follows:

a claim of X against Y.....................a no-claim of X against Y
a liberty of X in face of Y...................a duty of X to Y
an ability of X over Y......................a disability of X over Y
an immunity of X from Y ....a liability of X to Y

The legal advantages listed in the left-hand column are here contrasted with the logically contradictory legal positions, the legal disadvantages, listed on the right.

Hohfeld's table of correlatives also survives intact, although formulated in slightly different words.

a claim of X against Y $\longleftrightarrow$ a duty of Y to X
a liberty of X in face of Y $\longleftrightarrow$ a contrary no-claim of Y against X
an ability of X over Y $\longleftrightarrow$ a liability of Y to X
an immunity of X against Y $\longleftrightarrow$ a disability of Y over X

Once more the presumed legal advantages are listed on the left and the correlative disadvantages on the right. The logic of these pairs is such that each of the paired positions implies the other; that is, each position of X implies a correlative position of Y and vice versa.

My conceptual scheme is more complicated than Hohfeld's, however, for it contains a number of one-way implications. These may be listed in the following table:

a duty of X to
Y   → a duty of X
a liberty of X   → a liberty of X in face of (any) Y
a power of X   → an ability of X
a disability of X→ an impotence of X

In each of these pairs of concepts, the legal position listed on the left is logically stronger than that listed on the right. Thus, the former logically implies the latter, but the latter does not imply the former. Incidentally, just because not every duty of X implies a duty of X to Y, it is not the case that the concept of a legal duty implies the existence of some correlative claim of some second party, as Hohfeld presupposed.

Finally, there are two pairs of legal opposites in my conceptual scheme that are lacking in Hohfeld's.

a duty of X . . . . .a contrary liberty of X
a power of X . . . . .an impotence of X

These obviously reflect the introduction of the concept of an absolute duty and of a legal power in the narrower sense into my legal theory. Although the logic of my conceptual scheme is more complicated and less tidy than that envisaged by Hohfeld, this by no means undermines either the possibility or the desirability of applying the techniques of formal logic to legal language.

Legal Rights

Where do legal rights fit into Hohfeld's conceptual scheme? His answer is found in the following brief passage.

> As more fully shown in the former article, the word "right" is used generically and indiscriminately to denote any sort of legal advantage, whether claim, privilege, power, or immunity. In its narrowest sense, however, the term is used as the correlative of duty; and, to convey this meaning, the synonym "claim" seems the best. [1919, 71]

Remembering that Hohfeld has been seeking to identify fundamental legal conceptions, conceptions that denote simple and irreducible legal positions, we can discern a double thesis about legal rights in these words: strictly speaking only legal claims are rights, and a legal right is to be identified with a simple legal claim. Let us see how he attempts to establish this conception of legal rights.

First, Hohfeld maintains that strictly speaking only legal claims are rights. He argues for this thesis in a brief and enigmatic passage.

> Recognizing, as we must, the very broad and indiscriminate use of the term "right," what clue do we find, in ordinary legal discourse, toward limiting the word in question to a definite and appropriate meaning? That clue lies in the

correlative "duty," for it is certain that even those who use the word and the conception "right" in the broadest possible way are accustomed to thinking of "duty" as the invariable correlative. . . . If, as seems desirable, we should seek a synonym for the term "right" in this limited and proper meaning, perhaps the word "claim" would prove the best. [1919, 38]

What are we to make of this argument? We could read it either as an appeal to the correct use of the expression "a right," according to its established meaning in ordinary language, or as justifying a proposal to redefine the term for the special purposes of the theory and practice of the law.

Hohfeld finds a clue toward limiting "a right" to an "appropriate" and "proper" meaning in "ordinary legal discourse." This suggests that his argument is some sort of an appeal to ordinary language. He may be arguing that to use "a right" to refer to a liberty, a power or an immunity is to misapply the expression, much as the application of the term "socialist" to anyone who proposes to reform traditional laissez faire capitalism in some slight manner does violence to the established meaning of that term. Since the meanings of "a right" and "a duty" are logically correlative in ordinary language, the use of "a right" to denote any legal position that implies no correlative duty is inappropriate to the established meaning of that expression and linguistically improper.

If this is Hohfeld's argument, it is suspect. His evidence that the broad use of "a right" is improper is that "even those who use the word and the conception 'right' in the broadest possible way are accustomed to thinking of 'duty' as the invariable correlative." What evidence is there that this is so? Hohfeld does cite a number of jurists and judges who infer a correlative duty from some "right" in the sense of a liberty. It is striking, however, that his articles do not, as far as I can discover, contain a single example of the inference of a duty from "a right" as applied to a legal power or a legal immunity. This strongly suggests that our custom of thinking of rights and duties as correlative is far from invariable. Moreover, it is hard to believe that the inference from a liberty to a right, when it has occurred, has not often been challenged by an opposing lawyer. But suppose it were true that speakers and writers of ordinary legal discourse invariably did think of rights and duties as logically correlative. Then surely they would invariably apply the expression "a right" to claims only, and Hohfeld would have no need to recognize "the very broad and indiscriminate use of the term" at all. In the end, Hohfeld would probably not want his argument read as an appeal to ordinary language, for he laments the vagueness and ambiguity in ordinary legal discourse and intends to propose a more precise terminology more useful for the theoretical and practical purposes of lawyers and jurists.

Let us, therefore, read Hohfeld's argument as advancing one or more reasons for redefining the expression "a right" so that its application is limited to claims. One reason he advances is that the broad use of the term is "indiscriminate." How so? Often, he seems to be suggesting that the expression "a right" is ambiguous when used to refer to liberties, powers and immunities as well as to legal claims. After all, each of his legal conceptions is supposed to be fundamental, to refer to a simple indefinable legal element. If this is so, then they can share no common feature to which the expression "a right" could possibly refer. It is essential to avoid this ambiguity in our theory and practice of law because of the confusion it introduces. Excellent examples are the instances he cites in which jurists and judges have inferred legal duties from legal liberties, because they have failed to notice the fundamental conceptual distinction between a liberty and a claim.

I willingly grant, indeed I adopt and insist upon, Hohfeld's conceptual distinctions between legal claims, liberties, powers and immunities. But the fact that the broad use of "a right" applies the one expression to four classes of legal elements does not imply that the expression so used is ambiguous, for they may be species of a single genus. Indeed, Hohfeld concedes as much himself when he reports that "a right" is used "generically and indiscriminately to denote any sort of legal advantage" (p. 71). Although he never does explain what he means by a legal advantage, I believe that he is on the right track. What claim-rights, liberty-rights, power-rights and immunity-rights share is that the law sides with the possessor vis-à-vis some second party in a possible confrontation or conflict of wills.

But perhaps Hohfeld is lodging a milder, but far from trivial, complaint when he charges that the broad use of "a right" is indiscriminate. This general use fails to mark essential legal distinctions, precisely those he identifies and explains in his two articles. I fully agree. This is why I believe that any adequate theory of rights should be formulated in terms of Hohfeld's fundamental legal conceptions. But it does not follow that the expression "a right" should be limited to legal claims. We can, as indeed we should, mark Hohfeld's conceptual distinctions by using the distinct expressions "a claim," "a liberty," "a power" and "an immunity." It is a waste of our scarce linguistic resources to use two terms, "a claim" and "a right" to refer to one and the same legal reality. And for theoretical purposes, any such identification would be most unfortunate, for it would beg the issue against those theories that identify a right with a liberty or with a power.

In the passage I have quoted above, Hohfeld advances a second reason for adopting a more limited use of "a right," one in which only legal claims are rights. Only this narrower definition preserves the logical correlativity of rights and duties. But how much correlativity, if any, do we wish to build into our conceptual framework? Even if correlativity is firmly entrenched in our presystematic thinking, we might find it more useful for our juristic and philosophical purposes to use a terminology less laden with controversial implications.

Hohfeld, of course, presupposes a very strong correlativity thesis. Every right of X against Y implies some duty of Y to X and vice versa, and the essential content of the legal right and its correlative duty are the same. But the arguments of Joel Feinberg (1966, 140-142) and others have convinced many that not every duty implies some corresponding right. So-called duties of charity are the most usual counterexample, but others are also common. And if I am correct in defending the existence of absolute legal duties, duties that are not duties to any second party, then not every duty implies some correlative right.

One might, of course, wish to build a weaker correlativity thesis into one's theory of rights. Granted the existence of absolute legal duties, at least every legal right implies some correlative duty. Thus, one might preserve the inference from rights to duties but abandon the inference in the other direction. Even this weaker thesis, however, is far from uncontroversial. David Lyons has challenged this implication (1970, 53) by giving examples of legal rights that, although protected by legal duties, do not imply any correlative duty. Thus Alvin's right to free speech is protected by a legal duty of others not to silence him by the use or threat of force, but these duties are not logically correlatives of the content of Alvin's legal right; the content of these protective duties does not correspond conceptually or essentially to the content of the right they protect.

This still leaves open the option of building a very weak logical connection between rights and duties into our conceptual framework. We might wish to hold that any legal element or set of legal elements that implies no legal duties at all is too weak to be called "a right" in any significant sense of that term. But even if we should build this logical implication into our very concept of a legal right, identifying rights with legal claims would be the wrong way to accomplish this end, for the Hohfeldian conception of a legal claim carries with it a stronger, and more dubious, correlativity thesis.

Hohfeld has not proven, nor do I see any compelling reason to hold, that an adequate theory of rights will restrict the meaning of the expression "a right" in the strict sense to claims. To my mind, it is an open question whether rights should be thought of as claims or not. Feinberg defends a conceptual connection between legal rights and legal claims. I defend a theory according to which there are also liberty-, power-, and immunity-rights. Others ably defend still other conceptions of legal rights. My point is simply that any such theory stands in need of a philosophical defence. One cannot, as Hohfeld tries to do, dismiss any such conception of a legal right as a loose and inappropriate way of thinking and speaking.

The second half of Hohfeld's double thesis is that *a* legal right is to be identified with a *simple* legal claim. The argument for this thesis is developed more fully in opposition to John Austin's influential conception of a right *in rem* as a legal right that avails against other persons universally and imposes a single correlative legal duty upon persons generally.

> In opposition to the ideas embodied in the passages just given, it is submitted that instead of there being a single right with a single correlative duty resting on all the persons against whom the right avails, there are many separate and distinct rights, actual and potential, each one of which has a correlative duty resting upon some one person. Repeating a hypothetical case put above, let us suppose that A is the owner of Blackacre and X is the owner of Whiteacre. It may be assumed further that, in consideration of $100 *actually paid* by A to B, the latter agrees with A never to enter on X's land, Whiteacre; also that C and D, at the same time and for separate considerations, make respectively similar agreements with A. In such a case A's respective rights against B, C, and D are clearly rights *in personam*, or paucital rights. Surely no one would assert that A has only a single right against B, C, and D, with only a single or unified duty resting on the latter. A's right against B is entirely separate from the other two. B may commit a breach of *his* duty, without involving any breach of D's duty by D. For, obviously, the content of each respective duty differs from each of the others. To make it otherwise C and D would have to be under a duty or duties (along with B) that B should not enter on X's land. Even if that were the case, there would be said to be three *separate* duties unless B, C, and D bound themselves so as to create a so-called joint obligation. In the latter case alone would there be said to be a single right and a single (joint) duty. Going beyond this direct analysis of the situation, it seems clear that the three respective "right-duty" relations of A and B, A and C, and A and D respond to every test of separateness and independence. A might, e.g., discharge B from his duty to A, thus (in equivalent terms) creating a privilege of entering as against A (not as against X, of course); yet, obviously, the respective duties of C and D would continue the same as before. So on indefinitely.
>
> Point for point, the same considerations and tests seem applicable to A's respective rights *in rem*, or multital rights, against B, C, D and others indefinitely, that they, respectively considered, shall not enter on Blackacre. [Hohfeld, 1919, 92-93]

This is a very powerful argument that conclusively establishes an important conclusion about complex legal rights, such as a right *in rem*.

It is a serious mistake to conceive of a right *in rem* as (modifying Hohfeld's language slightly) a single claim with a single correlative duty resting on all the persons against whom the right avails. The landowner's right that others not enter upon his or her land imposes a logically distinct and legally separate duty upon each of the second parties against whom it avails. (1) The duty of one second party has a different content from the similar duty of every other second party. Thus, B is under a duty that B not enter upon the land, C is under a duty that C not enter upon the land, and so forth. (2) An act of entry upon the land by one second party does not constitute a breach of duty by any other second party. Hence, the respective duties bind the duty-bearers individually and independently. (3) Normally, there is no joint liability of the second parties for remedying any violation of the landowner's right that others not enter upon the land. Finally, and most dramatically, (4) the duty of one second party not to enter could readily be extinguished without affecting in any way the similar duties of the other second parties. Clearly any so-called right *in rem* imposes, not a single legal duty upon other persons generally, but a number of distinct and separate legal duties upon each of a number of second parties. But since legal claims and relative duties are logically correlative, a legal right *in rem* must really consist, not in a single legal claim holding "against the world," but in a large number of separate legal claims.

As long as one does not insist on using the expression "a right" as synonymous with "a claim," it does not follow, however, that it is a mistake to conceive of a right *in rem* as a single legal right. To be sure, one must be very careful to remember that this single claim-right really consists of a very large number of logically distinct and legally separate claims, each holding against a different second party. But it still may be true that this complex of legal claims has a unity in the law that can best be recognized by thinking of it as a single legal right. The invaluable lesson we can and must learn from Hohfeld is that one cannot understand any complex legal position without analyzing it into its simple and irreducible elements. But the other side of this insight, an aspect of Hohfeld's work that he too often forgets, is that one cannot adequately understand any complex legal position without recognizing how the constituent elements that make it up are structured in a complex whole.

It is not merely that Hohfeld's argument establishing the complexity of many legal rights fails to prove that a legal right must be simple rather than complex; one can recognize that a legal right must be a complex of Hohfeldian elements. A single legal claim, in and by itself, could not possibly constitute a legal right holding against any second party. Imagine that a creditor C has a legal claim to repayment against a debtor D, but that none of the other Hohfeldian elements normally associated with a legal claim-right is present. Could C's legal position be accurately said to constitute a legal right to repayment? D would lie under a legal duty to C to tender the amount owed on the due date, and C would have the legal power to take legal action in the courts in the event that D failed to fulfill this duty. But if this single claim were the *only* element in C's legal position, then, according to Hohfeld's own logic, C would lack the legal liberty to accept repayment if and when it is tendered by D. It strikes me as linguistically and conceptually odd to say that under these circumstances C has "a right" to repayment. Surely some element of liberty enters into any genuine legal right. Again, C's legal claim to be repaid in and of itself implies absolutely no sort of legal immunity against D. Let us imagine, therefore, that D has the legal power to extinguish C's claim simply by snapping his or her fingers in the creditor's face and repeating the legally prescribed formula "I hereby cancel my debt to you." Under these circumstances, C's legal claim to repayment would not hold fast against the debtor as any self-respecting legal right surely should. I conclude that only a complex structure of legal elements could possibly constitute a genuine legal right. Thus, although any adequate theory of rights should be articulated in terms of Hohfeld's fundamental legal conceptions, properly reinterpreted, Hohfeld's own conception of a legal right must be rejected.

Chapter 3

HART'S GENERAL THEORY

The nature of a right is, I believe, revealed to us most clearly through an examination of legal rights. This is because our legal system contains a wealth of readily identifiable rights that have been defined with considerable precision and in remarkable detail by the legal processes of legislation and, even more, judicial interpretation and application. Moreover, we can best understand these legal rights by interpreting them in terms of Hohfeld's fundamental legal conceptions, conceptions best defined as I have analyzed them. At the same time, we must reject Hohfeld's identification of a legal right with a single claim; only a complex of Hohfeldian elements could constitute a genuine right. But to what kind of legal complex does the expression "a right" properly refer? And how can an aggregate of logically distinct and legally separable Hohfeldian elements have the unity necessary to enable them to constitute a right? By far the most illuminating answers to these and other philosophical problems concerning legal rights are provided by the general theory proposed, and then retracted, by H. L. A. Hart in his insightful and influential essay "Bentham on Legal Rights."

Hart's Model

A revealing picture of a legal right is, perhaps unwittingly, projected by Hart's paradigm example, a man's right to look over his garden fence at his neighbor (Hart, 1973, 175). This picture shows us those features of a right that are essential to Hart's conception. The garden is a limited area within which the man is free to move about as he wishes; every right involves some defined sphere of activity within which the right-holder has freedom of choice and action. The man is standing in *his* garden; every right is possessed and may be exercised by someone so that the concept of a right is an essentially distributive concept. The man is standing behind his fence, a fence that constrains any neighbor who might wish to interfere with the man's freedom to act as he chooses; every right limits the freedom of action of one or more second parties by imposing duties, at least of noninterference and sometimes of performing positive services, upon others. This picture does not drop out of sight in Hart's essay, for it is implicit in the very language he uses to explain his analytical model of a right. His expressions "a protective perimeter" (1973, 179) and "perimeter of obligations" (1973, 180) vividly recall the picture of a fence around a garden.

When Hart is speaking literally, rather than figuratively, he uses Hohfeld's legal conceptions.

> In England and in most other countries a man has a right to look over his garden fence at his neighbor; he is under no obligation not to look at him and under no obligation to look at him. In this example the liberty is therefore bilateral; both the obligation not to look and the obligation to look are in Bentham's phrase 'absent'. [1973, 175]

At the center of Hart's paradigm of a legal right is a bilateral legal liberty, and protecting the exercise of this liberty are one or more surrounding legal duties.

> For he [the neighbor] has certain legal obligations or duties, civil or criminal, or both, which preclude some, though not all forms of interference, and these in practice more or less adequately protect the exercise of the liberty-right. Thus he cannot enter the next-door garden and beat up his tormentor, for this would be a breach of certain duties not indeed correlative to his tormentor's liberty-right to look at him, but correlative at least in the case of civil duties to certain other rights, which his tormentor has and which are not mere liberties. [1973, 176]

Thus, Hart's model of a legal right consists of a central bilateral legal liberty together with a protective perimeter of legal duties. Notice that although part of this protective parameter may be made up of duties to the right-holder, other parts may be legal duties imposed by the criminal law.

On the basis of this model, Hart defines the meaning of the expression "a right" as properly used in the language of the law.

> On this view there would be only one sense of legal right—a legally respected choice—though it would be one with different exemplifications, depending on the kind of act or act-in-the-law which there is liberty to do. [1973, 197]

Thus, in typical liberty-rights, the act would be a natural act such as looking over one's fence at one's neighbor. In power-rights, the act would be an act-in-the-law, such as alienating one's property. And claim-rights would be a special case of power rights in which the right-holder is at liberty to waive or enforce or leave unenforced the obligation of some second party. Since Hart's general theory is the culmination of his continuing search for a common denominator of Hohfeld's legal advantages, it is appropriate to test the philosophical adequacy of his model by seeing how well it can deal with liberty-rights, power-rights, claim-rights and immunity-rights respectively.

Liberty-Rights

There is, I am convinced, a very important lesson we can learn from Hart's treatment of liberty-rights: only a complex structure of Hohfeldian elements could constitute a real legal right. Hart advances a two-stage argument for the complexity of rights. First, a bilateral legal liberty would not, in and of itself, be "a right," in any interesting sense of that expression.

> But it is not at all clear that lawyers or anyone else would speak of a completely naked or unprotected liberty as a right, or that any useful purpose would be served if they did. The state of nature, if worth describing at all, can be described adequately in other terms. So far as organized society is concerned there would be something not only strange but misleading in describing naked liberties as rights: if we said, for example, that a class of helots whom free citizens were allowed to treat as they wished or interfere with at will, yet had rights to do those acts which they were not forbidden by the law to do. [1973, 181-182]

In short, the application of the expression "a right" to a naked legal liberty, even a bilateral liberty, would serve no purpose and would mislead. It would serve no purpose because this use of language would be redundant; the legal situation could be completely described in the language of duties, for liberties consist in the absence of contrary duties. It would mislead as shown by his counter-example of the helots. But precisely how would it mislead? After all, they are perfectly free, are they not, as far as the law is concerned, to do those acts not forbidden by any law? Quite true, but their legal liberties would not hold against any second parties, for others could treat them as they wished or interfere with them at will. Since it is an essential feature of any right that it hold against one or more second parties, naked liberties cannot be genuine rights.

Those who take most seriously the fact that any genuine right must hold against second parties tend to make the opposite mistake, that of identifying a liberty-right with its protective perimeter. But Hart insists that one must not ignore either the liberty or the perimeter.

> Both are required in the analysis of many legal phenomena including that of economic competition. Two people walking in an empty street see a purse

lying on the pavement: each has a liberty as far as the law is concerned to pick
it up and each may prevent the other doing so if he can race him to the spot
[1973, 180]

What Hart is doing here is giving a very powerful counterexample to
refute those who, like Hohfeld, maintain that a liberty-right, strictly
speaking, should be identified with a claim against interference with
one's action. Imagine a society in which competition for scarce resources
is so intense that it often breaks out into violence resulting in serious
injury and even death to one or more of the competitors. Accordingly,
the legal system forbids, in addition to the usual acts of murder, assault
and theft, any attempt of any individual to take possession of any
tangible object—even one apparently lost, abandoned or unowned.
Surely it would be a mockery to say that such a legal system confers upon
the individual the liberty-right to pick up a purse lying on the pavement
simply because the usual duties not to interfere with one's doing so by
hitting one, tripping one up or threatening one with violence exist.
Without the central liberty of picking up the purse, the claim against
interference surely does not constitute any sort of liberty-right.

Thus, neither an unprotected bilateral liberty nor a protective perimeter with no liberty to protect can properly be said to constitute a legal
liberty-right. Both those who identify legal rights with liberties and those
who identify them with claims fail to recognize that only a complex
structure of Hohfeldian elements could be a legal right. Hart has shown
us the essential complexity of any genuine right.

I am not convinced, however, that he has correctly described the
structure of a legal right. In his model, at the center of a legal right
stands a bilateral liberty. Indeed, this would seem to be essential to the
general theory he is proposing, for he insists that all three kinds of legal
rights discussed by Bentham are rights in the sense of legally recognized
choices. It is surprising, therefore, to find him admitting that there are
some unilateral liberty-rights.

> In the ordinary case, where the law imposes general obligations, e.g., to pay
> taxes, or to abstain from assault or trespass, it would be pointless or even
> confusing to describe those who had these obligations as having rights to pay
> taxes or to abstain from assault. Yet there undoubtedly are certain specific
> contexts where unilateral liberties are intelligibly spoken of as rights to do
> actions even where there is also an obligation to do the same action. Among
> these are cases where individuals by way of exception to a general rule are not
> merely permitted but also legally required to do some act generally prohib-
> ited.
>
> Thus a policeman ordered to arrest a man might be asked "What right have
> you to arrest him?" and might well produce his orders as showing that he had
> a right to arrest. In general the query "What right have you to do that?" invites
> the person addressed to show that some act of his which is prima facie

wrongful because generally prohibited is one which in the particular case he is at liberty to do. [1973, 182-183]

Now I heartily agree with Hart that in the ordinary case it is a mistake to describe a unilateral legal liberty as a right and that the language of rights is intelligibly applicable only in certain specific contexts. This passage remains puzzling, however: the way Hart characterizes these contexts—as "cases where individuals by way of exception to a general rule are not merely permitted but also legally required to do some act generally prohibited" (1973, 182)—does nothing at all to explain why this case is not a clear counterexample to his model of a legal right. Equally fascinating is the way in which he goes on to describe the context in a most revealing manner as one in which the policeman, if challenged, can appeal to his unilateral liberty-right. The context in which the language of rights is intelligible is that in which the right-holder con-fronts one or more second parties in a conflict of wills. What is essential is not that the law respects the choice of the right-holder but that the law favors the will of that party vis-à-vis the will of the party against whom the right holds. Hart has provided a beautiful test case in favor of my model of a legal right and against his own. But I am ahead of myself.

Hart's other example of a unilateral liberty-right comes closer to fitting his model.

> Further examples of unilateral liberties spoken of as rights are afforded by cases where duties in Bentham's phrase are "superadded" to liberty-rights. Thus a trustee who has equitable duties to put the trust property to a certain use may be said to have a right to do this since the equitable duty is for historical reasons conceived as something distinct grafted on to his still persistent legal bilateral liberty-rights, though its actual effect is to render the liberty-right unilateral. [1973, 183, note]

Hart recognizes that this sort of unilateral liberty-right is anomalous, at least when viewed in the light of his legally respected choice theory. But he insists that his model of a legal right can be extended to cover the trustee's legal right to put the trust property to a certain use: this unilateral liberty-right can be interpreted as the residue of a bilateral liberty-right to put the trust property to the use of the trustee's choice, restricted by a superimposed duty derived from equitable law. I can well understand how our contemporary use of the language of legal rights might mirror or reflect the legal history of our society; but I would think that, even granted the historical background supplied by Hart, the continuing application of Hart's model—centuries after the legal system, including equitable law, has ceased to recognize the choice of the trustee—is misleading at best.

An even more revealing counterinstance to Hart's general theory is provided by Joel Feinberg's paradigm case of what he labels a mandatory right.

> Jury service, whether in czarist Russia or in the United States, can be quite intelligibly described both as a duty *and* as a right, though it is more likely to be described as the former by a harrassed and annoyed citizen grudgingly performing the service, and as the latter by the victim of discrimination who is excluded from the process. [Feinberg, 1978, 109]

Jury service has probably been introduced into most legal systems, not as a bilateral liberty but as a duty imposed upon the citizens in order to institutionalize a practicable system of trial before a jury of one's peers. Much as witnesses were subpoenaed to constrain them to testify, so individuals were constrained by the imposition of the legal duty to serve on juries. What makes it intelligible to speak of jury service as a legal right is not some preexistent bilateral liberty in the historical past but certain specific contexts such as the one in which the victim of discrimination will be excluded from serving on juries, and thus denied full status as a citizen, unless he or she can appeal to his or her protected unilateral liberty-right in the face of some second party attempting to discriminate against him or her. My conclusion is that although Hart quite rightly insists that only a complex structure of Hohfeldian elements could constitute a legal right, there need not be a bilateral liberty at the center of one's model of a legal right. What is essential to the language of rights is not some respected choice but some adversarial context.

Power-Rights

Hart believes that legal power-rights fit his analytical model because they are special exemplifications of liberty-rights, those in which the action one has a liberty-right to do is the exercise of a legal power. Hart's paradigm is the owner's legal right to alienate property. The owner can exercise this right, for example, by selling a piece of real estate to a willing buyer. On Hart's model, what makes it appropriate to speak of the owner's "right" to sell the land is the owner's legal position consisting of a bilateral liberty of selling or refraining from selling the land, presumably protected with a perimeter of duties of others not to interfere with the exercise of this central liberty.

As Hart himself recognizes, however, not every legal power-right contains a bilateral liberty at its center.

> As in the case of liberty-rights, duties may be superimposed on rights which are powers and such duties will render the liberty to exercise the power unilateral (a simple example from property law is where an owner of property binds himself by contract either to sell or not to sell it). [1973, 196]

In this example, the owner who contracts to sell a piece of real estate does indeed superimpose a contractual duty to sell upon a preexisting bilateral liberty to sell or refrain from selling as he or she chooses. This might even explain why we apply a respected choice conception of a right to a legal position that used to, but no longer does, contain a bilateral liberty. But this historical explanation of our linguistic usage would not show that the *present* legal position of the owner fits Hart's model.

Moreover, there are other examples of unilateral power-rights where Hart's historical explanation seems out of place. A presiding judge has a legal power-right to decide any case properly before his or her court. But in our legal system, at least, it is not the case that the judge has a bilateral legal liberty of issuing or refraining from issuing a legally valid judgment in the case as he or she chooses; with the exception of cases that can be declared moot, the judge has a legal duty to exercise his or her power of deciding the case at hand. Nor is it plausible to suppose that this duty to decide even the hardest case has been superimposed upon a preexisting bilateral liberty. Similarly, the sheriff has a legal duty to execute a writ of the court. The act of executing such a writ may involve the exercise of a legal power-right, for example, when a sheriff executes a judgment of sale by selling a debtor's property and turning the proceeds over to the creditors. There is no bilateral liberty of executing or refraining from exercising the writ lurking in the background to justify, or even pretend to justify, the application of Hart's legally respected choice model to this unilateral power-right. Hart recognized that not every legal right has a bilateral liberty at its center. What he failed to appreciate is that this requires one to reject his analytical model of a legal right.

Even where a bilateral liberty is present, Hart's model fails to reveal the real structure of a power-right. Recall that his model consists of a bilateral legal liberty, together with a protective perimeter of duties of others not to interfere with the exercise of this central liberty. This model does not even do justice to his own paradigm, the right of an owner to sell a piece of land. To be sure, the owner normally has a bilateral liberty to sell or refrain from selling his or her property; and presumably the exercise of this liberty is protected by duties of others not to interfere by assault, murder or the threat of violence. But where does the legal power of alienating the property fit in?

> Thus in all three kinds of right the idea of a bilateral liberty is present and the difference between the kinds of right lies only [N.B. the "only"] in the kind of act which there is a liberty to do. . . . In the case of rights which are powers, such as the right to alienate property, the act which there is a bilateral liberty to do is an act-in-the-law, just in the sense that it is specifically recognized by

the law as having legal effects in varying the legal position of various parties. [1973, 196]

It strikes me as most peculiar to interpret "the case of rights which are powers" in such a way that the legal power involved is not even an element within the complex legal position that constitutes the power-right.

If, however, one were to decide to add a legal power to the central bilateral liberty and peripheral duties in Hart's model of a legal right, there is the question of where it would fit into the model. Are we to add the power to the protective perimeter of the right or place it at the center of the right? If choice is of the essence of the concept of a right, as Hart presupposes, then presumably a bilateral liberty belongs at the center of every legal right. But if what is essential to the concept of a legal right is that the law favors the will of the right-holder in the context of some possible confrontation with some second party, as I have suggested, then presumably any sort of legal advantage could be at the center of a legal right. There are at least three reasons that support the second hypothesis about the structure of a legal right. As Hart himself admits, not every legal right contains a bilateral liberty; there are unilateral liberty-rights and power-rights. As Hohfeld shows us through the detailed examination of judicial decisions and jurisprudential texts, the expression "a right" is in fact used indiscriminately to refer to liberty-rights, power-rights, claim-rights and immunity-rights. Let me add only that it is the legal power, and not any bilateral liberty, that identifies the party against whom a power-right holds. The right to sell a parcel of land holds only against one who has made an offer to buy it, for the owner's power to sell can be exercised only by accepting such an offer. Since the power is a power *over* the offerer, while the bilateral liberty is an absolute (that is, *non*relative) liberty, only the power can determine any second party against whom the power-right as a whole holds.

The structure of a legal power-right is better represented as a complex structure with a legal power at its center. But if we must displace the bilateral liberty at the center of Hart's model, we do not wish to remove it entirely from the owner's legal right to sell the land. This bilateral liberty, and the free choice it confers upon the right-holder, is part and parcel of his or her right. It must, then, find its place somewhere in the perimeter of the right; it must be one of the elements surrounding the central legal power to alienate the property. But it surely does not protect the exercise of that power in anything like the same way that duties of noninterference protect the exercise of the central liberty in a liberty-right. We must, I believe, replace Hart's conception of a protective perimeter of duties with the notion of associated Hohfeldian elements of various kinds. Just how these surrounding duties, liberties, and so on are associated with the central element in any legal right remains to be explained.

Claim-Rights

Just as Hart construes a power-right as a specific exemplification of a liberty-right, so on his general theory a claim-right is a special case of a power-right. In the case of a right correlative to obligation, the right-holder is at liberty to waive or extinguish or to enforce or leave unenforced another's obligation.

> The idea is that of one individual being given by the law exclusive control, more or less extensive, over another person's duty so that in the area of conduct covered by that duty the individual who has the right is a small-scale sovereign to whom the duty is owed. The fullest measure of control comprises three distinguishable elements: (i) the right holder may waive or extinguish the duty or leave it in existence; (ii) after breach or threatened breach of a duty he may leave it "unenforced" or may "enforce" it by suing for compensation or, in certain cases, for an injunction or mandatory order to restrain the continued or further breach of duty; and (iii) he may waive or extinguish the obligation to pay compensation to which the breach gives rise. [1973, 192]

Thus, if I have ordered and paid for a shirt from Sears & Roebuck catalogue, then I have a claim-right to the delivery of this merchandise and Sears has a correlative obligation to deliver the ordered shirt to me. According to Hart's model, my claim-right consists in: my bilateral liberty of waiving or not waiving Sears' duty to deliver the shirt, my bilateral liberty of suing or not suing for compensation in the event that Sears fails or refuses to deliver the merchandise I have ordered and paid for, and my bilateral liberty, in the event that Sears fails or refuses to deliver, of waiving or not waiving Sears' duty to compensate me for this wrong—together with a perimeter of duties that protect my exercise of any of these central liberties.

There is surely something paradoxical in the fact that although the idea central to Hart's conception of a claim-right is a small-scale sovereignty consisting of certain legal powers, these legal powers have no place in his model of a legal right. Central to his model of a claim-right are bilateral liberties, and the remainder of his model consists entirely of protective duties. The legal powers essential to his conception of a right correlative to obligation remain outside of the right itself, merely defining the kind of action the right-holder is at liberty to do.

But perhaps I am unfair to Hart. Let me, therefore, test the adequacy of his analysis of claim-rights by measuring it against his own account of its strengths.

There are I think many signs of the centrality of those powers to the conception of a legal right. Thus it is hard to think of rights except as capable of *exercise* and this conception of rights correlative to obligations as containing legal powers accommodates this feature. Moreover, we speak of a breach of duty in the civil law, whether arising in contract or in tort, not only as wrong, or detrimental to the person who has the correlative right, but as *a wrong to* him and a breach of an obligation *owed to him;* we also speak of the person who has the correlative right as *possessing* it or even *owning* it. The conception suggested by these phrases is that duties with correlative rights are a species of normative property belonging to the right holder, and this figure becomes intelligible by reference to the special form of control over a correlative duty which a person with such a right is given by the law. [1973, 192-193. Hart's italics]

Since this passage is as complex as it is compact, we will do well to examine it bit by bit.

First, Hart's general theory of legal rights is supposed to explain how a claim-right can be exercised. There does indeed seem to be a problem here. If the content of every claim-right, that to which the claimant has a right, is always the performance of the correlative obligation, a service to be performed by the duty-bearer, then how on earth could a claimant possibly exercise his or her claim-right? Obviously *I* do not exercise my right to delivery of the shirt I have ordered and paid for when *Sears* delivers the merchandise. And when I accept the tendered shirt, I am exercising my liberty-right to accept merchandise from Sears rather than my claim-right that Sears deliver the merchandise to me. The difficulty is to find some other act I might perform that could be construed as an exercise of my right to delivery against Sears. Hart suggests that I could exercise my claim-right by, among other things, waiving my claim to delivery and thereby extinguishing Sears' duty to deliver. But strictly speaking, in waiving delivery I would be exercising my power-right to waive delivery and not my claim-right to have a shirt delivered by Sears.

Confusion arises from our failure to formulate the content of many legal rights in clear and precise terms. When we follow Hohfeld's advice and Hart's practice of expressing the content of a legal right in terms of a verb describing the relevant action, we notice a striking asymmetry. Liberty-rights and power-rights are defined by a verb in the active mood; claim-rights and immunity-rights are defined by a verb in the passive mood. Thus, to use Hart's own examples, one has a right "to look at his neighbor over the garden fence" and one has a right "to alienate property," but one has a right "not to be assaulted" by another or "not to be taxed" by the Oxford City Council. This asymmetry is no mere idiom of our language; it reflects two very different ways in which rights bear upon human conduct. The defining application of a liberty-right or a power-right is to the conduct of the right-holder; the practical applica-tion of a claim-right or an immunity-right is essentially to the conduct of some second party, the duty-bearer or the party lacking the specified legal ability. What this implies is that the concept of exercising a right, while essential to the conception of a liberty-right or a power-right, is out of place with respect to claim-rights or immunity-rights. These sorts of rights are enjoyed, not exercised. I agree that "it is hard to think of rights except as capable of *exercise*," but I urge clear thinkers to resist this temptation.

Second, Hart's model of a legal right is supposed to explain the sense or way in which relative duties are relative. "Moreover, we speak of a breach of duty in the civil law . . . as *a wrong to* him and a breach of an obligation *owed to* him." Presumably any explanation of how a correlative obligation is owed *to* the right-holder will also explain how a legal claim holds *against* the duty-bearer. Hart argues against the beneficiary or interest theory of relative duties and maintains that the correct explana-tion lies in the special standing of the claimant, consisting in certain legal powers conferring upon him or her control over the correlative obliga-tion. This is a profound insight. For reasons I have tried to explain in the previous chapter, the correlative concepts of relative duties and legal claims can be properly analyzed only with the help of the concept of a legal power.

At the same time, I do not believe that Hart has fully grasped the implications of his own insight. His line of reasoning suggests, although it does not prove, that control is as essential to legal rights as freedom is. From his inaugural lecture in 1953 through his most recent papers on rights, Hart has insisted that there is something distinctive about the concept of a right. Accordingly, one of his main arguments against the beneficiary analysis of claim-rights is that it makes the language of rights redundant, because on this analysis the language of rights says nothing that cannot be said as well or even better in terms of the language of duties. Precisely what he takes to be distinctive is best explained in his paper "Are There Any Natural Rights?": "The concept of a right belongs to that branch of morality which is specifically concerned to determine when one person's freedom may be limited by another's" (1955, 177). That this notion of the distribution of freedom equally underlies his conception of a legal right is indicated by this passage from his paper "Bentham on Legal Rights."

> . . . I shall use instead of Bentham's expression "right resulting from obligation" the more familiar "right correlative to obligation" for his second sort of right, which arises when the law imposes a duty not on the right-holder, but on another and thus restricts the other's freedom to act as he chooses. [1973, 175]

Thus, in his model of a claim-right, Hart continues to think of rights as determining a distribution of freedom, for a claim-right both confers a bilateral liberty of action on the right-holder and confers upon the right-holder control over the duty-bearer's obligation, an obligation that limits the latter's freedom of action. Right and duty, however, are correlated by legal powers that confer control over that duty upon the claimant. What this suggests to me is that legal rights confer, not merely a certain distribution of freedom, but a certain distribution of freedom *and control.*

Although Hart's insistence that legal claims must be analyzed in terms of legal powers is entirely correct and richly suggestive, his proposed analysis is unnecessarily and undesirably complex. This complexity arises from two features of his model of a legal claim. In his paradigm case, three distinct legal powers are built into a claim—the power to waive the claim, the power to sue in the event of actual or threatened breach of the claim, and the power of waiving compensation for any breach of the correlative obligation. Since he takes a claim-right to be a special exemplification of a liberty-right, every paradigm legal claim involves three bilateral legal liberties, together with all the duties of noninterference that make up the protective perimeter(s) around these liberties.

Now it seems to me that the power to waive payment of any compensation is extraneous to the concept of a relative duty, and hence to the correlative concept of a claim. Since a legal duty is to be understood in terms of legal constraint, only powers directly concerning legal constraint are essential to relative duties in the law. Although the power to waive compensation no doubt releases the violator of a claim-right from any constraint to compensate the right-holder, it does not release him or her from the correlative obligation to respect that right as long as the primary claim, as opposed to the secondary remedial claim, has not been waived. The power to waive a legal claim is relevant to the constraint imposed upon the duty-bearer, for it can release the duty-bearer from that constraint. But it does not seem essential to the existence of a claim. As MacCormick points out (1977, 197), one's claim not to be assaulted by an opponent in manly sports or by a surgeon conducting an operation is surely no more a paradigm of a claim than one's claim not to be assaulted by one engaged in "unmanly" pastimes or by an unqualified person operating upon one. The latter sustain legal actions against the duty-bearer as fully as the former and hold against the duty-bearer, if anything, even more steadfastly since there can be no pretence of a defence arising from the consent of the claimant. I conclude that my own simpler analysis of a legal claim in terms of the power to initiate legal proceedings to enforce the correlative duty is preferable to Hart's more complex analysis.

Moreover, on Hart's model every legal claim is an entire right, and a liberty-right at that. This requires him to build bilateral liberties and protective perimeters into every legal claim. This strikes me as undesirable for at least two reasons. The complexity of legal claims threatens to introduce an unmanageable complexity into many liberty-rights. Notice that some, although not all, of the duties that constitute the protective perimeter of a liberty-right are typically duties to the right-holder. For example, protecting a man's right to look at his neighbor over the fence are his neighbor's duties not to enter on his land and not to beat him up. Thus, Hart must build claims against entry and against assault into his liberty-right. But as soon as claim-rights conceived of as liberty-rights become constituents in liberty-rights, the complexity of liberty-rights becomes multiplied in an alarming manner. Indeed, his model threatens to generate infinite regresses of liberty-rights within liberty-rights within liberty-rights. Moreover, Hart's model of a legal right is an effort to reveal the nature and structure of a legal right by analyzing it into Hohfeldian elements. For this analytic purpose, for this purpose of displaying a complex legal phenomenon as a complex of simpler constituents, one prefers the simplest possible analysis of those elements that are legal claims. My conclusion is that although Hart's analysis of a legal claim should be rejected as overly complex, he has proposed the right sort of analysis, an analysis in terms of legal powers, and that his suggestion that a right confers control is even more insightful than he recognized.

Third, Hart's analysis of a claim-right is supposed to explain the sense in which such a right is possessed by the right-holder. From first to last Hart has insisted upon the essentially distributive nature of rights, the way in which they confer freedom (I would add control) upon *each* individual covered by the right-conferring law. This feature is reflected in our language of rights. "We also speak of the person who has the correlative right as *possessing* or even *owning* it." (He might well have italicized the "has" as well. He could have added that we speak of *someone's* right as *his* right or *her* right.) Hart suggests that "this figure becomes intelligible by reference to the special form of control over a correlative duty which a person with such a right is given by the law." Thus, the very same legal powers that explain in what sense a correlative duty is owed to a right-holder are supposed to explain the sense in which that holder owns the right to performance of this duty.

I must confess that I cannot understand how the right-holder's control over the correlative obligation is supposed to explain his or her ownership of the claim-right. Presumably this control explains the sense in which the right-holder possesses or owns the right by analogy with the control that an owner has over his or her possessions. But then the legal control over the correlative obligation should lead us to speak in the first place of the right-holder as possessing or owning the obligation and only derivatively, if at all, of his or her possessing the correlative right. We do not, however, speak of the right-holder as possessing or having the obligation; on the contrary, it is the duty-bearer's duty owed to, but not owned by, the right-holder. Moreover, even if this explanation worked in the special case of claim-rights, it would not explain the sense in which the right-holder possesses or owns liberty-rights or power-rights, since these do not necessarily involve any comparable control over correlative obligations. Just because the concept of a right, whatever the kind, is essentially distributive, Hart needs a more general explanation of the sense in which one has, possesses or owns a right.

Fourth, what most needs explaining is the correlation between a legal claim-right and its corresponding relative duty. The very label that Hart chooses for a claim-right, "right correlative to obligation" (1973, 175), shows that to his mind it is this correlativity that is definitive of this kind of right. The crux of his explanation of the relation between right and duty is "the special form of control over a correlative duty which a person with such a right is given by the law" (1973, 193). But his model of a legal right undermines his attempt to explain, or even preserve, this correlativity, because it requires him to construe every claim-right as a special kind of a liberty-right.

When Hart characterizes Bentham's conception of a claim-right, he does so in a manner that makes clear the logical correlativity of legal claim and corresponding relative duty: "All rights correlative to obligations are rights to services which consist in the performance of their correlative obligation. . . ." (1973, 176-177). Thus the individual's right not to be assaulted and the duty of others not to assault the individual are logically correlative simply because the content of the individual's claim-right, that *to* which the claimant has a right, is defined as and thus consists in the performance of the corresponding relative duty. Right and duty are logically correlative when the content of one must— logically must—match the content of the other, because one is defined in terms of the other.

Now that we understand the correlativity of right and duty, let us see what happens to this correlativity when a claim-right is analyzed in terms of Hart's general model of a legal right. My right not to be assaulted, to take his paradigm example, turns out to be a liberty-right with three bilateral liberties at its center: my liberty to waive or not waive the duty of others not to assault me, my liberty to sue or not sue for compensation in the event that another person assaults me without my consent, and my liberty to waive or not waive payment of compensation awarded me for wrongful assault. According to Hart's own explanation of the nature of an obligation correlative to a liberty-right, the obligation correlative to this complex liberty-right would consist in three matching duties of noninterference: the duty of others not to interfere with my waiving or not waiving performance of the duty not to assault me, the duty of others not to interfere with my suing or not suing for compensation in the event that some person assaults me without my consent, and the duty of others not to interfere with my waiving or not waiving payment of compensation awarded me for wrongful assault. But surely none of these can plausibly be regarded as logically correlative to my right not to be assaulted, for surely an assailant who beats me to a pulp without my consent violates my claim-right not to be assaulted even if he or she has not interfered with my exercise of any of the three liberties Hart places at the center of his model of a claim-right. Because Hart's general theory of legal rights misinterprets the essential content of a claim-right, it misplaces and misinterprets the content of the correlative obligation. Only if one recognizes, with Bentham, that the defining content of a claim-right is a service of the duty-bearer owed to the right-holder can one explain the logical correlation of my right not to be assaulted and another's correlative obligation not to assault me.

Immunity-Rights

Hart has proposed a general theory of legal rights as legally respected choices and offered a model of a legal right that, he believes, is applicable to liberty-rights, power-rights and claim-rights alike. But what of the other kind of rights identified by Hohfeld, immunity-rights? One might, I suppose, deny that there are any genuine immunity-rights, but Hart does not do this.

> The chief, though not the only employment of this notion of an "immunity right" is to characterize distinctively the position of individuals protected from such adverse change by constitutional limitations or, as Hohfeld would say, by disabilities of the legislature. Such immunity rights are obviously of extreme importance to individuals and may usually be asserted in the form of justiciable claims that some purported enactment is invalid because it infringes them. [1973, 199]

Hart concedes that his analytical model cannot explain such fundamental constitutional rights of the individual and concludes that his general theory of rights is adequate to account for only "the rights of citizen against citizen; that is of rights under the 'ordinary' law (1973, 198). But is it adequate even for this? Before we turn to an examination of constitutional rights, let us see whether Hart's model can be extended to cover ordinary immunity-rights.

Hart observes that "immunities against divestment of various kinds are involved in the notion of ownership" (1973, 199, note). Accordingly, a paradigm example of an immunity-right is my right that my neighbor not sell my house and lot while I am away on vacation. The law confers this right upon me, in part, because it does not recognize any act of my neighbor as constituting a legally valid sale of my property. Now Hart's *express* reason for admitting that his analytical model cannot deal with immunity rights is that it consists entirely of liberties, duties, acts and acts-in-the-law, thus having no place for immunities. But his model does not contain any claims, either; yet he extends his model to deal with rights correlative to obligations by using the notion of "the individual's legal powers of control, full or partial, over that obligation" (1973, 196). Recalling that an immunity is the correlative of a disability immediately suggests dealing with a right correlative to disability analogously, by using the notion of the right-holder's legal powers of control, full or partial, over the correlative disability of the second party.

It seems quite possible to extend Hart's model to immunity-rights in this way, because the law does confer upon me various sorts of legal control over my neighbor's disability analogous to those Hart uses in his analysis of claim-rights. Presumably I can waive my immunity-right and extinguish my neighbor's disability simply by authorizing my neighbor to act as my agent in the sale of my property. In the event that he purports to sell my house without my authorization, I have the legal power to assert my right by petitioning the court to declare the "sale" of my property null and void or legally invalid and to order the "buyer" to return possession of my property to me. And I have the legal power to waive my claim that the "buyer" vacate my property and return possession to me. Thus on Hart's model, at the center of my immunity-right that my neighbor not sell my property stand my bilateral liberties of waiving or not waiving my neighbor's disability, of suing or not suing to have any purported sale declared invalid and possession returned to me, and of waiving or not waiving my legal claim against the ostensible buyer. Each of these bilateral liberties is protected by a variety of duties of noninterference.

That such an extension is possible does not show, however, that it would provide an adequate interpretation of immunity-rights. As one might expect, this analysis misrepresents the essential content of my right that my neighbor not sell my house and lot in a manner analogous to that in which Hart's treatment of claim-rights misrepresents their content. That to which I have a right is that my neighbor not do something, but *what* my neighbor is not to do is to sell my property rather than interfering with my exercise of certain related liberties of mine. Recall that my immunity-right is taken to be a "right correlative to disability" rather than a right correlatives to obligations of noninterference. What makes my right an immunity-right, rather than a claim-right, is that the correlative burden or disadvantage the law imposes upon my neighbor is a disability of selling my house, rather than one or more relative duties owed to me. Thus, Hart's general theory of legal rights is not general enough to deal with immunity-rights, even under ordinary law.

When one turns from ordinary immunity-rights of one citizen against another to constitutional immunities of the individual against the state, even Hart admits the inadequacy of his analytical model. His reason for believing that his choice theory of rights cannot be extended to constitutional immunities is that the individual citizen has no legal powers that give him or her control over the correlative disability of the legislature. There is nothing I can do, analogous to my act of authorizing my neighbor to sell my house on my behalf, that could waive my immunity against state legislation denying me equal protection of the laws, or extinguish the disability of Congress to make any law abridging my freedom of speech. Constitutional law simply does not respect my choice regarding these fundamental immunities.

I believe, however, that these examples of constitutional rights do not refute Hart's theory quite as simply or in precisely the manner he imagines. Consider, first, my constitutional right to the equal protection of the laws. This is conferred upon me by the Fourteenth Amendment, which reads in part: "nor [shall any state] deny to any person within its jurisdiction the equal protection of the laws." This does indeed confer upon me a constitutional immunity against "discriminating and partial legislation . . . in favor of particular persons as against others in like condition" (*Minneapolis Railway Co.* v. *Beckwith,* 129 U.S. 26 (1889)). And it is entirely true to observe that I have no legal powers conferring upon me control over my immunity from such legislation. But these legal facts do not immediately refute Hart's theory unless one takes this immunity to define the essential content of this right. I suggest that Hart is too quick to concede the inadequacy of his theory because he misinterprets rights such as these.

My constitutional right to the equal protection of the laws is primarily and essentially a claim-right and not an immunity-right. Its defining function in our legal system is, as Hart himself suggests in other passages, to secure for me a "benefit" consisting in "equality of treatment in certain respects" (1973, 198). At its center is my legal claim holding against any state in our country acting toward me in a partial or discriminating manner. This constitutional right has reference to "state action," and although state action includes legislation, it equally includes the administration of laws not in themselves discriminatory, the operations of state courts, and even the administrative acts of state officials such as boards of education or the Regents of the University of California. Thus Brown was alleging a state obligation to integrate a system of public schools, and Bakke alleged that the University of California had violated his claim to equal treatment in its admissions process. It is a mistake to assume that just because some constitutional right includes an individual immunity against legislation among its constituents that it necessarily constitutes an immunity-right of the individual against state legislation. This mistake led Hart to a premature confession of inadequacy.

But if my constitutional right to equal protection is not an immunity-right, then just where does my constitutional immunity against discriminatory state legislation fit into my right? The clue lies in this pregnant sentence: "Such freedoms and benefits are recognized as rights in the constitutional law of many countries by Bills of Rights, which afford to the individual protection even against the processes of legislation" (Hart, 1973, 197). Whatever Hart may have meant when he wrote these words, what they say to me can be explained in this way. The underlying and presupposed purpose or function of my constitutional right to equal protection is to secure to me a specific benefit, equal and nondiscriminatory treatment by any and every state within our country. Accordingly, the Constitution of the United States recognizes my legal claim to such treatment as a fundamental legal right. This defining claim is *protected by* my immunity against any state legislation that would deny me equal protection of the laws. In the end, then, Hart's analytic model is inadequate to explain my constitutional right to equal protection. But the reason is not that I have no legally respected choice regarding and no legal control over an immunity at its center. It is that Hart's model has no place for immunities in the "protective perimeter" of a right. A more adequate model of a legal right will enrich the notion of a perimeter of duties of noninterference to encompass a variety of Hohfeldian elements associated with the essential core of a right.

A paradigm case of a freedom recognized as a right in our constitutional law is the freedom of speech. The First Amendment reads in part: "Congress shall make no law . . . abridging the freedom of speech." Clearly this provision does confer upon the individual subject to the jurisdiction of the United States an immunity against legislation abridging freedom of speech, an immunity beyond any control the individual might choose to exercise. But once more, this fact in and of itself does not render inapplicable Hart's choice theory of legal rights because the right to free speech need not and should not be construed to be an immunity-right. As the language of the amendment suggests, the function of this Congressional disability is to protect a presupposed right, the traditional right of Englishmen to "the freedom of speech." Why else use the expression "*the* freedom of speech" rather than the simpler and more natural "freedom of speech"? This reading is supported by the way in which the Supreme Court has extended the application of this constitutional right to the states via the Fourteenth Amendment.

> The First Amendment to the federal Constitution provides that "Congress shall make no law . . . abridging the freedom of speech or of the press. . . ." While this provision is not a restraint upon the powers of the states, the states are precluded from abridging the freedom of speech or of the press by the force of the due process clause of the Fourteenth Amendment. . . . The word "liberty" contained in that amendment embraces not only the right of a person to be free from physical restraint, but the right to be free in the enjoyment of all his faculties as well. *Grosjean* v. *American Press Co.* 297 U.S. 243-244 (1936)

Since the constitutional right to free speech is a liberty-right, rather than an immunity-right, it does not automatically constitute a counterexample to Hart's choice theory. Indeed, it has at its center, as his model would require, a bilateral liberty. *West Virginia State Board of Education* v. *Barnette,* 319 U.S. 633-34 (1943) established the fact that the right to free speech confers a liberty of remaining silent as well as a liberty of speaking out. Moreover, this right incorporates protective duties of noninterference of other private individuals as well as official agents of the federal and state governments, as both Black and Douglas recognized in *Feiner* v. *New York,* 340 U.S. 326-27, 330-31 (1951). Thus, Hart's analytical model is almost adequate to explain the constitutional right to free speech. The immunity against Congressional and state legislation abridging free speech belongs in the "protective perimeter" of that right, not at its center.

Are there, then, no constitutional immunity-rights of the sort that Hart imagined to be immediate and compelling counterexamples to his legally respected choice theory of legal rights? There probably are a few of them. Perhaps the clearest example is the right of federal judges, conferred by Article III, Section 1, of the *Constitution,* not to be removed from office except on impeachment and conviction. The defining function of this right in our constitutional law is not to protect some presupposed liberty-right, claim-right or even power-right, but to render federal judges independent of political control by making them immune from any action of Congress, the Executive or the public that might purport to remove them from their judicial office. Again, the constitutional right of the individual person not to be enslaved or reduced to involuntary servitude conferred by the Thirteenth Amendment is best construed as an immunity-right. Its legal effect is not to impose any duty not to enslave upon governments or other persons, but to make legally invalid any contract, status or statute that purports to enslave anyone. Hart's analytical model, even with a protective perimeter enriched to include immunities, cannot be extended to immunity-rights such as these, because at their center stands a defining constitutional immunity over which the individual right-holder has no legal powers of control.

But do these constitutional immunities constitute genuine rights? Might Hart not allege that here the language of rights is redundant upon the language of disabilities, much as he charges the beneficiary theory of claim-rights with rendering the language of rights redundant upon the language of duties? Very wisely, Hart not only refrains from alleging this, he explains why such a charge would be out of place: "Such immunity rights are obviously of extreme importance to individuals and may usually be asserted in the form of justiciable claims that some purported enactment is invalid because it infringes them" (1973, 199). In effect, constitutional immunity-rights can properly and illuminatingly be spoken of as genuine legal rights, not because one or more choices of the right-holder are respected by constitutional law, but because the right-holder can assert them in justiciable claims against some second party attempting to infringe them. What is essential to this use of the language of rights is not some central choice but an adversarial context in which the will of the right-holder conflicts with the will of some second party.

Our extended critical examination of Hart's general theory and analytical model of legal rights yields a number of valuable insights. No single Hohfeldian element, such as a naked liberty, could constitute a genuine right; a legal right must consist of a complex of such elements. The unity of such a complex of Hohfeldian elements arises from its structure, consisting of a center that defines the essential content of the right and a perimeter of additional elements. The center of a legal right need not, however, be a bilateral liberty. There are unilateral liberty-rights, and there are also rights with legal powers, claims and even immunities at their centers. Thus, what is distinctive and essential to the concept of a right is not the choice of the possessor, but a context in which the will of the right-holder might confront the conflicting will of some second party. Hart's choice theory of rights must be replaced by some sort of adversarial conception of rights. Since a variety of Hohfeldian elements can give advantage to the will of the right-holder in a confrontation with some second party, Hart's protective perimeter must be enriched to include associated elements in addition to duties of noninterference. My task, thus, is to pick up where Hart left off and develop a more adequate model of legal rights.

Chapter 4

INSTITUTIONAL RIGHTS

Having rejected H. L. A. Hart's general theory of legal rights, I must provide a more adequate account of my own. My purpose in this chapter will be to preserve his many and profound insights while at the same time avoiding his errors. I will follow his example by constructing a Hohfeldian model of legal rights, by conceiving of a right as a complex structure of legal positions. But while his was a choice model focusing upon freedom, mine will be a confrontation model centering upon dominion, or freedom-control. Finally, I will generalize my theory even further by explaining how my legal model can be extended to apply to other species of institutional rights, such as the academic rights conferred by the rules and regulations of Washington University or the morality rights defined by the conventional morality of our society.

Defining Core

Only a complex of Hohfeldian elements could constitute a genuine legal right. But how can an aggregate or collection of fundamental legal positions, each of which is logically distinct and legally separable from all the rest, constitute *a* legal right? The challenge presented by Hohfeld's conceptual analysis of legal positions is to explain the unity of any complex legal position. The response suggested by Hart is that each right is unified by some central Hohfeldian element. I call this element "the core" of the legal right. This core is logically central to the complex right because it, and it alone, defines the essential content of the right. Thus, the creditor's right *to be repaid* has as its core the legal claim of the creditor against the debtor to be repaid, and the citizen's right to *free speech* has as its core the citizen's bilateral liberty to speak out or remain silent on a wide range of controversial matters. Because this core element defines the content of the right, to change the core in any way is to extinguish the old right and create a new and different right. To add, subtract, or modify an associated element, however, is usually merely to change a continuing legal right in some nonessential way.

Although every legal right contains Hohfeldian elements in addition to its core, the core unifies the right because each of these additional elements is associated with this core. Thus, an aggregate of Hohfeldian elements constitutes *a* single complex legal position, because each associated element belongs to the right only *via* its relation to the single core element. Although it is made up of many elements, each right is a unified structure, and it is its defining core that stands at the center of this complex structure.

There are at least three important aspects of the defining core, for the core determines three distinguishable yet related aspects of the nature of any right. First, it specifies the essential practical relevance of the right. This is because every Hohfeldian element involves some specified action, such as the act of repaying a debt or the act of speaking out on a controversial issue. Second, it identifies the holder of the legal right as a whole. Although a legal right may contain legal positions of parties other than the right-holder, the possessor of the right is necessarily the party whose legal position stands at its logical and functional center. Third, the core determines the modality of the right. Although the creditor's right to be repaid contains associated liberties, powers, and other Hohfeldian elements, it is a claim-right because its core is a legal claim of the creditor against the debtor.

Is the core of a legal right ever a complex of Hohfeldian elements? That is, does more than one legal position ever define the essential content of a legal right? Although I see nothing logically inconsistent in thinking in this way, I would rule it out of my theoretical framework as an unnecessary and undesirable complication. Why it is unnecessary to admit any complex cores into one's theory of legal rights is revealed by an ambiguous passage in Hart:

> In England and in most other countries a man has a right to look over his garden fence at his neighbor; he is under no obligation not to look at him and under no obligation to look at him. In this example the liberty is therefore bilateral; both the obligation not to look and the obligation to look are in Bentham's phrase "absent." [1973, 175]

Since Hart speaks of two obligations, "both the obligation not to look and the obligation to look," as being absent, one might imagine that he places a pair of legal liberties, both the liberty to look and the liberty not to look, at the center of his model of this paradigm of a legal right. Instead, he says that "*the* liberty is bilateral," implying that the core of this right is, not a pair of liberties, but a single liberty to look-or-not-look. Hence, it is usually unnecessary to incorporate several Hohfeldian elements into the core of a single right, for when the law suggests such a model, one can ordinarily picture the right as having a single complexly defined Hohfeldian element at its core.

Of course, it would be a mistake to link any and every pair of liberties in this way. Under United States law I have both a legal liberty of sleeping until noon and a legal liberty of not shaving before I leave my home. But it would be preposterous to speak of my legal liberty of sleeping-until-noon-or-not-shaving-before-leaving-my-home. It would be accurate to consider these two liberties as part of a single complexly defined liberty only if they were somehow linked *in* the law of the land. And even if they were linked by common legal sources or as spelling out the legally accepted meaning of some legal formula, such as freedom of personal life-style, one would not want to take a complexly defined legal liberty to be the core of a single legal right unless the other legal elements associated with this pair of liberties were related to them as a pair, rather than to each independently and somewhat differently. Suppose, then, a situation where there is some connection between more than one Hohfeldian element close enough so that one might be tempted to treat them as cores of a single right yet not tight enough so that one could treat them as a single complexly defined legal position. It is still not necessary to admit rights with more than one core element, for one can treat them as rights-packages, as clusters of rights rather than as single complex rights. Generalizing Feinberg's conception (1973, 70), we can define a rights-package as a set of rights all relating to some particular activity or subject matter. A paradigm case is the right to life which probably contains at least a claim-right not to be killed and a liberty-right of self-defence and might, more controversially, be thought to include a claim-right to be provided with the means of sustaining one's life and/or a liberty-right of ending one's own life. Given the alternatives of a complexly defined legal position and a rights-package, it is never necessary to picture any legal right as having more than one Hohfeldian element at its core.

Moreover, it would be theoretically undesirable to admit models of rights with more than one core element into one's theory of legal rights. The primary function of the core of any right is to define the essential content of that right. To admit the possibility of a core consisting of more than one Hohfeldian element would, therefore, be to conceive of some rights as having several logically distinct and legally separate contents. How, then, could they be core elements in a single legal right? Moreover, the unity of the core is theoretically important in order to meet Hohfeld's challenge that no mere aggregate of legal elements can constitute *a* legal right. If the core of a right is to unify the complex structure of the right, then it needs to have a very tight unity of its own. Ideally, it should be a single legal element. Finally, to admit rights with more than one core is to allow for the possibility that the various associated elements bear on these different core elements in different ways and that some elements may be associated with one of the cores but not with another. In this case, the complexity of the structure is brought out much better by taking the whole to be a rights-package rather than a single right with several cores. Accordingly, in my model of a legal right, the core is always a single Hohfeldian element, although sometimes a complexly defined legal position.

What kinds of Hohfeldian elements can function as the core of a legal right? In Hart's model, a bilateral liberty stands at the center of every paradigm case of a legal right. But I have argued that what is essential to any legal right is not some choice respected by the law, but that the law sides with one party vis-à-vis some second party in a possible conflict of wills. Thus, in my model only a legal advantage can function as the core of a genuine right.

Hohfeld appears to hold that there are four and only four sorts of legal advantages. Is it really true that *all*—and *only*—legal claims, liberties, powers and immunities are legal advantages? This might seem to be the case if one limits attention to confrontations in the courts. But as soon as one recognizes that the law is applied outside the courtroom as well as within it, one recognizes that Hohfeld's generalization breaks down in both respects. Not all legal powers, for example, are legal advantages for their possessor. Indeed, having a legal power becomes a legal *dis*advantage upon occasion. Suppose that I sue my surgeon for medical malpractice and allege that at the time I ostensibly gave my consent to the operation he performed I was legally incompetent to give free informed consent. I may lose my case and my legal adversary may have his way just because the court decides that I did have the legal power at issue. Also, Hohfeldian elements other than claims, liberties, powers or immunities are sometimes legal advantages. Imagine that a widower dies intestate, leaving one son and one married daughter. Imagine also that according to the law of the land married women cannot hold property in their own names and that their holdings automatically become vested in their husbands. The son demands his father's entire estate on the grounds that since his sister is legally incapable of owning property it is impossible for ownership of any part of the estate to pass from the father to daughter upon the death of the former. The daughter, however, demands one-half of the estate on the ground that the executor of an estate of one who dies intestate has a legal duty to divide the estate equally among the surviving heirs and that as a surviving child, she is one of his heirs. Now if the daughter can establish her liability to inherit, she wins her case. Here even a legal liability, so often a legal disadvantage, can be a legal advantage. I am not prepared to go so far as to assert that every kind of Hohfeldian element can, upon occasion, be a legal advantage. I do suggest that one should be cautious about generalization and examine the way in which any legal position bears upon the confrontation at hand on a case by case basis.

Nevertheless, it is surely true in every case that a legal advantage of one party vis-à-vis some second party must, by the very adversarial conception of a legal advantage I accept, be some sort of relation under the law. Is Hohfeld correct, therefore, in presupposing that a legal position can be a legal advantage of X in face of Y only if it is a relational position between X and Y, such as a claim of X against Y or a power of X over Y? Imagine a man intent upon rape confronting a woman who very much desires that he not have his way with her. In this conflict of wills, the criminal law sides with the woman and against the man by virtue of the duty not to rape it imposes upon the man. Yet the correlative legal claim is not a legal claim of the woman but of the state. Again, consider my legal power to alienate my own property, for example to divest myself of ownership of an expensive watch that is no longer keeping accurate time but quite readily repairable, by abandoning the watch. If I can establish that I really do have this legal power *over myself* in face of my objecting wife who alleges that I lack any such unilateral power because spouses own all property in common, then I can show that the law sides with me and against my wife in our conflict of wills. Thus, a legal advantage of X vis-à-vis Y need not be a legal position between X and Y, the adversaries in the confrontation within which it is an advantage.

Still, although the cores of legal rights are not as restricted as the traditional Hohfeldian analysis would suggest, there are important limits upon the kinds of legal positions that can function as the cores of rights. At the center of every legal right of X there must be some legal advantage of X. Moreover, it must be the sort of legal advantage concerning which X can have dominion. This is because rights concern a very special sort of legal advantage, an advantage consisting in the allocation of a system of freedom and control to the right-holder rather than the second party. Thus, although the state's claim against the would-be rapist that he not rape a woman is a legal advantage to the woman confronting a potential rapist, it cannot stand at the center of any right of the woman not to be raped, because the law does not confer upon her any dominion concerning the criminal duty not to rape. If it did, it would be her private claim not to be raped rather than the state's criminal claim that the man not rape her.

In the end, then, what conclusion can we draw about the kinds of Hohfeldian elements that can be cores of legal rights? Claim-rights and liberty-rights are so frequent in the law that one need hardly mention the fact that claims and liberties typically, although not inevitably, function as the cores of rights. Nor does it take much imagination to think of legal powers, such as the power to make a will or to enter into contractual agreements, that are central to everyday legal rights. Immunity-rights are probably much less common, and certainly less often recognized, but they do exist in most legal systems. My legal right against all other persons that they not sell my car has at its core my immunity against any act of another that would purport to transfer title to my car from me to a willing buyer. Again, the immunity-right not to be enslaved conferred upon every person by the Thirteenth Amendment has as its core the immunity of each individual from any contract, status or statute that purports to reduce the right-holder to involuntary servitude. Thus we are back to Hohfeld's fourfold classification of claim-rights, liberty-rights, power-rights and immunity-rights.

This is not, however, the whole story. Some years ago, Herbert Hart remarked to me in conversation that his model of legal rights could be extended to cover ordinary immunity-rights and liability-rights. Only much later did it dawn upon me what an extraordinary suggestion this was. I cannot recall in the entire philosophical or legal literature on rights a single reference to a liability-right as such. Hart's examples were a legal right to inherit property and a right to be given something. I shall discuss a less ordinary example of a liability-right, however, because it illustrates so well the importance of this neglected species of rights.

A number of recent cases in the United States concern the legal right of same-sex couples to be married. I suggest that the central, although not the only marriage right, at issue in these cases is a liability-right. James Hallahan, Clerk of the Jefferson County Court, refused to issue a marriage license to Marjorie Jones and her female friend. Jones *et al.* contended that this refusal denied them their constitutional right to marry. Now the right to marry previously recognized by the Supreme Court in *Loving* v. *Virginia* is presumably a liberty-right, and at its core is a bilateral liberty to marry or not marry the eligible individual of one's choice. But according to the judicial reasoning in *Jones* v. *Hallahan*, Ky., 501 S.W. 2d 588, this is not the legal right at stake in confrontations between same-sex couples wishing to marry and state officials opposing their wills.

> It appears to us that appellants are prevented from marrying, not by the statutes of Kentucky or the refusal of the County Court Clerk of Jefferson County to issue them a license, but rather by their own incapability of entering into a marriage as that term is defined. . . . If the appellants had concealed from the clerk the fact that they were of the same sex and he had issued a license to them and a ceremony had been performed, the resulting relationship would not contitute a marriage. [*Jones* v. *Hallahan*, 589]

In other words, what the same-sex couple lack is not a legal liberty of marrying one another but a legal liability of being married to each other. Because of the way in which marriage is defined, the laws authorizing court clerks to issue licenses and ministers and magistrates to perform marriage ceremonies do not confer upon them any legal power to issue valid licenses or perform valid ceremonies in the case of same-sex couples. Correlatively, same-sex couples lack a legal liability to be married in the United States.

In this respect, the cases concerning same-sex marriages are in striking contrast to the cases relating to interracial marriages. The legal right at issue in *Loving* v. *Virginia,* (388 U.S. 1), is a liberty-right to marry the eligible individual of one's choice and not a liability-right to be married. Richard Loving, a white man, and Mildred Jeter, a black woman, were married in the District of Columbia and then returned to Virginia and established their marital abode in Caroline County. They were then indicted and convicted of violating paragraph 20-58 of the Virginia Code:

> *Leaving State to evade law.*—If any white person and colored person shall go out of this state, for the purpose of being married out of it, and with the intention of returning, and be married out of it, and afterwards return to and reside in it, cohabiting as man and wife, they shall be punished as provided in § 20-59, and the marriage shall be governed by the same law as if it had been solemnized in this State. The fact of their cohabitation here as man and wife shall be evidence of their marriage.

At no time did the State of Virginia, or any other party to the case, suggest in any way that the Lovings were not legally married because they lacked the capacity to marry one another—that is, the legal liability to be married. Quite the contrary, just because their interracial marriage had taken place, they were guilty of a felony and sentenced to one year in jail, a sentence suspended on condition that they leave Virginia and not return for 25 years. And the legal right of the interracial couple upheld by the Supreme Court was their liberty-right to marry, their "freedom to marry" (388 U.S. 12) guaranteed to them by the Equal Protection and Due Process Clauses of the Fourteenth Amendment.

The contrast between the interracial cases, in which the liberty to marry is at issue, and the same-sex cases, in which the liability to be married is at stake, is brought out most clearly by comparing *Loving* v. *Virginia,* where a couple are appealing a conviction for having married in violation of a criminal prohibition, and *Anonymous* v. *Anonymous,* 325 N.Y.S. 2d 499, where a same-sex couple who had ostensibly been married were declared to have never been married at all. The plaintiff, a non-commissioned officer in the United States Army, sought a declaration as to his marital status with the defendant, whom he first met as a prostitute. Thereafter, the defendant followed the plaintiff to Fort Hood, Texas, where they later took part as groom and bride in a marriage ceremony. At 2 o'clock the next morning the plaintiff discovered that his "wife" was a male. The obvious practical question is whether the parties were legally married. The underlying and central legal question is whether a same-sex couple have the legal liability to be validly married by a minister or magistrate authorized by state law to perform marriage ceremonies. The decision of the court is directly to the point at issue:

> The instant case is different from one in which a person seeks an annulment of a marriage or to declare the nullity of a void marriage because of fraud or incapacity to enter into a marriage contract or some other statutory reason. Those cases presuppose the existence of the two basic requirements for marriage contract, i.e., a man and a woman. Here one of these basic requirements was missing. The marriage ceremony itself was a nullity. No legal relationship could be created by it. . . . Accordingly, the court declares that the so-called marriage ceremony in which the plaintiff and the defendant took part in Belton, Texas, on February 22, 1969 did not in fact or in law create a marriage contract and that the plaintiff and defendant are not and have not ever been "husband and wife" or parties to a valid marriage. [325 N.Y.S. 2d 501]

In other words, same-sex couples cannot be parties to a valid marriage because they lack the legal liability to be married.

All that remains is to become a little clearer about the nature of this legal liability and about how it can function as the core of a legal right. According to North Carolina General Statutes, paragraph 51-1, for example, the essential requirements for a valid marriage are:

> The consent of a male and female person who may lawfully marry, presently to take each other as husband and wife, freely, seriously and plainly expressed by each in the presence of the other, and in the presence of an ordained minister of any religious denomination, minister authorized by his church, or of a magistrate, and the consequent declaration by such minister or officer that such persons are husband and wife, shall be valid and sufficient marriage. . . .

For our purposes, it is important to notice that the prescribed marriage ceremony has two distinct stages—the consent of a male and female person and the *consequent* declaration by a minister or magistrate that the persons are husband and wife. This is why one must distinguish between the couple's legal *power* to consent to be married and their legal *liability* to be subsequently married, a liability logically correlative to the legal power of the minister or magistrate to perform the ceremony. Strictly speaking, it is the declaration that effects or brings about the marriage. Such a declaration has this legal consequence, however, only if the person making the declaration is legally authorized to do so and hence has the legal power to marry couples, and if the persons being married are legally eligible to marry and hence have the legal liability to be married. This legal liability is the core of a legal right because the eligible couple have legal dominion concerning its enjoyment. Thus, they acquire this legal liability to be married only if they first freely consent to be married to each other; no minister or magistrate has the legal power to marry reluctant couples dragged in off the streets, or even out of their bedrooms. And presumably the couple retain the legal power to withdraw their consent at any time during the marriage ceremony before the declaration has been completed. And individuals have the legal power to take legal action, as Marjorie Jones and Anonymous did, to establish their liability to be married or their lack of it. Although same-sex couples have not yet vindicated their liability-right to be married in the courts, their cases show very clearly that legal liability-rights are both conceptually coherent and practically important.

There are, then, at least five sorts of Hohfeldian elements that can and do function as cores of legal rights—claims, liberties, powers, immunities and liabilities. But how does one identify the core of a legal right? If we are to answer this question, it is essential that we recognize the problem it poses. This is *not* the problem of deciding which one of a given set of Hohfeldian elements constituting a right is the core of that right. Complexes of legal elements do not come in bundles; one never is given a set of Hohfeldian elements, knowing that they are all constituents in a right but not knowing just which one defines the essential content of that right. The real problem has two distinguishable aspects. First, what may be given is some part of the language of legal rights. Legal language contains many expressions such as "the right of marriage" or "the right to free speech." The problem then is to interpret the meaning of such expressions. Obviously the "plain meaning" of these expressions, especially when they occur in authoritative legal sources such as statutes or judicial decisions, must be taken seriously. But one must also consider any evidence of legislative intention and the line of reasoning used to justify any relevant judicial decision. One may even need to attempt the Herculean task of interpreting the legal norms in which the language of this right occurs in the light of the entire body of law. Since the language of rights has meaning only relative to possible confrontations, in the end one must interpret any rights expression in the light of its bearing upon adversarial conflicts between an alleged right-holder and some second party against whom the right might hold. This is why I propose a model of legal rights formulated in terms of Hohfeldian legal positions. Second, one may begin at the other end. What is given may be some confrontation in which one adversary is appealing to the law vis-à-vis some second party. The problem then is to identify and define the way in which the law might favor the party alleging some right in face of the contending party—that is, the alleged legal advantage upon which the conflict or dispute hinges. To do this, of course, one must pick out of the body of applicable legal norms those crucial to just this confrontation and interpret their language in the appropriate manner. Although one may find the problem of identifying the core of a legal right posed in either of two ways, by given language of rights or by some given confrontation of two parties under the law, it is one and the same problem in both instances. And the solution is suggested by the nature of the problem. The language of legal rights must be interpreted in terms of its application to confrontations of parties under the law, *and* the way in which the law favors one party vis-à-vis the other must be read in the language of the authoritative legal sources.

Let me illustrate what I mean by continuing my discussion of two distinct marriage rights. Clearly *Loving* v. *Virginia* established some sort of right of interracial marriage. But precisely how should we define this right? Just what legal position constitutes its defining core? I have suggested that it is a liberty-right. I shall now be more specific and assert that its core is a bilateral legal liberty to marry or not marry a person of another race. This interpretation is strongly, although not conclusively, supported by the language of Chief Justice Warren's opinion of the court:

> To deny this fundamental freedom on so unsupportable a basis as the racial classifications embodied in these statutes, classifications so directly subversive of the principle of equality at the heart of the Fourteenth Amendment, is surely to deprive all the State's citizens of liberty without due process of law. The Fourteenth Amendment requires that the freedom of choice to marry not be restricted by invidious racial discriminations. Under our Constitution, the freedom to marry, or not marry, a person of another race resides with the individual and cannot be infringed by the state. [*Loving* v. *Virginia,* 388 U.S. 12]

Although the language of judicial decisions, even when written by chief justices, cannot be taken at face value, my interpretation of this language fits the crux of the confrontation in this case. Virginia was attempting to punish the Lovings for having violated a statute prohibiting interracial marriages; the Lovings were defending their liberty of marrying each other on the ground that their alleged duty not to do so could not exist consistently with the Fourteenth Amendment.

When one turns to the leading cases concerning same-sex marriages, one finds that Baker appeals to "the right to marry without regard to the sex of the parties" (*Baker* v. *Nelson,* 191 N.W.2d 186) and Jones alleges "the right to marry" (*Jones* v. *Hallahan,* Ky., 501 S.W.2d 589). This language strongly suggests the liberty-right previously established in

Loving. No doubt this is no accident. Presumably the appellants wished to argue that legal restrictions on same-sex marriages are just as discriminatory, and hence unconstitutional, as prohibitions of interracial marriages. But both the logic of these judicial decisions and the nature of the confrontations in these two cases shows us that the relevant right they needed to establish to prevail is not the liberty-right to marry but the liability-right to be married. Unlike the State of Virginia, neither Minnesota nor Kentucky had enacted a statute prohibiting same-sex marriages. Neither state was seeking to punish the appellants for the violation of some alleged legal duty. Thus, no legal liberty was at issue in these cases. Instead, Nelson and Hallahan had refused to issue marriage licenses to the appellants on the grounds that they were not *authorized* to issue such licenses to couples legally *incapable* of being married. Hence, the relevant right the appellants needed to establish is their liability-right to be married without regard to the sex of the parties. This interpretation is confirmed by the reasoning of the justices in both cases.

> The questions for decision are whether a marriage of two persons of the same sex is authorized by state statutes and, if not, whether state authorization is constitutionally compelled. [*Baker* v. *Nelson,* 191 N.W.2d 185]

> A license to enter into a status or relationship which the parties are incapable of achieving is a nullity. If the appellants had concealed from the clerk the fact that they were of the same sex and he had issued a license to them and a ceremony had been performed, the resulting relationship would not constitute a marriage. [*Jones* v. *Hallahan,* Ky., 501 S.W.2d 589]

In these confrontations concerning same-sex marriages, the law failed to side with these appellants, not because it imposed upon them any legal duty not to marry, but because the law failed to confer upon them any legal liability to be married to another person of the same sex.

Thus, one can and should distinguish between the liberty-right of interracial marriage, recognized by the courts, and the liability-right to same sex marriage, not so recognized. I do not present my brief discussion of these problematic rights as instructive to practicing lawyers; their interpretation of our law is far more precise and reliable than mine. My purpose has simply been to illustrate how one can identify the defining core of any legal right by an examination of the language of the relevant authoritative legal sources and of the way in which these sources are applied to confrontations between parties by the courts.

Associated Elements

A legal right, such as a man's legal right to look over his garden fence at his neighbor, is a complex legal advantage to which the right-holder can appeal in the event of some possible confrontation with one or more second parties. It is a legal advantage, not necessarily because its possession is beneficial to the right-holder, but in the sense that it favors the right-holder's will vis-à-vis the opposing will of any second party. A right is *complex* in that it is constituted by a number of Hohfeldian elements in addition to its defining core. It is a complex because these associated elements belong to the right only by virtue of their essential relation to that core.

Since a legal right is a complex legal advantage, each of the associated elements must itself be a legal advantage to the right-holder in face of the second party or parties of the right. I use the word "to" advisedly. Although each associated element must be a legal advantage to the right-holder, it need not be some legal position *of that first party*. As Hart observed, the neighbor's criminal duty not to prevent a man from looking over his garden fence at her by any act of murder or criminal assault "protects" the exercise of the man's core bilateral liberty of looking or not looking. Nevertheless, since this duty is not the correlative to any legal claim of the right-holder, it is not possessed by the right-holder in any sense. Most of the associated elements in any right probably are, however, legal positions of, as well as legal advantages to, the possessor of that right. Thus, a man's core bilateral liberty of looking or not looking over his fence at his neighbor is "protected" by his legal claims against his neighbor not to be prevented from looking or forced to look by entering his garden or by any assault or battery upon his person.

Not every legal advantage of the right-holder in face of the second party belongs to a specified right. Let us imagine, for example, that a man has purchased an easement over his neighbor's property so that he now possesses a right of way from his garage to the street in front of his neighbor's house. The man's consequent claim that the neighbor not interfere with his driving from his garage to the street is a legal advantage to the man in the event that the man wants to drive across the neighbor's property and she wants to stop him from doing so. But it is obviously not part of a man's right to look over his garden fence at his neighbor, for it has no essential connection to the defining core of this legal right. Only legal advantages concerning the exercise or enjoyment of the core of a specified right are associated elements in that right. A complex of distinct Hohfeldian elements can have the unity required to constitute a legal right only if each and every element in addition to the central core is essentially tied to that core.

Precisely how must any associated element be related to the defining core in order to belong to or be an element in the right defined by that core? H. L. A. Hart provides us with clues to the solution to this problem, although he failed to appreciate fully their significance. In "Are There Any Natural Rights?" he remarked that a very important feature of a moral right is that it concerns "a certain distribution of human freedom" (1955, 178). Although he emphasized the centrality of freedom, and therefore developed a choice theory of rights, on my confrontation model of rights it is the notion of distribution that is more central. Rights concern the distribution of freedom *to* the right-holder *rather than* the second party in some possible confrontation of wills. Moreover, they necessarily involve the distribution of more than freedom. Once more Hart provides the clue when he notes that the metaphor of a person possessing or having a claim-right "becomes intelligible by reference to the special form of control over a correlative duty" given to that person by the law (1973, 193). Thus, rights also involve the distribution of control *to* the right-holder *rather than* the second party in some possible confrontation. It is not merely that the creditor is free to accept repayment while the debtor is legally constrained to repay the debt; the creditor has legal powers the debtor lacks, such as the power to cancel the debt or sue for repayment, that give him control over the duty correlative to his right.

Accordingly, each associated element belongs to the specified legal right by virtue of distributing some sort of freedom or control to the possessor of its core rather than to any second party. It follows that a man's right to look over his garden fence at his neighbor includes a variety of associated Hohfeldian elements other than any "protective perimeter" of duties of noninterference. For example, it includes a man's legal power of restricting his core bilateral liberty by contracting with his neighbor not to look at her over his garden fence, for this gives him some measure of control over the core of the right. The right-holder's bilateral liberty to exercise or not exercise this associated legal power confers on the possessor of the core one kind of freedom essentially connected with the exercise of that core. A very different sort of associated element is a man's legal immunity against his neighbor's terminating his core liberty to look or not to look by any unilateral act of her own. To say that the right-holder has this legal immunity is to say that the second party lacks any corresponding legal power. In this way the law is distributing control between the right-holder and the second party by withholding this sort of control from the second party. In a variety of ways, each associated element in a legal right confers some relevant kind of freedom or control upon the possessor of that right or withholds some relevant freedom or control from the second party.

It is essential, however, that the associated element contribute some measure of freedom or control directly. Hohfeldian elements that indirectly, through the effects of their exercise or enjoyment, do so are not constituents in the specified right, for their connection with its defining core, when it occurs, is merely accidental. One of the associated elements in a man's legal right to look over his garden fence at his neighbor is his legal claim against his neighbor not to be prevented from looking by any act of assault or battery. This Hohfeldian element directly protects his exercise of a man's core liberty of looking or not looking at his neighbor, because not being battered or even assaulted in itself leaves one more free to exercise that liberty. Let us imagine, however, that the neighbor disobeys the law and repeatedly attempts to stop the man from looking at her over his garden fence by acts of assault or battery or both. A court order that the neighbor cease and desist from any and all such acts upon the man might well enable his will to prevail over hers in this confrontation. But in order to obtain any such writ of mandamus, the man must go to court, and this costs money. Let us imagine further, however, that the man has loaned Jones $5,000 in the past and that the time for repayment has arrived. The man's legal claim against Jones to be repaid is in its way a legal advantage in the man's conflict with his neighbor, for it would enable the man to obtain the money needed to hire a lawyer to obtain a writ of mandamus, prohibiting any further acts by his neighbor of interference with his exercise of his liberty of looking at her over his fence. Still, it is surely not an element in the man's legal right to look at his neighbor over his garden fence, for it is only indirectly and accidentally tied to the defining core of that right.

One additional proviso is required. I have said that each associated element confers upon the right-holder some sort of freedom or control concerning the exercise or enjoyment of the core of the specified right. The possession of some legal liberty does not imply the freedom to exercise it, for freedom of action is restricted by many constraints other than the constraints imposed by the law. Again, the possession of a legal power does not automatically guarantee actual control, for the possessor may, like the man without sufficient funds to hire a lawyer, not be in a position to exercise his or her legal power. It is only *if respected* that any associated element actually confers freedom or control upon the right-holder. It remains true, however, that the point or purpose of each associated element is to confer such freedom or control and that in any viable legal system legal positions are respected often enough so that legal advantages are very often practical advantages as well.

How, then, are the associated elements in a legal right tied to its defining core? They are functionally tied by the way in which any associated element, if respected, confers upon the possessor of the core some sort of freedom or control concerning the exercise or enjoyment of that core. These ties confer a tight unity upon any right because this functional connection must be direct rather than indirect.

Dominion

Indeed, the unity of a right is even tighter than my account so far would suggest. I have argued that a legal right is a complex structure of Hohfeldian elements consisting of a defining core together with a variety of associated elements. Each associated element is tied to the central core by conferring upon the right-holder, at least if respected, some sort of freedom *or* control concerning the exercise or enjoyment of the core. One must not imagine that freedom and control are two independent aspects of human life. Although they are conceptually distinct, they are inseparable in fact. I cannot have any genuine freedom to take an afternoon walk through the woods unless I have control over anyone who would lock me in my study or block my path by standing in my way. Conversely, I cannot have any real control over my young son unless I am free to issue orders to him and to impose punishments for disobedience if necessary. What a respected legal right confers upon its possessor, then, is a two-sided freedom-control.

Can we find a single word and a unified concept to sum up this freedom-control? As usual, Hart supplies a revealing insight.

> The idea is that of one individual being given by the law exclusive control, more or less extensive, over another person's duty so that in the area of conduct covered by that duty the individual who has the right is a small-scale sovereign to whom the duty is owed.

Shall we call this freedom-control "sovereignty"? To do so would be doubly misleading, for sovereignty is by definition a supreme power or authority and the sovereign is often thought to be a lawgiver above the law. To possess a legal right, however, is to have a position under the law and to be subject to those who make and enforce the law.

Still, Hart's language points to the word and the concept we need. The word is "dominion." In order to avoid unnecessary confusion, let us immediately resolve the ambiguity between the sense in which dominion is the power of governing and that in which it is the right to govern. The latter is useless for our purposes, for it would be circular to explain the concept of a right in terms of the right to rule. The concept we need is that of dominion in the sense of the power of governing. Paradigm examples of those who have dominion are the Roman *dominus* and the feudal lord.

The *dominus* was far from sovereign in Roman society; he typically held a subordinate position in society and was always subject to the law.

But he was master of his household, that is, he was master of the property of the family and master over the other members of the family. Within the household, the *dominus* had almost unlimited freedom and control vis-à-vis the others, who were constrained by and had virtually no control over their master.

The dominion of the feudal lord displays the same essential features. He was subject to his king under whom he held his fiefdom. Thus, his dominion was subordinate and limited. But he was lord of his manor and could lord it over his vassals. In relation to his vassals, the lord possessed the largest measure of freedom and control, while their wills were predominantly constrained and impotent.

The dominion conferred upon a right-holder by a respected legal right is essentially similar. It is a two-sided freedom-control concerning a limited domain defined by the core of the right and in face of the second party or parties to that right. To the extent that it is realized, this dominion enables the will of the right-holder to prevail over the will or wills of the second parties in any confrontation to which the right is relevant.

Thus, the essential function or defining purpose of legal rights is to determine the distribution of dominion among those subject to a legal system. They accomplish this aim by allocating legal positions between the parties to potential confrontations so that the law favors the will of the right-holder vis-à-vis the opposing will of the second party. On this view, a legal right is a system of legal advantages that, if respected, confers upon the right-holder dominion within a domain defined by its core and over his or her potential adversaries.

The Parties to a Right

The language of rights is essentially adversarial, for it presupposes some possible confrontation to which the specified right is applicable. Accordingly, there are three parties, or classes of parties, to every legal right. A first party is a person who possesses the right, a right-holder. A second party is a potential adversary in a confrontation to which the right is relevant, the person against whom the right holds. A third party is anyone other than the principals, the right-holder and the second party, and who could intervene to side with one principal against the other. Let us reflect upon each kind of party in turn.

A first party is a right-holder, a possessor of the given right. Who is the possessor of any specified legal right? It is the party whose legal position constitutes the defining core of that right. Thus, it is the creditor who is the first party of the right to be repaid, for it is the creditor who has the legal claim to repayment against the debtor. And it is the owner who has the right to drive the car without the permission of another because it is the owner who has the legal liberty to use an item of tangible property as he or she wishes within the bounds of law.

Although one usually speaks of *the* possessor of a legal right, a right can have more than one first party. The constitutional right to free speech is possessed by each and every citizen of the United States. This is why it is so natural, and appropriate, to speak of "our" right to free speech. No doubt, Hohfeld would object to saying that we are all possessors of the right to free speech. Strictly speaking, each citizen has his or her own constitutional right to free speech because the constitutional law of the United States confers upon each individual citizen a bilateral legal liberty of speaking out or not speaking out on controversial matters, and each such legal position is the defining core of a distinct legal right. Still, there is no linguistic or conceptual impropriety in speaking of a single right to free speech with many first parties provided that we do not forget that this is a convenient shorthand for speaking about a set of similar legal rights of separate individuals.

On rare occasions, however, a legal right may have more than one first party and yet it cannot be analyzed into separate rights of the several parties. Consider a bank account in the name of John Doe *and* Jane Doe, rather than in the name of John Doe *or* Jane Doe. Although neither John Doe nor Jane Doe has any legal right to write checks against this joint bank account individually, John Doe and Jane Doe do have such a right together. Here two first parties possess the same right, numerically not just qualitatively the same.

A first party to a legal right is a possessor of its defining core. But a right is more than its core; it also includes a variety of associated legal elements that confer freedom-control concerning the exercise or enjoyment of that core upon the right-holder. We have noted, however, that not all of these associated elements need be legal positions of the right-holder. Hence, it would be inaccurate to say that the first party of any right is the possessor of every element in that right. What one can and should say is that the possessor of any specified legal right is the party that (1) possesses the legal position that constitutes the core of the right and (2) possesses a balance of legal advantages in face of some unspecified adversaries in any conflict concerning the exercise or enjoyment of that core.

But in precisely what sense does a first party possess a legal position or a legal advantage and hence possess a right? It is often supposed that one possesses a right in the sense of holding it as property, owning it as one might own an automobile. I venture to suggest that while we very often speak of a possessor of a right, of someone possessing a right or a right being possessed by someone, we very seldom speak of an owner of a right, of someone owning a right, or of a right being owned by someone. Hence, one must be very cautious about assuming that the language of possession, including possessive nouns or pronouns like "the creditor's right to be repaid" or "her right to privacy," is correctly interpreted as asserting or presupposing ownership.

Moreover, any such interpretation would lead immediately to an infinite regress that would render impossible any explanation of the concept of possessing a right. I own the typewriter upon which I am writing this paragraph. Presumably my ownership of my typewriter consists in either a very complex legal right or a complex set of legal rights concerning my typewriter. Now shall we say that I possess these rights in the sense that I own them? Well, then, presumably my ownership of my rights concerning my typewriter consists of a set of rights concerning my rights concerning my typewriter. Shall we say once more that I possess these rights in the sense of ownership? If we do we shall never be able to explain what it means to say that one has any right at all.

Let us return to the language of rights. Philosophers sometimes speak of a right-holder, and lawyers often say that someone holds this or that right. This reminds us of another sense of the verb "possess" defined as having possession of, in contrast to ownership. For example, a pickpocket may possess my wallet and its contents even though I still own them in the eyes of the law; again, a squatter may be in possession of a house I own. Possession in this sense seems to amount to a physical control over the property consisting in either physically occupying a piece of real estate or physically holding and manipulating a tangible object. A right-holder does not, of course, physically control his or her legal rights. Although a right-holder does typically possess one or more legal powers that, if respected, confer control, one cannot explain what it is to possess a legal right in terms of the possession of such legal powers without engendering another infinite regress. One holds a right, just as one owns a right, only in some figurative sense.

Can one give any literal interpretation to the language of possessing a legal right? One can if one turns to the Oxford English Dictionary (OED) and notes its definition of another sense of "possess" as "To have as a faculty, adjunct, attribute, quality, condition, etc. (often meaning no more than the simple *have*)." Precisely what is this "simple *have*"? It is simply another idiom of predication. Thus "She has intelligence" means no more than "She is intelligent" and "He has great strength" simply means "He is very strong." Rights are a kind of property, not in the sense in which real estate is a kind of property but in the sense in which color attributes are a kind of property. Unfortunately, this idiom in which we speak of substances having properties is philosophically misleading, for it prompts one to ask what kinds of entities properties are and just how one thing, a substance, possesses other things, its properties. All that is really involved in this idiom is asserting various predicates of some subject. To be sure, there are questions to be asked about the nature of subject and predicate and about their relation, but these are linguistic and not metaphysical questions.

Let us see, then, how the idiom of having rights can be translated into the idiom of simple predication. To say that X possesses a specified legal right is to say that (1) X possesses a legal position that is the defining core of that right *and* that (2) X possesses a number of legal advantages that on balance and if respected give X dominion over some unspecified adversary in any confrontation concerning the exercise or enjoyment of that core position. To say that a person has some legal position is to characterize that person in terms of how the law applies to him or her. For example, to say that X has a legal duty is to say simply that X is constrained by the law, and to assert that X has a legal ability is to assert that the law enables X to effect legal consequences. And to say that a person has some legal advantage is to say that in some way the law sides with or favors the will of that person in face of some presupposed or potential adversary. In this way, the idiom of possessing rights can and should be understood as nothing more than a way of speaking about how the law applies to a first party under the law and of the way the law favors that party's will in some possible confrontation with some second party.

A second party to any specified legal right is any person, natural or artificial, against whom the right holds. Is a second party, like a first party of a given right, identified by its core? Not directly because, *pace* Hohfeld, not every legal position is a relation between two persons under the law. Although every Hohfeldian element is necessarily someone's legal position, not every legal position is a relative one. Still, a second party to a right is indirectly identified by its core, for a party against whom the right holds is an adversary in a potential confrontation concerning that core. More precisely, a second party to a specified legal right is anyone whose will could conflict with that of the right-holder concerning the exercise or enjoyment of its core *and* who would be disadvantaged on balance by the law in any such confrontation. The qualification "on balance" is important, for no single legal advantage would hold against another party; only a complex of Hohfeldian elements could constitute a legal right. How many such elements must there by? There must be enough to tip the balance in most confrontations concerning the core of the right.

What does it mean to say that some legal right "holds against" one or more second parties? The paradigm case, I suppose, is a legal claim-right that holds against some duty-bearer. This suggests that for a right to hold against a second party simply means for it to impose a duty upon that party, but this suggestion will not do. For one thing, not every legal right is a claim-right, and other species of rights do not imply any correlative duty. Thus, what is central to their holding against some second party is something quite different. For example, a liberty-right holds against anyone who would try to use the law to prevent the right-holder from exercising his or her liberty right; for it constitutes a legal defence in any suit or prosecution aimed at that action. For another thing, even a legal claim would not hold against any second party were it not protected by an immunity against termination by the duty-bearer. Thus, the creditor's legal claim against the debtor to be repaid would hardly hold against the debtor if that debtor, like the creditor, had the legal power to cancel the debt whenever he or she wished.

The relevant sense of the verb "to hold" is defined as "to maintain one's position (against an adversary)." Thus, the notion of holding against a second party has two aspects. A legal right holds *against* a second party in the sense that it disadvantages that party in the relevant confrontation with the right-holder. That is to say, when X has a legal right in face of Y, the law sides with X and against Y in some potential conflict of wills between these potential adversaries. Also, a legal right *holds* against a second party in the sense that it stands fast in the face of resistance by that second party. It is for this reason that one hesitates to say that my privilege of entering on my neighbor's land, conferred upon my by her permission revokable at will, is a legal right in face of my neighbor. It is too fragile to be more than a privilege, to be a real right holding against my neighbor.

A party to a right is any potential party to or participant in the possible confrontation that right presupposes and to which it is relevant. A *third* party is, following the OED, "a party or person besides the two primarily concerned, as in a law case or the like." In other words, a third party is one other than a first or second party (the principal adversaries) who might intervene to side with one and against the other.

A very important aspect of the way the law sides with a right-holder against a second party in any relevant confrontation consists in the legal rules governing interventions by third parties. Suppose that I observe a teenager being beaten up by a drunken man. The victim's claim-right under tort law not to be battered is being violated by a second party, a man against whom the claim-right holds. Even if I believe that the teenager deserves a beating, the law imposes a duty upon me not to join with the man in hitting the boy, or even to hold the victim so that he provides a better target, for either form of intervention would be itself a battery. On the other hand, the law permits me to prevent the aggressor from continuing his beating, either by physically restraining him or by striking him with my powerful fists or big stick if necessary; for although such an act of touching without consent would under normal circumstances constitute a battery against the man, in the present situation I could plead defense of others were the case ever to come to court (Prosser, 1971, 112). I might even have a legal duty thus to intervene, if I happen to live in a jurisdiction that has enacted duty-to-rescue legislation, or if the child is one to whom I have a special duty of care.

Probably duties of third parties not to intervene in such a way as to side with the second party against the right-holder are more common than positive duties of intervention. Consider, for example, the claim-right of a creditor holding against a debtor and imposing upon that second party a legal duty to repay the loan on the due date. Every third party has a legal duty not to intervene in such a way as to cause the debtor to fail to perform his or her duty of repayment, for the common law recognizes a tort of inducing breach of contract (Prosser, 1971, 929). Thus, the law sides with the first party and against the second party, not only in giving the creditor a power of taking legal action in the event that the debtor refuses to repay the loan and by imposing a duty of repayment upon the debtor, but also by imposing a duty upon all third parties to refrain from any interference with the contract between the principals.

It is of some importance to notice that third parties fall into two classes, legal officials and private citizens. Although the law, conceived of as a system of legal rules and principles and precedents, can be said to side with a right-holder vis-à-vis a second party, the law actually intervenes in any confrontation between them only through the actions of some legal official, such as a policemen preventing an armed robbery or a judge rendering a decision for the first party and against a second party. Private citizens are also permitted, and sometimes required, to intervene under the law, but typically in somewhat different ways. Although private citizens as well as officers of the law have the legal authority to arrest without a warrant, the situations in which these two classes of third parties have a legal power, a legal liberty or a legal duty to make an arrest differ somewhat (Prosser, 1971, 131-36). No private citizen, of course, has either a legal power or a legal duty to render a legally binding decision in any dispute between a right-holder and a second party.

Some of these legal positions of third parties will, if respected, contribute to the right-holder's freedom or control concerning the exercise or enjoyment of the core of a legal right. Accordingly, some third-party Hohfeldian elements will be constituents in a legal right. But in order to maintain the unity of the right, only third party positions that, if respected, *necessarily* contribute to the first party's dominion in face of a second party should be taken to be associated elements in a specified right. For example, a person's right not to be battered would include a policeman's legal duty to arrest any second party observed battering the right-holder but not a private citizen's liberty of restraining such an observed batterer. In any event, the complete articulation of a legal right will include three distinct parties or classes of parties—one or more first parties who possess the right, one or more second parties against whom the right holds, and third parties who are in a position to intervene in the presupposed confrontation and side with one of the adversaries against the other.

Model and Meaning

Having rejected H. L. A. Hart's legally respected choice model of a legal right, I have now completed the construction of my alternative, a dominion-if-respected model. On my interpretation of the language of rights, every assertion or denial of a right presupposes some possible confrontation to which the right is relevant. At the center of any right stands a defining core, a legal position that defines the essential content of the right, that to which the possessor has a right. Around this core cluster a variety of associated elements, other Hohfeldian elements that, if respected, confer upon the right-holder freedom and control concerning the exercise or enjoyment of the core. There are three parties or classes of parties to any right. A first party is anyone who possesses the right. A second party is anyone against whom the right holds. A third party is anyone in a position to intervene in the presupposed confrontation between a right-holder and a second party and side with one principal adversary against the other. The essential purpose or function of any legal right is to confer upon its possessor a specific sort of dominion over one or more potential adversaries. The right achieves its purpose only if the legal norms that define and confer it are respected by those subject to the law—hence, my dominion-if-respected model, constructed out of Hohfeld's fundamental legal conceptions, somewhat reinterpreted.

Perhaps a sample analysis of a familiar legal right into Hohfeldian elements would serve to illustrate and illuminate my model. The defining core of the creditor's legal right to repayment is the creditor's legal claim against the debtor that the debtor repay the amount borrowed, plus any interest that may have been agreed upon, on or before the due date. This core claim can itself be analyzed into the debtor's duty to repay together with the creditor's legal power of taking legal action in the event of threatened or actual nonpayment. Tied to this core are a variety of associated elements that, if respected, confer upon the creditor dominion over the debtor concerning repayment of the debt. These include at least the following: (1) The creditor's bilateral liberty of exercising or not exercising the core power to sue, (2) the creditor's power to waive the core claim and thus cancel the debt, (3) the creditor's bilateral liberty of exercising or not exercising this power to waive the core claim, (4) the creditor's legal power of accepting payment from the debtor or some third party and thereby terminating the claim to repayment, (5) the creditor's legal liberty of accepting payment tendered, (6) the creditor's legal immunity against the cancellation of the debt by any unilateral act of the debtor, (7) the creditor's claim against every third party that they not induce the debtor to breach his or her contract with the creditor, and so on. Thus, a legal right is not a single legal advantage but a complex structure of legal advantages that, if respected, together confer upon the right-holder dominion in some specific domain over one or more second parties to a potential confrontation.

Does my analytical model constitute an adequate interpretation of the meaning of the language of legal rights? Can some specified legal right accurately be said to consist in some such set of Hohfeldian elements? Neil MacCormick has argued that this is not so.

> During the whole period when the 1974 [Trade Union and Labour Relations] Act was in force, any individual who was a worker had the right conferred by Section 5(1) of the Act. For any worker at any moment of time his having that right would have entailed a large set of Hohfeld-type atomic relationships with other individuals in a position to affect his membership (actual or projected) of some union. But although such individual atomic relationships are derivable from the existence of the right conferred by the Act, the converse is not true. The legislature can establish that vast myriad of atomic relationships by establishing the right to non-exclusion and non-expulsion. It could not establish the latter by establishing the former. (Of course, the legislature could establish a whole set of such "atomic" relationships, but no particular set would be equivalent to the right actually established, which, depending on the circumstances which emerge, results in a variable set of claims, powers, etc.). [MacCormick, 1977, 206]

This passage contains two distinct, although related, arguments. A specified legal right cannot be identified with any particular set of Hohfeldian elements because one and the same legal right can entail different sets of Hohfeldian elements at different times. Also, no finite set of Hohfeldian elements can exhaust the meaning of legislation enacting a specified right, because it is always possible for valid judicial reasoning to infer a new Hohfeldian element as the courts decide new cases arising in unanticipated circumstances. Let us examine each of these arguments in turn.

It is true that the Hohfeldian elements entailed by the statement that some legal right exists vary over time. This happens both through the development of common law and through new legislation designed to improve the protection for some preexisting legal right. But my model is entirely adequate to explain such temporal changes in continuing legal rights. As long as the defining core of a legal right persists, associated elements can be added, subtracted or modified without changing the essential content of the right. Thus, my distinction between the defining core and the associated elements can readily explain how a given legal right can remain essentially unchanged and yet entail different sets of Hohfeldian elements at different times.

It is also true that, given any particular set of Hohfeldian elements entailed by the legal recognition of a specified right, it is always possible for the courts to infer new Hohfeldian elements as they decide new cases arising from unanticipated circumstances. MacCormick is entirely correct when he argues that no finite set of Hohfeldian elements can exhaust the meaning of legislation or judicial decision establishing the existence of some specified legal right. Thus, what I have proposed in this chapter is an analytic *model* of legal rights, not a definition of the meaning of the legal language of rights. The "and so on" in my sample analysis of the right to repayment represents more than the incompleteness in my knowledge of the various ways the law applies to creditors and debtors; it reveals an ineliminable logical richness in the language of legal rights.

Does the fact that no complete translation of the language of legal rights into Hohfeldian legal conceptions is possible undercut my Hohfeldian model of legal rights? Not, I believe, if my analysis is understood to be a model rather than a definition. Although it would be inaccurate to imagine that a legal right literally *is* a complex of Hohfeldian elements, it is entirely proper to maintain that a legal right can best be thought of *as* such a complex structure. But what is the point of interpreting the language of legal rights on this model if that language is not formulated in terms of Hohfeld's fundamental legal conceptions? It is just because a model does differ from what it models that it has the capacity to show us features of the original we are unable to discern, or to notice so clearly, when we pay attention only to the original itself.

The language of legal rights is not always clear and precise, and its relevance to human conduct often remains implicit in its formulation. The law, however, serves its regulative purpose only insofar as it is applied to those subject to it, and much of our interest in the law is a very practical interest, whether this be an interest in pursuing gain and avoiding loss or a more scientific interest in understanding forms of practice. When the language of the law is formulated in terms of Hohfeldian legal conceptions, its practical relevance is made explicit and expressed in more precise and unambiguous language. And to the extent that the interpretation of the law has been determined by previous judicial applications of the language of legal rights, such a Hohfeldian interpretation can be entirely accurate.

But the judicial interpretation of the law is not merely a process of finding a preexisting meaning given to legal language and fixed as long as the legal sources remain unchanged; judicial interpretation is in considerable measure a process of giving new meaning to the language of the law by resolving ambiguities and reducing vagueness in the old language and, at the same time, adding new language in the form of written decisions of the courts. There is no way to know in advance which Hohfeldian elements the courts will validly infer from the given legal sources. Thus, there is no way to complete the translation of the language of legal rights according to my model. But even here the model remains useful, for it indicates the *kind* of meaning that the courts can sensibly ascribe to the language of legal rights. The "and so on" in my analysis of the legal right to repayment indicates more of the same. Thus, it is more indicative of the open-endedness of the process of applying the law to those subject to it than it is indicative of a weakness in my model.

Knowing the kind of meaning that the courts must ascribe to the law enables one to use a Hohfeldian model of legal rights to formulate alternative interpretations that could be given to the law. Hohfeld's distinctions between the different legal positions suggest different ways in which the ambiguity of legal language could be resolved, and spelling out legal formulae in terms of specific legal positions of the several parties to a right suggests how vague language could be more precisely interpreted. This is useful both for the lawyers and judges actively involved in the judicial processes through which the meaning of the law develops and for moral philosophers or politicians actively seeking to improve the law.

My model of a legal right is also theoretically illuminating because it reveals the essential presupposition of the language of rights, the adversarial context in which its use alone makes sense. The three parties to any right, parties distinguished and made explicit in my model, are the three kinds of parties in the possible confrontation to which the given right is relevant. In order to understand properly the meaning of the language of legal rights, one must be aware of this central presupposition of its meaningful use.

Finally, the structure of my Hohfeldian model reflects the essential function of a legal right. Each associated element in my model is tied to the defining core of the specified right by the way in which, if respected, it confers upon the right-holder some sort of freedom or control concerning the exercise or enjoyment of that core. Thus, the structure of a legal right reflects the way in which a right functions to confer dominion in some limited domain upon the right-holder in face of one or more second parties. Understanding the point of a legal right is helpful in molding legal rights that perform their function well rather than badly. It is also helpful to the social scientist trying to explain why certain sorts of complexes of Hohfeldian elements tend to go together in any legal system. In these various ways, then, a Hohfeldian model of legal rights can be helpful as a model, even though it is only a model and not a genuine definition.

Would it be better if one could define a legal right in the way in which my model suggests? Even while rejecting the identification of a legal right with any particular set of Hohfeldian elements, MacCormick admits that "Of course, the legislature could establish a whole set of such 'atomic' relationships." If legislative enactments and judicial decisions were carefully formulated in Hohfeldian terms, there would be a marked gain in the clarity, precision, and unambiguousness of the language of legal rights. This linguistic gain would produce a marked increase in the certainty of the law, a very practical improvement. But this genuine value would be purchased at a price, the price of inflexibility as the law is applied to new circumstances that change in unanticipated ways. The vagueness and ambiguity of legal language have very real values of their own, for they enable legislators to hedge their bets and judges to adapt old law to new cases. Therefore, although I recommend my Hohfeldian model as an instrument for understanding the language of legal rights, I do not propose it as a substitute for the more traditional legal language.

It might, however, be possible to define this traditional language in the light of the model. Perhaps "X has a legal right to R" means simply "the law on balance sides with X and holds against one or more potential adversaries in any confrontation concerning R." This definition seems to be accurate enough. And it is general enough to cover both very simple legal rights consisting of a few Hohfeldian elements and more complex structures of legal advantages, even entire rights-packages. On the other hand, it is not very illuminating, for it leaves the notions of the law siding with one party, holding against some second party, doing so on balance, and just how a confrontation might concern the content of the right unexplained. Any such definition is more useful as a slogan to remind one of a Hohfeldian model than as an independently adequate analysis of the meaning of the language of legal rights.

Moreover, if the definition is to reflect accurately the entire range of such language, it must be an ambiguous formula, for the language of rights is systematically ambiguous. There are both sentences *in* the law that ascribe or deny rights and sentences *about* the law that report the existence or nonexistence of some right in the legal system. For this reason, there must be two ways of reading the proposed definition: "the law (hereby) on balance sides with X and holds against one or more potential adversaries in any confrontation concerning R" and "the law (in fact) on balance sides with X and holds against one or more potential adversaries in any confrontation concerning R." What this shows is that a fundamental and philosophically important ambiguity in the language of legal rights remains entirely unresolved and unclarified by my Hohfeldian model. This is simply because the same ambiguity infects the Hohfeldian vocabulary itself. Thus, the word "a duty" is used both in the law to impose constraint upon those subject to the law and in reporting the law to describe the existence of such constraint by the legal system. Similarly, the expression "a power" is used in the law to enable those under the law to effect specific legal consequences and also used in the social sciences to describe an ability to effect legal consequences. This ambiguity need not mislead us provided, and this is a crucial proviso, that we bear in mind this ambiguity of our Hohfeldian vocabulary as we use my model of a legal right.

Other Institutional Rights

Our most familiar and intelligible examples of rights are legal rights. To talk about a legal right is to talk about how the law applies to potential adversaries in some presupposed confrontation. I use the expression "the law" advisedly, for seldom if ever can a law, a single statute or judicial decision, create and define the entire complex of legal positions that constitutes a genuine legal right. Also, the proper interpretation of any given law depends in part upon how it fits into the entire body of legislative, judicial, constitutional and customary law recognized in the given jurisdiction. But the law exists only insofar as it is incorporated into the practices of a functioning legal system. Analytical philosophers often think of a legal system as a set of legal norms; social scientists more often think of it as a social system constituted by a set of officials such as legislators, judges, policemen and wardens, each performing some specialized function within a social institution. The law, the body of legal norms applicable within a given jurisdiction, is real only as it is recognized and applied within an organized institution defined by such interrelated social roles as that of the legislator, the judge, and so on. Thus, legal rights are rights instituted by one sort of social organization.

There are many other sorts of organizations that also institute their own sets of norms governing the conduct of their members. An organization, as I am using that term, is any organized social institution. To be organized, according to the OED, is to be "formed into a whole with interdependent parts; coordinated so as to form a system or orderly structure; systematically arranged." Thus, a social organization consists of some body of persons that is divided into subordinate bodies performing specialized functions; the individuals that make up a social organization play distinct but related social roles in it. We are all familiar with a wide range of organizations that create and apply their own bodies of norms. Churches often make and enforce their own laws; canon law has its own sphere of validity even when it is no longer recognized as valid by the legal system in a country. Private clubs often have their own constitutions and bylaws. Academic institutions typically enact and apply some set of rules and regulations governing the academic community. Business corporations normally institute their own bodies of rules to define their internal offices and regulate the business activities of the individuals who make up the corporate body. And organizations like the United States Tennis Association and the International Chess Federation promulgate and enforce the rules of specific sports or games.

Presumably every body of organizational norms brings into existence its own set of normative positions, for to assert the existence of any specified normative position is simply to describe how some presupposed set of norms applies to the person who has that position. Since it would not make sense to speak of a norm that does not apply to anyone's conduct at all, there can be no sets of actual norms without corresponding positions under those norms. It does not follow, however, that every body of organizational norms confers some sort of rights. A set of norms would do so only if it defined normative positions analogous to the legal positions Hohfeld identified. We have seen that ultimately the law applies to those subject to it by constraining their conduct or by enabling them to effect legal consequences. The various Hohfeldian legal positions can all be defined in terms of legal duties or legal abilities. Therefore, we can generalize my Hohfeldian model of legal rights and apply it to other sorts of organizational rights only where the norms instituted by some other organization are such as to impose duties and confer abilities upon those to whom they apply.

Academic institutions, such as Washington University, do establish rules and regulations of the sort that impose duties and confer abilities upon the members of its academic community. Examples of duties come readily to mind. The dean of the faculty has the duty of presiding at meetings of the Faculty of Arts and Sciences. The chair of each department has an academic duty to provide each tenure-track faculty member of the department with an annual evaluation of his or her progress or lack of it towards achieving tenure. The academic duties of the members of the faculty of Washington University are specified in a list of responsibilities promulgated by the Washington University Board of Trustees; these include a duty to meet announced classes regularly, a duty to hold office hours at times convenient to one's students, and a duty to perform services to one's department and to the University such as advising departmental majors or serving on university committees. Students have various duties imposed by the official Code of Student Conduct jointly approved by the student body, the faculty and the administration. That the various rules and regulations of Washington University impose academic duties upon the members of its academic community is hardly news.

That these same rules and regulations confer academic abilities and powers upon those subject to them has, however, received less attention. For example, the dean of the faculty has an academic power to recommend to the provost that an untenured member of the faculty of Arts and Sciences be granted tenure by Washington University. This is an important power, for it renders such a member of the faculty eligible for tenure since the Board of Trustees grants tenure only on the recommendation of a dean transmitted by the provost of the university. The Judicial Board has the academic power to sit in judgment upon and decide cases involving alleged violations of the Code of Student Conduct by undergraduate students at Washington University. Within the university community this is surely analogous to the legal power of a court to find an indicted defendant guilty or not guilty, and in the former event to sentence the party found guilty. A student has the academic power to render himself or herself liable to a grade in a course by enrolling in that course. A student has an academic ability, but not a power in the strict sense, to render himself or herself liable to being put on probation or being dropped by the university by achieving unsatisfactory grades in his or her courses. Any member of the faculty teaching a course in the University has an academic power to grade the students enrolled in that course. Others could, of course, read and evaluate the examinations and papers of the students or fill out and send in the forms upon which grades are reported, but their acts would not constitute actions of grading under the rules and regulations of Washington University.

It seems clear that an organization such as Washington University institutes a body of academic norms rich enough to confer academic rights upon those subject to them. Since its norms define normative positions analogous to legal positions, my Hohfeldian model of a legal right can be extended to apply to the organizational rights of a university. I can illustrate this by giving a somewhat rough analysis of the academic right to an accurate grade in each course. The core of this right is the academic claim of an undergraduate student at Washington

University against a member of its faculty teaching a course in which the student is enrolled that the teacher report an accurate grade of the student's performance in that course. This core claim consists of the academic duty of the faculty member to report an accurate grade of the student's performance in the course, together with the student's academic power to appeal to the dean of the college for performance or remedy in the event of threatened or actual nonperformance of this duty by the second party. Associated elements include at least the following: (1) The bilateral academic liberty of the student to exercise or not exercise his or her power of appeal; (2) the academic power of the student to enroll in any course offered in the college, provided that the course is not already filled and the student has completed its prerequisites; (3) the student's bilateral academic liberty to exercise or not exercise this power of enrolling; (4) the student's academic power of withdrawing from any course before the tenth week of the semester without the permission of the teacher; (5) the student's bilateral academic liberty to exercise or not exercise this power of withdrawing; (6) the student's academic immunity against termination of his or her core claim by any unilateral action of the member of the faculty teaching the course; (7) the academic duty of the chair of the department under whose auspices the course is offered to use his or her influence in favor of the student and to put pressure upon any faculty member of the department who fails to report an accurate grade for the student. If something like this analysis of the undergraduate's academic right to a fair grade is accurate and illuminating, then my Hohfeldian model of a legal right can profitably be extended by analogy to apply to the rights instituted by organizations such as Washington University. Just which sorts of organizations do in fact establish and recognize bodies of norms rich enough to confer rights obviously cannot be determined a priori; one must examine the normative system of each organization on its own terms. But wherever a body of instituted norms does define normative positions analogous to those identified by Hohfeld, organizational rights may exist and can be interpreted on a Hohfeldian model.

Not every set of norms is instituted by some organization. In addition to the rules of baseball officially recognized by the American League, there is the set of rules informally accepted and applied by those who play sandlot baseball in this or that area. No doubt the latter tends to conform to the former, but they are not the same, either in content or in validity. It may take some time for a change in the official rules of baseball to become known and generally accepted on sandlots around the country, and those who play on sandlots in some limited area may agree to depart from this or that rule of major league baseball to improve their rather different game. Again, the validity of the official rules is derived from their acceptance, promulgation and enforcement by the organizations, such as the American League and the National League, that control the major leagues. The validity of the rules of sandlot baseball depends upon the fact that they are generally accepted, both as standards to govern one's own play and as authoritative bases for settling disputes between players, by those who participate in this sport, either as players or as spectators or as unofficially appointed umpires. There is a similar contrast between the *Principles of Medical Ethics,* adopted by the American Medical Association in 1957, and the standards of good medical practice generally accepted by those who practice medicine in the United States today. The latter are recognized by the members of a profession in our society even though they are not instituted by their professional organization.

Bodies of norms such as the rules of sandlot baseball or the standards of good medical practice are not organizational, but conventional. They are instituted by convention in the sense defined by the OED as "general agreement or consent, deliberate or implicit, as constituting the origin and foundation of any custom, institution, opinion, etc., or as embodied in any accepted usage, standard of behavior, method of artistic treatment, or the like." Such norms are not created by any special body of legislators, are not applied to disputes by any official judges, and are not sanctioned by public bailiff or penal warden. They arise from psychological and sociological processes that somehow result in a widespread consensus and they are valid because they are accepted, applied and sanctioned by, as Bentham put it, *"chance* persons in the community" (Bentham, 1970, 35). They are the norms of some unorganized (not disorganized) group—that is, a group that as such has no organs, no specialized subgroups with distinct official normative functions to play in the whole. They are the norms of the group insofar as they are generally accepted as valid by the individual members of the group.

There surely are bodies of conventional norms of some logical complexity and practical importance. A clear example is any positive morality. A morality consists of the mores of some society. The mores, as conceived of by social scientists, are not coextensive with the customs of a society as the Latin term would suggest. The mores are those customary ways of acting that are generally regarded as so important as to be imperative and are informally sanctioned in serious ways by the members of the society. Thus, although it is customary in our society to eat three meals a day, one can eat more or less frequently without violating any of our mores. In order to distinguish between such conventional norms of morality and the "true" moral norms philosophers such as myself seek to discover, I shall call the former "morality" and the latter "morals." I shall similarly distinguish between morality duties and moral duties, morality rights and moral rights. What sorts of conduct are required, forbidden or approved by the mores of any given society is a matter to be established by anthropological investigation and not philosophical speculation; but philosophical analysis is required to explain the essential features of any positive morality.

The mores of any society serve as a very special sort of standard of conduct because implicit in them is a very special sort of norm. These norms of positive morality have four defining features. (1) Morality norms are instituted by convention. Unlike legal rules, they are not legislated by any special authorities, such as the king, a legislature or a judge, and are not enforced by any authoritative courts. They are norms, not of some organization, but of society in general. Morality norms are issued by the members of any society in moral education and in the criticism of the conduct of others; they are followed or disregarded by the individual agents in the society; and they are informally sanctioned with penalties imposed for deviation and rewards given for conformity. All of this presupposes some more or less definite awareness of the content of the norms of morality; and this in turn presupposes some conceptualization of one's mores, a conceptualization that will be expressed in the language of education and criticism. Thus, although there is no authoritative formulation of any such norm, morality norms are typically expressed in language and tend toward definite formulations, much as the proverbs or legends in any society are often expressed in something like formulae. Morality norms exist only as they are implicit in the practices of any society, but the nature of these practices of criticism, being guided by and sanctioning require that these standards of conduct be made explicit in language as well.

(2) Morality norms, at least the primary ones, are rules. They necessarily take the form of universal but specific directives. Since they are standards for human conduct, they would normally be formulated in sentences with directive meaning. They tell human agents what to do or not to do. In order to function to regulate individual choice and to occasion informal penalties for deviation or rewards for conformity, they must specify what sorts of actions are called for under what circumstances. Thus, "If asked an awkward question, never lie except to prevent some disaster" could be a morality norm, but "Always maximize utility" is too general and indeterminate to become embedded in the mores of any society. The norms that define any positive morality must be fairly specific in content.

At the same time, they must be universal in logical form. No individual norm, such as "Richard Roe open that window," could possibly capture the normative content of any mos, for it could not become *generally* accepted, taught, followed and sanctioned in any society. To be sure, the application of some universal morality norm to some particular situation might well imply some individual norm of conduct. But this individual norm would be derivative from and would presuppose the universal norm embedded in the mores of the society. Accordingly, the fact that morality norms are constituted by convention, that they exist only insofar as they are incorporated into certain sorts of social practices through an entire society, implies that the primary norms of morality must be formulated with a specific content and in a universal logical form.

(3) Morality rules are dual-aspect norms. They are standards for individual action *and* for reaction to the actions of others. They apply in the first instance to any individual member of the society choosing how to act, whether to break a promise or to perform an act of charity, for example. But since the mores of any society are by definition informally sanctioned, the rules of positive morality are also standards to govern the ways in which others are expected to respond to agents they observe deviating from or conforming to any morality rule. It is not just that others do in fact generally respond negatively to deviation and positively to conformity; they do so intentionally and in order to penalize disobedience or reward obedience to the morality norms accepted in their society. Moreover, they are expected to do so; these sanctioning activities are built into the social practices that constitute any positive morality. Accordingly, the rules of morality have two distinct, but essentially interrelated, applications. They apply to the conduct of the individual members of the society and to the reaction of other members of the society who observe or become aware of any individual following or deviating from the mores of their society.

(4) Finally, morality norms are nonelective. They are social rules that apply to one's conduct willy-nilly. There is nothing the individual can do to render them inapplicable to his or her conduct. In this respect, they differ radically from the equally conventional rules of sandlot baseball. If one chooses to play sandlot baseball, then one is required to abide by the rules recognized by the participants, and deviation from the prescribed modes of conduct will be sanctioned by them in the usual ways. But playing baseball is itself optional. If one chooses not to play the game, then the rules are inapplicable to one's actions. But morality is not regarded as a game by any society, perhaps because the members of the society regard these norms of conduct as so critically important that deviation should not be tolerated. Therefore, there is nothing the individual can do to opt out of morality; one cannot render the norms of morality inapplicable to one's conduct. One can, of course, refuse or fail to conform to the morality rules of one's society; one cannot choose not to be subject to those rules.

It is this that distinguishes the norms of morality from the code of etiquette practiced in any society. Etiquette consists of the conventional rules of personal behavior to be observed in the intercourse of polite society. It probably originated in the prescribed ceremonial in a royal court or elite circle and gradually became broadened to include socially prescribed proprieties for all ladies and gentlemen. The upper class connotations of the terms "ladies" and "gentlemen" remain. Accordingly, the norms of etiquette are elective. Since one need not participate in polite society (one is not required to go to dinner parties or attend formal weddings), one is allowed to opt out of the code of etiquette. No doubt one pays a price for such a choice, but the rules of etiquette do not demand that others punish one for thus withdrawing from the best circles. The elective nature of the norms of etiquette is confirmed by our use of the expression "good manners." A manner is a way of doing something. Etiquette mainly prescribes how one must do something if one chooses to do it at all, for example, how one must hold one's knife and fork if one accepts an invitation to dinner. Morality norms, on the other hand, specify *what* one must or must not do, not simply *how* one ought to engage in some optional activity.

The norms of any positive morality consist of a set of nonelective dual-aspect rules instituted by convention in some society. Whether any given morality has a code of rules logically rich enough to confer rights is a contingent empirical matter. Let us leave any general conclusions on this issue to anthropologists and reflect briefly upon the morality norms of our own society. Our mores surely forbid acts of murder, theft, lying, inflicting unnecessary bodily injury, rape, cruelty, gratuitous insult, and malicious gossip, to give but a few familiar examples. Moreover, our morality rules probably require keeping one's promises, caring for one's dependent children, aiding someone in distress, provided one can do so without undue sacrifice, and doing one's fair share in any cooperative enterprise. Moreover, these conventional norms constrain our conduct for many reasons ranging from noninstitutional moral considerations to a prudent regard for the informal but very real social sanctions frequently inflicted upon those who deviate from the mores. Accordingly, we have morality duties not to murder, not to steal, not to lie, and so on, as well as morality duties to keep our promises, care for our children, etc.

Not only do our morality norms define morality duties and liberties; they also enable us to effect normative positions under positive morality. This is because of the way in which specified acts enter into the internal logical structure of the norms. One norm might be expressed roughly, "if a parent tells a dependent child to do something, then the child ought to do it." Thus, a parent has a morality power to impose morality duties upon her or his young children. Another morality rule is something like "it is wrong for a male to have sexual intercourse with a female unless she consents." Hence a female has the morality power of making an act of intercourse that would have been morally prohibited rape without her consent into an act that is morally permissible, at least as far as this particular morality norm applies. In addition to morality powers in the strict sense, we have morality abilities in the more general sense. For example, a person capable of having a child has the morality ability of acquiring a morality duty to care for a child by fruitfully engaging in an act of sexual intercourse. Again, one has a morality ability to acquire a morality duty to remedy or compensate by one's act of inflicting bodily injury upon the person of another or doing damage to the property of another. Accordingly, our body of morality norms is rich enough to confer morality rights.

A very useful example is the promisee's morality right that the promisor keep his or her promise. Although this has a structure very similar to the creditor's legal right to repayment, it is neither identical with nor dependent upon any such legal right, for the promisee may have this right under our morality norms even when the promise at stake does not constitute a legally valid contract.

The defining core of this right is the morality claim of the promisee against the promisor that he or she act as promised. This claim is itself composed of the morality duty of the promisor to act as promised together with the morality power of the promisee to take his or her case to one or more morality judges in the event that the promisor threatens or fails to keep his or her promise. I use the word "power" in this context advisedly, for the right-holder's act of appealing to a morality judge changes the position of that person under the norms of our morality. Our morality condemns meddling in the affairs of others, but intervening in response to an appeal from one of the parties is no longer meddling. Thus at the very least, the promisee's act of appealing to a morality judge effects a morality liberty of that judge to intervene. It may, although I am less confident of this, also bring into existence a morality duty to render judgment. If so, this may be because our morality norms are dual aspect rules, conventional rules that not only require specific sorts of actions, but also call for the imposition of sanctions for disobedience.

I have spoken of the promisee's power "to take his or her case to one or more morality judges." Obviously I mean to assert that the promisee has a morality power that is strictly analogous to the creditor's legal power of bringing suit against the debtor. No doubt there is some analogy between taking legal action in a court of law and appealing to one or more bystanders for a judgment of how morality bears on one's confrontation, but is this analogy really close enough to sustain the extension of the concept of a claim from law to morality? (1) The morality judge is not an official in an organization with a special standing to decide cases and with a limited jurisdiction like a judge. A morality right-holder can appeal to any bystander, any chance member of the community. Still, it can be accurately said that there is an office of morality judge, an office held by every normal adult member of the community, for the social role of the morality judge is defined by generally accepted norms of the society. (2) The appeal is of a very special sort. It is not simply begging for help or inviting the intervention of brute force. In taking his or her case to a morality judge, the promisee is asking for a judgment, that is for a decision as to how the norms of morality apply to his or her situation. Similarly, in taking legal action one is not simply asking the court to act on personal preference or intervene with arbitrary force; one is petitioning for a judgment concerning how the norms of the legal system apply to one's situation. (3) In both sorts of appeal, one takes "one's case" to court. That is, one argues one's case by trying to establish the facts of the situation and citing those norms that one takes to favor oneself in the confrontation at issue. And both in a court of law and in the forum of morality, it is understood that one's adversary has the right to defend himself or herself by arguing the opposing case. (4) Unlike the decision of a court of law, the morality judge's decision is not authoritative. It is merely his or her personal opinion; it does not constitute an addition to the body of morality norms in the way in which a judicial decision, at least in a commonlaw system like our own, becomes a legally valid precedent for future cases. A morality judge's opinion may, however, be a small-scale unauthoritative precedent to the extent that it becomes generally known and respected by other members of the morality community. (5) Although the morality judge's decision is not authoritative, it may be binding upon the parties to the dispute in ways that are strictly analogous to those in which a judicial decision is binding upon the parties involved. The parties may be constrained to submit both by the sanctions that enforce our morality norms and by whatever nonprudential reasons they may have to abide by those norms. (6) Although the decision of a court of law is presumedly backed by the entire legal system, the morality judgment of some chance member of the community is not backed by the combined force of the entire morality community. It is customary to say that the norms of positive morality are enforced with "social sanctions." But this expression might mislead, for it is not society as a whole that binds the individual to obedience to its mores. The sanctions of morality are social in a somewhat looser sense. They are imposed generally within a society by the individual members of that society, and they are imposed in accordance with generally accepted norms in that society. Still, the crucial analogy remains. Just as one who takes legal action sets the machinery of legal enforcement in action, so the individual who takes his or her case to a morality judge sets in motion a process typically culminating in the sanctions that lie behind our morality norms. (7) Moreover, just as legal sanctions are imposed in accordance with legal norms, so the imposition of morality sanctions is governed by norms of our positive morality. Our morality norms include one or more norms of justice; including the morality rule that one ought to treat others as they deserve, specifically by rewarding the moral action and punishing the immoral agent. Implicit in our society's norms of justice are standards of what kinds of sanctions may justly be imposed for violations of various morality norms and in what degree. These range from scolding (in private or in public), through withholding favors, to the silent treatment or ostracism, and even to the deprivation of liberty or the infliction of suffering. But to inflict such evils upon a person as a consequence of a morality judgment, whether of one's own or of some respected member of the community, can be justified by our morality norms in a way in which other acts of harming others cannot. It seems to me that the analogy between taking one's case to court and taking one's case to a morality judge, in spite of the very real and important differences, is close enough to justify my contention that there are morality claims strictly analogous to, although not the same as, legal claims. What is crucial is that in appealing for a morality judgment, one is appealing to a body of norms through the judge and that the entire process of appeal and decision and subsequent enforcement is governed by the norms binding upon both parties and the judge alike.

The promisee's right that the promisor keep his or her promise is, of course, more than an isolated morality claim. Associated elements within this morality right include at least the following: (1) the promisee's bilateral morality liberty of exercising or not exercising the core power of appealing to a morality judge; (2) the promisee's morality power to extinguish the promisor's duty to keep the promise by releasing him or her from that promise; (3) the promisee's bilateral morality liberty to exercise or not exercise this power of release; (4) the promisee's morality immunity against the promisor's terminating the duty to keep his or her promise by any unilateral act of the promisor; and probably (5) the morality duty of third parties to side with the promisee and against the promisor in the event that the former refuses to release the latter from the promise but the promisor refuses to keep his or her promise. Thus, given the logical richness of the norms of our positive morality, a Hohfeldian model of rights can be applied to morality rights.

It is important to distinguish between organizational and conventional rights. The former are conferred by a body of norms created, applied and enforced by some organization; the latter are conferred by a body of norms generally accepted, followed and sanctioned informally within some community. It is equally important to recognize that both organizational and conventional rights are institutional rights, for both arise from and depend upon some "institution," in the very general sense defined by the OED as "An established law, custom, usage, practice, organization, or other element in the political or social life of a people; a regulative principle or convention subservient to the needs of an organized community or the general ends of civilization." The concept of an institution has two aspects, each essential to any adequate understanding of institutional rights.

First, an institution is something that is instituted; it is introduced or set up, established or founded, brought into use or practice. Thus, every human institution is the product of human activity. In this way, the concept of an institutional right captures the essential meaning of the more traditional term "an artificial right" in contrast to "a natural right." Although the distinction between institutional and noninstitutional rights preserves the *point* of the distinction between natural and artificial rights, it does so without the misleading suggestion that institutional rights are somehow contrasted with a set of rights that exist as objects in the natural world or are possessed by individuals in a state of nature.

Second, an institution, in the sense defined, is necessarily social. This social dimension of institutional rights is essential for the significance of their application to confrontations between adversaries. If a right is the justification for siding with one party against an adversary, if a right is to consist of elements that bind and enable the parties to a confrontation, then they cannot be instituted by the parties themselves on an *ad hoc* basis. They must be conferred by social norms that are independent of the parties to them, because they are established in the ongoing practices of some larger group to which the adversaries belong. The kinds of rights we have been examining are not merely instituted; they are instituted by or in some sort of a society.

In the process of moving from our paradigm of a right, a legal right, to other sorts of rights, we have discovered the beginnings of a useful classification of rights. One family of rights consists of institutional rights. This family has two distinct and coordinate genera—organizational rights and conventional rights. Species of organizational rights include legal rights, academic rights, club rights of officers in or members of some private club, and the game rights of those who play in matches under the auspices of some organization like the International Chess Federation. Species of conventional rights include morality rights, the comparable but less compelling etiquette rights conferred by the code of etiquette of any society or some class within a society, and the game rights of those who play informal games like sandlot baseball.

One family of rights consists of all institutional rights. Is this the only family of rights? Are all genuine rights conferred by some set of norms instituted by a society of some sort? It is high time that we investigated the reality of noninstitutional rights, and, if they exist, the possibility that our Hohfeldian model can be extended to apply to them also.

Chapter 5

MORAL POSITIONS

A morality, as I conceive of it, consists in the mores of any society, customary ways of acting that are generally regarded as imperative and are informally sanctioned by the members of some society. Morality norms are instituted by convention and are binding upon the members of the group instituting the positive moral code. "Morals," as I shall use the term, is the noninstitutional counterpart of positive morality. Morals consists of a body of norms of conduct and character that are noninstitutional, objectively valid, and specifically moral. Thus moral norms differ from morality norms in that they are not created, modified or extinguished either by any social organization or convention. They differ from the equally noninstitutional norms of prudence or technical efficiency in some way yet to be explained.

Some philosophers deny that there really are any moral norms in this sense. They believe that, for any number of reasons, specifically moral norms of conduct cannot be both noninstitutional and objectively valid. They may, of course, be correct. But this issue, important as it is, is far too large to be discussed here. I shall simply assume that it is possible for a member of a society to make moral judgments that are not simply expressions of his or her society and that sometimes, at least, it is possible for such moral judgments to be rationally justified. If the arguments I have advanced in *Challenge and Response* are insufficient to establish the objective validity of moral judgments, then I can hardly hope to do better in the limited space available here.

Although I shall ignore any general moral scepticism here, I cannot simply assume the existence of moral rights. There are special reasons to doubt the reality of any noninstitutional rights and these cannot be ignored in any systematic theory of rights. Even granted the existence of morals as I have defined it, it might well be that this body of moral norms does not define any positions in the sense that the law defines the positions of those subject to its jurisdiction, or that although "morals" does define some moral positions, these are not analogous to the Hohfeldian positions constituting a genuine right. What shall we say, then, of moral positions?

Morals

Whether there really are any moral positions, and if so of what kinds, depends, of course, upon the nature of morals. Morals, as I have defined it, consists of that body of norms that are noninstitutional, objectively valid, and specifically moral. But how can moral norms be both independent of social institutions and still objective? A traditional answer is that they are the rules of natural law, a body of rules of conduct somehow built into the nature of our universe or ourselves. To my mind this sort of theory, at least in its traditional forms, should be rejected because it is laden with dubious ontological and epistemological presuppositions. A more fruitful approach is via a consideration of the objective validity of scientific theories. How can science claim to be objective if it is not an expression of a social consensus? The answer is that the theories of science are grounded in and based upon empirical evidence. Indeed, in nonscientific as well as scientific belief, thinking something to be the case does not make it so because there is a distinction between correct and incorrect belief arising from the reasons that justify accepting some factual statements and rejecting others. Similarly, moral judgments are objectively valid because they, too, are capable of rational justification. Thus, it is the existence of moral reasons that ultimately explains the objectivity of morals.

I will go even farther and suggest that moral norms *are* moral reasons. This is to say that the primary moral standards against which any person's action is to be measured simply are those facts about each individual act which constitute morally relevant considerations for or against doing that action. Recall the law, the body of legal norms. Lawyers and social scientists, not to mention ordinary citizens, make legal judgments every day. But these judgments, unlike the decision of a judge, are not included in or incorporated into the law because, unlike the judgment of a court, they are not authoritative. They are judgments about the law but not themselves legal norms within the law. Similarly, the moral judgments you and I—not to mention moral philosophers—make are judgments about morals but are not themselves possessed of moral authority. It is the practical reasons to which one appeals to justify a moral judgment that have normative force.

There are many kinds of norms. Just as a judicial decision or a morality rule is a norm of conduct, so a practical reason is a norm. A practical reason is a norm in that it is both a guide for choice of a moral agent and a standard for criticism of moral action. In arguing "you ought not to keep on kicking him because it hurts badly" or "you really ought to help her move because you promised," one is appealing to practical norms. In the end, then, morals consists of a body of practical reasons.

But not every practical reason is a moral one. In arguing "you ought not to keep on kicking him because he is bigger than you are" or "you really ought to help her move because she will reward you handsomely," one is appealing to prudential rather than moral reasons. What is it that distinguishes specifically moral reasons from other species of practical reasons such as those that support prudential or technical ought judgments? It is, I suggest, that they are essentially connected to positive morality. Our concept of the moral is historically derived from and remains logically tied to social morality; morals is by very definition a counterpart of a conventional code of morality. Moral reasons as norms and morality rules as norms share two essential features.

First, moral reasons, like morality rules, are dual-aspect norms. By this I mean that they are both norms for action and norms for reaction. The mores of a society are standards that govern the choices and conduct of all members of that society. At the same time, they are standards to govern the reaction of all members of that society to any action that conforms to or deviates from those mores. This is because morality norms are sanctioned informally by the reactions of any chance member of the society to one who lives up to or violates their society's morality code. Similarly, a morality reason is not simply a reason to do or not do some sort of action; it is equally and essentially a reason for reacting to the doing or not doing in an appropriate manner. Thus, "you are hurting him" is both a reason for the moral agent to stop kicking his victim and a reason for any moral bystander to respond with disapproval, condemnation and even penalties such as isolation or the withdrawal of favors. I have tried to capture this essentially dual-aspect nature of specifically moral reasons by saying that they are reasons for acting and for reacting, but reacting is, of course, itself a form of acting. What distinguishes specifically moral reasons is not that they are norms for something in addition to action; it is that they are norms for the actions of moral agents playing two rather different roles. One role is that of the moral agent simply deciding what to do and in living his or her own life; the other role is that of a moral agent observing another moral agent acting, acting as a moral judge of that agent, and acting on that agent in the light of that agent's conduct. Notice that one reacts to the agent, not the act. One does not disapprove, blame or punish an action; one disapproves, condemns, or penalizes an agent for doing the action. It is in this sense that morals, like morality, is essentially social; it necessarily involves the interactions of individuals within a group because it consists of norms governing the reaction of one person to another as well as governing the conduct of any individual actor.

This dual-aspect feature of moral reasons helps to explain something that has always bothered me. I am convinced that W. D. Ross is correct when he distinguishes the morally right act from the morally good action or agent. Yet it is somehow very difficult, almost impossible, to separate these two concepts in moral philosophy or in everyday moral judgment. I have long wondered why this confusion is so pervasive and persistent. I now see that it is not a mere muddle. It is of the essence of any genuinely *moral* judgment of human conduct that it be at one and the same time a judgment of the agent and of his or her action because specifically moral reasons are reasons for action and for reaction.

To speak of the sanctions of morality or of morals is to borrow a term from the law and use it in its extended sense. The OED defines a sanction as "The specific penalty enacted in order to enforce obedience to law. . . . Extended to include the provision of rewards for obedience, along with punishments for disobedience, to a law." Thus, one can and should distinguish between negative and positive sanctions. The negative sanctions of morality and morals include disapproval, condemnation and informal penalties; the positive sanctions include approval, praise and informal rewards. Moral reasons justify the imposition of such sanctions. It is worthy of note, however, that just as negative and positive sanctions are seldom incorporated into the same morality rule, so they are seldom justified by a single morality reason. Thus, the duty-imposing norms of positive morality are sanctioned by disapproval, blame and punishments for disobedience and the virtue-defining morality norms are sanctioned by approval, praise and informal rewards for conformity. Similarly, one should distinguish between duty-imposing moral reasons that justify reacting to any action contrary to such a reason with negative sanctions, and, on the other hand, ideal-projecting moral reasons that justify reacting to any agent who acts in conformity with them with approval, praise and informal rewards.

A second essential feature that moral reasons share with morality rules is that they are nonelective. One cannot opt out of morals any more than one can opt out of the mores of one's society. It is this that distinguishes specifically moral reasons from merely technical reasons. Since technical reasons concern the most effective means to achieve a chosen end, one can evade the force of a technical reason by abandoning that end. Since our neighborhood is holding a beautiful lawn contest, I ought to put weed-killer on my lawn. Why? One reason is that this is the most effective way to rid my lawn of weeds and thus enhance my chances to win the contest. But this is a merely technical reason. I can render this reason inapplicable to my conduct simply by opting out of the contest. I have, however, a second and very different sort of reason for putting weed-killer on my lawn. I promised my wife that I would do so. I cannot render this moral reason inapplicable to my conduct simply by deciding not to try to keep my promises as I might decide not to try to win a contest. Similarly, I have a very strong moral reason not to put weed-killer in my wife's tea. It would probably kill her. This sort of reason is nonelective; its relevance does not depend upon my projects. It remains a practical reason applicable to my conduct whether I have chosen to rid myself of my wife in order to marry a younger woman or to preserve her life in order to prolong our happy marriage. Thus, moral reasons share two of the essential characteristics of morality rules. They are norms that are both dual-aspect and nonelective.

Although I shall not pause to provide here any extended defense of my conception of morals, I must respond to one obvious objection to it. To define a moral reason as one that justifies the imposition of sanctions, as I have done, is to make the proposition that morals ought to be enforced in the same way that positive morality is enforced analytic. But David Lyons has argued that it is objectionable to connect moral and external sanctions by very definition (Lyons, 1982, 57). Moreover, there is a very long tradition that holds that enforcement is not only extraneous to morals but subversive because of the way in which it interferes with the motivation essential to moral virtue. To my mind this worry springs from misunderstanding. To begin with, notice that my conception of morals does not imply that the legal enforcement of morals is justified; this would follow only with the addition of some sort of normative premise. What would be justified by definition is the imposition of the informal sanctions characteristic of morality. Also, it may be that when one is worried about justifying the social "enforcement" of morals by definition, one is thinking primarily of the ideal-projecting norms rather than the duty-imposing ones. But remember that ideal-projecting reasons justify only positive sanctions such as approval, praise and informal rewards. I doubt that one need worry about encouraging moral virtue in these ways. Nor do I seriously doubt that it is appropriate to impose disapproval, censure and informal penalties short of force upon those who fail to act as moral duty-imposing reasons require. Lyons himself is quite prepared to connect the concept of a moral duty analytically with the internal sanctions of individual conscience. But I fail to see how moral reasons could justify internal sanctions without justifying, at least prima facie, external sanctions as well. And to omit any reference to sanctions from the definition of morals would be to eliminate part of what is distinctive of the specifically moral.

The primary virtue of my conception of morals is that it can explain, as lamentably few moral philosophers do, what makes a moral duty or a moral virtue *moral*. It accomplishes this end by defining morals in terms of two of the essential features of morality, so that the specifically moral is conceptually tied to positive morality. But there is an alternative conception of morals that promises this same theoretical advantage because it, too, defines morals in terms of morality, but in a manner that seems more natural. Some philosophers distinguish between positive and critical morality. The former consists of that actual body of rules for conduct and character generally accepted and informally sanctioned in any given society; the latter consists of an ideal body of morality rules that it would be rationally justified for any given society to accept and sanction. This way of looking at morals as the moral law or the completely rational morality is as appealing as it is widespread. It is similar to my conception in the way in which it takes morals to be justified by reason in contrast to a morality instituted by social convention. It differs primarily by thinking of morals as a body of rules rather than a body of reasons. It is very natural to think of morals in this way, as an ideal set of rationally justified morality rules, because our conception of morals is derived from and conceptually tied to positive morality, a social institution consisting of conventional rules.

Nevertheless, I urge that we reject this identification of morals with critical morality. Why not define morals as the body of rationally justified morality rules? One reason is that this conception of morals is a poor explanation of the difference between morally right and morally wrong actions. Any adequate philosophical theory of morals ought to explain, at the very least, why some acts are morally wrong and others morally right. I find it more efficient and agreeable to schedule my activities so that I work on campus most mornings and at home most afternoons. Accordingly, when I was recently asked whether I could meet with the Faculty Council next Wednesday at 4:00 p.m., I falsely replied that I was leaving town just after noon. My ruse paid off, for our meeting was scheduled for Thursday morning, a time convenient for me but inconvenient for several of the others involved. Still, my act was morally wrong. Why? The explanation is supposed to be that it violated a rationally justified morality rule such as "Never lie except to avoid disaster or spare someone's feelings in a relatively harmless way." How good is this explanation?

Well, it is not necessary to appeal to any rule of critical morality in order to explain why my act was morally wrong. Certain facts about my act spring to mind as being morally relevant. I lied to those who trusted me and who relied upon my honesty. I seriously inconvenienced my colleagues to gain a small advantage for myself. These facts about my action are reasons for me not to act as I did and for others to react to my conduct with negative sanctions. In short, these facts are the moral reasons in terms of which I have defined morals. It is only by virtue of such facts about my particular action that any universal rule of critical morality would be applicable to my conduct at all. But since one can explain the wrongness of my action by saying that I acted contrary to these moral reasons, there is no need to appeal to any rationally justified morality rule as an explanation. It seems to me that something like Ockham's razor applies here. One ought not to complicate any philosophical explanation beyond necessity.

It may be imagined that I have overlooked a simple, but fundamental, logical point. What I call a "moral reason" would not be a reason in the absence of a moral rule. What makes any feature of an act, perhaps that it is a lie, morally relevant is that this feature subsumes the act under some moral rule, perhaps that one ought never to lie except to avoid disaster or spare feelings. But this is not so at all. What makes it seem so is that we tend to presuppose a deductive model of moral reasoning. But as I have argued at length in chapter 1 of *Challenge and Response,* this model is both unnecessary and misleading. The logical validity of a moral argument does not require some presupposed moral rule under which the moral reason can be subsumed.

Not only is the appeal to a rule of critical morality unnecessary to explain why my act was morally wrong; it is insufficient. The existence of some ideal moral rule against lying is not a sufficient reason to conclude that any individual act falling under that rule is morally wrong, for in exceptional circumstances there may be countervailing moral reasons that override the moral rule. Thus, a lie may not be morally wrong, even though it is neither necessary to avoid disaster nor a little white lie, but because the questioner insists on an answer when he or she has no right to know the truth. But, it may be objected, all this shows is that my formulation of the relevant moral rule is incomplete.

One must reformulate the rule to say that it is always morally wrong to lie except to avoid disaster or to spare someone's feelings in a relatively harmless way or to deny a questioner some truth he or she has no right to know. The real true moral rule has each and every exception written into it. Hence, the existence of a genuine moral rule is a sufficient condition to conclude that any act falling under it is morally wrong. Agreed. Since moral reasons, like every other species of reasons, are universalizable, there is in principle some moral rule derivable from every moral reason. Presumably God would be able to formulate these unexceptionable moral rules. But as I reflect upon all the attempts by mere human beings to formulate moral rules, I inevitably find exceptions to every formulation. It seems to me, therefore, that for us mere human beings it is an empty gesture to insist that it is moral rules that make any act morally right or wrong. Moreover, how do we and how does God know when to write some additional exception into a moral rule? We recognize the inadequacy of some formulation of a moral rule when and only when we recognize some moral reason sufficient to override that rule in some situation to which it applies. But then moral rules must be derived from moral reasons. I conclude that in morals it is moral reasons that are primary in moral reasoning and that best explain what makes any action morally right or wrong.

This suggests a second reason why it is inappropriate to conceive of morals as a body of moral rules. In making a moral decision or in making a moral judgment of some act of another, one frequently has to weight conflicting moral considerations against one another. For example, a doctor might have to weigh the chances that a comforting lie will improve the patient's chances of recovery or enable the patient to die in peace against the facts that even a benevolent lie is a betrayal of trust and may be destructive of a doctor-patient relationship essential to therapeutic effectiveness. This feature of morals, brought home most vividly in any conflict of moral obligations, cannot be accommodated in any rule model of morals. The very point of any duty-imposing rule is to "rule out" alternative choices for the moral agent subject to the rule. As G. J. Warnock observes "What the rule does, in fact, is to *exclude* from practical consideration the particular merits of particular cases, by specifying in advance what *is to* be done, whatever the circumstances" (Warnock, 1971, 65). By the very nature of rules, valid rules cannot conflict. When rules threaten to conflict, either one must be rejected or one must be revised to eliminate the conflict. Since no body of rationally justified rules could apply to any action in conflicting ways, there can be no place for weighing one rule against another. One might, of course, have to decide which of two conflicting rules to adopt or to obey. One would not, however, make this decision on the grounds that one rule outweighed the other; one would make the decision between rules on the grounds that the reasons for adopting or following one rule outweighed the reasons for adopting or following the other. One should reject the conception of morals as a body of moral rules in order to explain how it is that moral decision or judgment may involve the balancing of conflicting moral considerations.

One could, however, reject the model of rules without accepting my conception of morals as a body of moral reasons. One might take as the appropriate model of morals, not legal rules, but legal principles. One would then identify morals as a critical morality consisting of an ideal set of moral principles justified by reason. The distinction between a legal principle and a legal rule is explained by Ronald Dworkin in two crucial passages.

> The difference between legal principles and legal rules is a logical distinction. Both sets of standards point to particular decisions about legal obligation in particular circumstances, but they differ in the character of the direction they give. Rules are applicable in an all-or-nothing fashion. If the facts a rule stipulates are given, then either the rule is valid, in which case the answer it supplies must be accepted, or it is not, in which case it contributes nothing to the decision. . . . But this is not the way the sample principles in the quotations operate. Even those that look most like rules do not set out legal consequences that follow automatically when the conditions provided are met. [1977, 24-25]

and

> This first difference between rules and principles entails another. Principles have a dimension that rules do not—the dimension of weight or importance. When principles intersect (the policy of protecting automobile consumers intersecting with principles of freedom of contract, for example), one who must resolve the conflict has to take into account the relative weight of each. [1977, 26]

Precisely because principles combine the universality of rules with the dimension of weight, conceiving of morals as a body of moral principles promises to retain the advantages of the model of rules while accommodating the weighing of conflicting moral considerations.

Unfortunately, this is not so. One of the theoretical advantages of the model of rules is that it seems to explain how legal or moral reasons are relevant to legal or moral judgments. Specific features of the case at hand are logically relevant because they can be subsumed under a rule in such a way that the legal or moral conclusion can be deduced from the rule as major premise together with the facts of the case as minor premise. Now this is precisely what principles cannot do because, as Dworkin notes, they "do not set out legal consequences that follow automatically when the conditions provided are met." How on earth, then, can a legal or moral principle "point to particular decisions"? Dworkin does nothing whatsoever to solve this mystery; but until it is solved, his model of principles cannot perform anything like the logical function of the model of rules in legal or moral theory.

This glaring weakness might, however, be offset by the ability of his model to explain the weighing of conflicting considerations in legal or moral reasoning, for he builds the dimension of weight into his definition of a principle. But in precisely what way do principles have weight? When Dworkin speaks of "weight or importance," this suggests that one principle might be more important than another. For example, the particular decision in *Henningsen* v. *Bloomfield Motors, Inc.* might be explained in part by the fact that principle (d) "In a society such as ours, where the automobile is a common and necessary adjunct of daily life, and where its use is so fraught with danger to the driver, passengers and the public, the manufacturer is under a special obligation in connection with the construction, promotion and sale of his cars" is more important than principle (a) "in the absence of fraud, one who does not choose to read a contract before signing it, cannot later relieve himself of its burdens" (Dworkin, 1977, 24). But if the dimension of weight attaches to a principle because of the importance *of the principle,* then it is the principle *as a universal principle* that has more or less weight. This would imply that in valid legal reasoning principle (d) ought always to outweigh principle (a). Not only does this implication fly in the face of judicial practice; it is surely a recipe for cooking up unreasonable decisions. No doubt, in any case where the danger to the driver, passengers and the public is great and the burden on the manufacturer of voiding the contract is relatively minor, principle (d) ought to outweigh principle (a). But in any case in which the danger to drivers, passengers and the public is slight and the burden on the manufacturer of voiding all such contracts is considerable, principle (a) ought to outweigh principle (d) in the decision of any reasonable judge. What this shows is that it is not the principles as principles that have weight but the considerations mentioned in the principles that have different weights in different cases. This solves the problem of how principles can "point to particular decisions." Principles point to relevant considerations by mentioning them; these considerations are then weighed against one another to arrive at a decision. But this means that it is reasons, the relevant considerations in each particular case, and not the universal principles that have the dimension of weight. If we wish to explain the weighing of conflicting moral considerations, then, we must abandon both the model of rules and the model of principles and conceive of morals as the body of moral reasons.

Does morals define any moral positions analogous to the legal positions identified by Hohfeld? A legal position is the position of some party under the law or, less figuratively, the way in which the law applies to some person subject to its jurisdiction. Remember also that legal norms apply to those subject to them by the way in which they bear upon their actions. Every Hohfeldian legal conception has a practical content. A duty is necessarily a duty to perform some specific action, and a legal power is the legal ability to effect specific legal consequences by some action. Thus, the law defines legal positions because of the various ways it applies to the actions of those subject to its jurisdiction.

Moral reasons clearly apply to moral agents in an analogous manner. Since moral reasons are a species of practical reasons, moral norms are reasons for or against some possible action. Accordingly, they apply directly to any moral agent choosing whether or not to do that action. But moral reasons are also reasons for reacting to specific actions with positive or negative morality sanctions. Since such prospective sanctions are also practical reasons, moral reasons apply to moral agents indirectly as well as directly. In this respect, moral norms are analogous to legal norms. The mere existence of a statute prohibiting one from driving more than 55 miles per hour may be directly a reason for not speeding on the highways, and the prospect that the statute will be enforced by the police and in the courts is indirectly an additional reason not to speed. Thus, morals does define moral positions in very much the same way that the law defines legal positions.

One difference worthy of note, however, is the range of those subject to these two bodies of norms. There are many legal systems, each with its own limited jurisdiction. Thus residents of the United States are subject to the law of the United States, and residents of France are subject to French law. The law of each land defines the legal positions of all and only those subject to its jurisdiction. But morals has a universality lacking in the law. Moral reasons apply to each and every moral agent, wherever his or her place in geography or history may be. In this respect, morality positions are like legal positions. Morality positions, and therefore morality rights, may differ from society to society. Moral positions, and moral rights if there are any, are the same for every moral agent in every society.

But are there any moral rights? On my model of a right as a complex of normative positions, this depends upon the nature of the positions defined by morals. Surely moral norms do define some sorts of moral positions. What remains to be seen is whether they are really analogous to the sorts of positions distinguished by Hohfeld.

Moral Duties

To have a duty of some kind is to be in a position to have one's choices constrained by one or more norms of the appropriate kinds. Thus, one has a legal duty when the law, the body of legal norms, applies to one so as to constrain one to act in one manner rather than any other. One has a morality duty when the conventional norms of positive morality impose constraints upon one's conduct. Similarly, one has a moral duty when morals constrain one's choice by the way in which it applies to the alternative acts one is in a position to choose among.

But just how does morals impose constraint upon the moral agent? Morals consists of the body of moral reasons, and moral reasons are by their very nature both reasons for or against acting and reasons for reacting to any moral agent who has chosen to act in a situation where moral reasons are applicable. Hence, duty-imposing moral reasons impose a double constraint—the constraint of any practical reason together with the specifically moral constraint of potential morality sanctions. Let us consider each of these constraints in turn.

Even the recognition of a merely technical reason, to borrow Kantian terminology, constrains the choices of a rational agent. If I want to win, or at least place high, in the local Memorial Day Run, knowing that sustained jogging and frequent hard sprinting are necessary to get one into one's best running condition will constrain a rational athlete to work out strenuously even on an inclement day when I am feeling very tired. Perhaps the tightest connection between required action and desired or desirable result exists when performing the act is a necessary condition of the occurrence of the result, as in von Wright's example of making a fire to heat a hut. But imagine that it is the evening before, it is dark with a chill wind outside and I am sitting comfortably in my hut burning the last of my firewood. Given that there will be a frost in the morning, "I can heat my hut in the morning only if I go out and gather some firewood now" may well constrain me to fight against the strong temptation to stay inside and then crawl into bed and choose, even against my desires for immediate comfort, to go out and, much against my will, to chop firewood for the morning. A somewhat looser connection between action and desired consequence exists when the action is conducive to, but not strictly a necessary condition of, achieving some desired end. Thus, "Using a word processor will make it much easier to revise my next manuscript" may constrain me to spend a week learning how to use our new technology, a week I would much prefer to spend relaxing beside our neighbor's swimming pool. Clearly, the constraint of practical reason is not limited to moral reasons.

Prudential reasons also constrain a rational agent; they imply that he or she ought to act in ways that may run directly counter to present inclination and contrary to intense immediate desires. The distinction between technical and prudential reasons is not, as Kant supposed, the distinction between reasons dependent upon a desire or goal that a given agent may or may not happen to have and reasons dependent upon a desire or goal (one's own happiness or well-being) that all agents do in fact have. It is the distinction between practical reasons conditional upon some optional end and practical reasons conditional upon the end of one's own well-being that is not optional, because it would be irrational for anyone to reject this end. In this way, technical reasons are elective and prudential reasons are, like moral reasons, nonelective. Thus reason enters into prudential reasons in two places, as rationally requiring the choice of some specific means to one's own welfare and as rationally requiring one to opt for or set as one's goal one's own welfare. Even if I do care about my own welfare and strongly desire to maximize it, I may find prudential reasons highly constraining and act upon them, when I have the strength of will or firm rationality to do so, very reluctantly. Although I know that overeating is bad for my health and causes me to appear physically repulsive to those whose friendship matters so much to my personal happiness, my appetite for fine food and good wines is usually overpowering. When I do restrain my appetites "in a cool hour," it is only because I am sufficiently rational to be constrained by prudential reasons. Similarly, "chain smoking greatly increases one's chances of having lung cancer" imposes the constraint of practical reason upon a moral agent trying to stop smoking primarily for this reason.

Moral reasons, since they are reasons for or against acting, share this constraint of practical reason with technical and prudential reasons. "I promised to shovel my neighbor's sidewalk while he is away" imposes a rational constraint upon me when I have just finished removing a heavy snow from my own walk and would much prefer to go back inside and rest my weary bones. Similarly, "your drunken driving endangers the lives of your passengers and any nearby pedestrians" is a reason why you ought not to drive drunk no matter how much you like to drink and how strong is your desire to drive yourself and your friends from one party to another. Moral reasons are like prudential ones and unlike merely technical reasons in that they are not conditional upon the adoption of any rationally optional end; if they depend upon ends or goals at all (and let us not reject deontological theories of obligation out of hand), the presupposed ends are ones, like the well-being of other persons, that it would be contrary to reason for any moral agent to reject.

Moral reasons are typically strong reasons. Since a moral reason is both a reason for action and a reason for reaction and reacting with morality sanctions would not be justified in the absence of some strong reason to act or not act in some way, moral reasons typically impose relatively stringent constraint upon the moral agent. To be sure, there are little white lies. But what is little in such cases is the importance of the truth that the speaker conceals. It is still a serious matter to lie because mutual trust is essential to acceptable relationships between persons.

One cannot, however, fully explain the constraint implicit in our concept of a moral duty by pointing out that as reasons for or against acting, moral reasons impose the constraint of practical reason in a relatively stringent form. Any adequate explanation must take note of the fact that moral reasons are also reasons for *re*acting to the conduct of the moral agent for whom they are practical reasons. The reactions definitive of moral reasons are the sanctions of positive morality. Only negative morality sanctions, however, such as blame or censure, the withdrawal of favors such as gifts or invitations to social occasions or desirable social positions, and the silent treatment on an individual level or informal ostracism by the group impose the genuine constraint involved in duty-imposing, as opposed to ideal-projecting, moral reasons.

Moral reasons as reasons for imposing negative morality sanctions resist the balancing of practical considerations in a way in which moral reasons as practical reasons do not. Consider, for example, a situation in which Jones has promised Smith to do something that is not really very important to Smith. Perhaps between the time of making the promise and the time of keeping it, Jones has discovered that it will be very inconvenient, although far from disastrous, for him to do as promised. Even if Jones now has practical reasons against keeping his promise that outweight the moral reason "Jones promised," this moral reason may continue to justify reacting with negative sanctions. This is typically, although not invariably so, because the rational justification for *re*acting to actions contrary to moral reasons, at least insofar as these reactions take the form of morality sanctions, is to reenforce the practical reason of the moral agent choosing how to act. Just as legal sanctions are appropriately imposed to enforce the law, so morality sanctions are justified *as* sanctions by the way in which they constrain the moral agent to take moral reasons seriously. Since they are out of place when almost everyone will act rationally anyway, moral reasons typically concern kinds of actions that run counter to inclination and where humans are often tempted to act contrary to practical reason. But in order to fulfil their function of countering the irrational impulses and motivations in human nature, the threat of morality sanctions must be built into the character of the moral agent. Hence, third parties may need to overreact, in a sense, in order to act effectively as enforcers of moral reasons, much as an actor may need to use somewhat exaggerated gestures on stage to project a realistic presence into the theater audience. The actor choosing between alternative courses of action quite properly balances one practical reason against another; and in this balancing a moral reason may be outweighed by contrary considerations, either stronger moral reasons or a number of nonmoral ones. As Kant recognized, for a holy will or a perfectly rational agent, this would be sufficient. Moral reasons are also reasons for others to react to an agent who has chosen contrary to practical reason and as such are appropriate to decisions of imperfectly rational beings. They are needed only when irrational dispositions come into play in the deliberating moral agent, and when such irrational dispositions are present, the practical reason of the individual needs to be reenforced sufficiently so that the motivational balance can coincide with the balance of practical reasons. To do this, it is usually necessary to counterbalance the irrational inclinations with extra reasons to act in conformity with moral reasons. Thus, moral reasons may justify reacting with negative sanctions even when they are outweighed by contrary practical considerations as reasons for acting.

The same point can be explained in a somewhat different manner. Moral reasons typically justify reacting with negative sanctions even when they are outweighed by contrary reasons for acting because as reasons for reacting they typically presuppose different background conditions from the background conditions they presuppose as reasons for acting. It is not self-evident that "Jones promised to do act A" is a reason for "Jones ought to do act A." This bit of practical reasoning presupposes certain background conditions such as the facts that the promisee usually wants the promise to be kept, that promises frequently facilitate mutually desirable cooperation, that breaking a promise tends to undermine trust, and so forth. "Jones promised to do act A" is also a reason for reacting to Jones by imposing negative morality sanctions in the event that Jones fails to do A. Here also certain background conditions are presupposed such as the facts that promisors are often strongly tempted to break promises and that moral agents are constrained by the prospect of negative sanctions.

Since these background conditions are somewhat different from those presupposed by the same moral reason as a reason for acting, a moral reason often stands firm as a reason for reacting even when it has been outweighed as a reason for acting. For example, even when "Jones promised" is not a sufficient reason for Jones to keep the promise in this special situation, it may still be a sufficient reason for bystanders to impose negative sanctions upon Jones in the event that he or she breaks the promise, either as an example to others or to mold the character of the agent. This helps to explain why moral duty-imposing reasons seem to speak to us in so stern a tone and with an external voice. They justify reactions by others as well as actions by oneself.

What remains to be explained is how moral reasons for *re*acting can constrain the moral agent who is acting rather than reacting. Moral reasons justify the imposition of sanctions. But negative sanctions such as censure or the silent treatment may be justified even when they are not actually imposed, either because third parties are unaware of the relevant moral reason or are unwilling to make the effort to uphold morals. Since justified sanctions need not be actual, how can they impose any actual constraint upon the moral agent? This is a serious problem because if a moral duty consists in a moral constraint, then a moral duty can be actual only when the constraint is actual also. It is crucial to note that what constrains is not the sanction, but the threat of sanction. Sanctions are imposed retrospectively, after a failure to act on some moral reason, as a penalty for this failure to do one's duty. But moral constraint is imposed upon the moral agent prospectively when deliberating about what action he or she will do. Since people tend to be rational, there will be a tendency for morality sanctions to be imposed by others whenever one acts contrary to any moral duty-imposing reason. Thus, some threat of sanction is always actual. Of course, there may be occasions when an agent knows that this threat is almost infinitesimal because the agent knows that others are not alive to some moral consideration. Such moral duties then have a status not unlike that of imperfect legal duties where the law imposes constraint even in the absence of the usual provisions for enforcement. Such moral duties would continue to impose the constraint of any reason for or against action. Notice also that even when the legal norms do provide for the imposition of legal sanctions, the law may remain unenforced in a great many instances and for a variety of reasons. The difference between the hard constraints of the law and the softer constraints of moral reasons are not as drastic as is often imagined.

In sum, the position of having a moral duty is the position of a moral agent whose conduct is constrained by morals, the body of moral norms. These moral norms consist of moral reasons, and duty-imposing reasons, in contrast to ideal-projecting ones, are both reasons for the agent to act or not act in some way and reasons for others to react with negative morality sanctions in the event that the agent chooses to act contrary to a moral reason. Thus, the duty-imposing moral reasons constrain the agent in two ways. They impose the constraint of any practical reason and this is reenforced with the constraint of the threat of sanctions imposed by rational bystanders.

Most, although not all, legal duties are relative duties, duties to some second party with the power to initiate enforcement either by suing or prosecuting. Are there also relative duties under moral norms? I believe that there are relative moral duties and that they can be defined analogously. A moral duty of X to Y consists of a moral duty of X, together with a moral power of Y, to claim performance or remedy in the event that X fails to fulfil that duty. Thus, the moral duty of the promisor to the promisee to keep his or her promise consists in the moral duty of the promisor to act as promised together with the moral power of the promisee to claim performance or remedy in the event that the promisor fails to keep his or her promise.

I have already explained the notion of a moral duty; it is the constraint imposed upon a moral agent by some applicable moral reason that is both a reason for the agent to act and for other members of the moral community to impose negative sanctions in the event that the agent fails to act in accordance with this moral reason. In the case of a relative duty, however, the imposition of negative morality sanctions is justified only if some second party appeals to some third party to impose such sanctions. Thus, the party to whom a relative moral duty is owed has a moral power of claiming performance or remedy. The act of petitioning some chance member of the moral community to intervene and impose sanctions upon a promisor who has failed to act as promised or refused to remedy this wrong to the promisee renders the third party's intervention morally justified, while the coercive act would have been morally wrong without this act of claiming. Of course, only the promisee, or someone authorized to act for the promisee, has this moral power to claim.

What gives the second party of any relative moral duty this special standing? What moral reason makes the imposition of morality sanctions without any appeal by the party to whom the duty is owed morally wrong? Colloquially put, it is the moral norm expressed as "Don't meddle" or "Mind your own business." Whether or not the promisor keeps his or her promise to the promisee is the business of the promisor and the promisee. Therefore, any imposition of negative morality sanctions by some chance member of the community would normally be meddling in their affairs. But if the second party appeals to some bystander thus to intervene, it is no longer an invasion of the privacy of the parties to the promise. Thus, a relative moral duty is a moral duty to some second party with a special standing consisting in the moral power to effect the moral liberty of third parties to intervene with morality sanctions.

But is there really any such moral power? One might deny the existence of any moral power to claim analogous to the legal power to sue or prosecute on either or both of two grounds. First, one might hold that the intervention of other members of the moral community is always rationally justified without any appeal from some second party. Indeed, just because a moral reason is by very definition a reason to react as well as to act, this must be so. But it is not so. To be sure, every duty-imposing reason is a reason for bystanders to impose negative morality sanctions upon any moral agent who chooses to act contrary to such a reason. But in the case of relative duties, this reason to intervene coercively is normally outweighed by the contrary reason that any such sanctioning would be meddling or invading the privacy of the parties immediately involved. To be sure, it would be morally permissible for third parties to disapprove of anyone for failing to perform his or her relative duty. Moreover, any such attitude of disapproval could quite properly be expressed by saying, even publicly, that the agent has acted immorally. But these mild reactions stop short of genuine morality sanctions. Negative morality sanctions begin with private condemnation or public censure. To condemn is to judge the agent morally reprehensible for his or her act, not just morally fallible; to censure is to assume the voice of the ancient Roman censor, a magistrate with the functions of supervising the moral conduct of the citizens and penalizing moral offenders. To intervene in these ways is meddling, a morally presumptuous act in the absence of any appeal from some second party. Other negative morality sanctions are the withdrawal of favors and informal ostracism. Again, it would be prima facie wrong to impose these as moral penalties without any appeal from a second party. One other qualification is necessary. A third party is sometimes morally justified in intervening to prevent serious harm even when one would not be justified in intervening to impose negative sanctions. Presumably each moral agent has a moral duty to every other person not to assault or batter that person. Now if Jones observes Smith beating up Williams, then Jones may well be morally justified in intervening in order to prevent Smith from injuring Williams seriously. But this intervention to prevent harm is quite different from a retrospective intervention to penalize Smith for having harmed Williams by some past action. It is this retrospective imposition of negative sanctions that would be prima facie morally wrong without any act of claiming by Williams.

A second ground for denying the moral power of any second party to render the enforcement of moral reasons justifiable is that coercive intervention is morally wrong even with the appeal of a second party. Presumably a debtor has a moral duty to the creditor to repay the debt. Now suppose that a colleague, who has borrowed ten dollars from me last week, now refused to repay me on payday as we agreed. Suppose also that I now go to our department chairperson and petition him to intervene and force the debtor to give me ten dollars, either by twisting his arm or by threatening to reduce his salary. Would my act of claiming performance before this chance member of the moral community render any such intervention morally permissible? Surely not—but this is because these forms of coercive intervention go too far. Just as interventions short of morality sanctions may be justified even without my act of moral claiming, so interventions beyond morality sanctions cannot be rendered morally permissible by any appeal by the second party. Our chairperson would be morally justified in censuring my colleague for his failure to fulfil his moral duty to me, and in withdrawing some favor or even giving him the silent treatment for some time. Thus, the second party in morals, like the second party under the law, does have a special standing concerning the constraint imposed upon the duty-bearer by the applicable norms.

This special standing is most readily apparent in situations in which one can distinguish clearly between some second party *to* whom a duty is owed and some other person *regarding* whom the duty-bearer is morally constrained to act. If I pay a barber to cut my son's hair, for example, the barber then has a moral duty to me regarding my son to cut his hair as we have agreed. That I have a moral standing my son lacks in this instance can be seen by comparing this example with the situation in which I pay a gardener to mow my lawn. Although the gardener now has a duty to me regarding my lawn, no one would dream of suggesting that the gardener has any duty to the lawn itself. Again, suppose that I hire a private eye to maintain surveillance over my wife and to collect evidence I can subsequently use to divorce her. Surely this is a duty to me regarding my wife and not a duty to my wife at all. Similarly, I have a moral duty to my close friend not to alienate the affections of his wife, either by causing her to fall in love with me or by reporting his misdeeds or revealing his inadequacies so as to cause her to fall out of love with him. This is a duty to him, but only regarding her, because it is he, and not she, who is in a position to complain of my disloyalty or betrayal in the event that I fail to perform my moral duty not to alienate the affections of my friend's wife. Finally, imagine that when I visited Oxford last spring, Professor Smith went to great pains and considerable expense to make my stay in this strange city philosophically profitable and personally enjoyable. Now, when I hear from him that his son will be visiting Saint Louis for the first time and alone, I doubtless have a duty to reciprocate and do what I can to make his son's visit to my home city a success. Surely I owe this much to my benefactor Professor Smith. It is a duty to my benefactor but only a duty regarding his son, for I owe nothing to the son himself, someone I have never met in my life. Examples such as these show that not everyone essentially involved in a moral duty is a second party to that duty. Clarity and perspicuity require that we distinguish between a moral duty to some second party and a moral duty regarding some person to whom the performance may or may not be due. Thus, when I pay a barber to cut my child's hair, the barber has a duty to me regarding my child; when I pay him to cut my hair, he has a duty to me regarding me. The fact that I can play two roles in such a situation, however, should not lead us to neglect the distinction between the second party to whom a duty is owed and the person regarding whom the duty is to be performed.

Are there also situations in which I can play the two roles of duty-bearer and second party of one and the same duty? That is, can one have moral duties to oneself? Kant asserts that one has a duty to oneself to develop one's talents, and others have asserted that one has a duty to oneself not to injure oneself analogous to one's duty to others not to injure them. Suppose that when I become frustrated, I often strike any available hard surface so violently that I frequently bruise my fist, sometimes sprain my wrist and occasionally fracture a bone or two in my hand, or that I smoke so heavily that I am rapidly destroying my health.

How should we interpret the allegation that I have a moral duty to myself not to continue to act in these injurious ways? Taken literally, this would mean that I have a moral duty not to act in these ways—that is, that there are duty-imposing moral reasons against treating myself in these ways—*and* that I have the moral power of claiming performance of this duty—that is, the moral power of appealing to other members of the moral community to impose negative morality sanctions upon me in the event that I fail to act in accordance with these moral reasons. Now there may well be specifically moral reasons against injuring oneself. Accordingly, I am prepared to admit that one can have moral duties *regarding* oneself. I probably do have a moral duty not to smash my hand against a wall or to smoke myself into chronic illness. But this may well be a moral duty to my wife and children who would suffer as a consequence of my imprudent actions. Could I also be said to have a duty to myself not to do these things? If so, I must be able to have a moral power of appealing to third parties to impose negative morality sanctions in the event that I continue to mistreat myself in these ways. Well, why not? There is some reason to doubt that my act of claiming would render the imposition of morality sanctions justified in this sort of situation. That one's act injures another is a reason to react to it with negative sanctions only against the background of certain presuppositions, such as that some reenforcement is needed because moral agents are often motivated to perform actions that injure others and that coercive intervention into such interactions will be reasonably effective and salutary. But it may be that one is much less tempted to injure oneself than one is to injure others and, if the standard arguments against paternalism are sound, that intervening to save a moral agent from himself or herself is far from salutary. But even if these doubts could be overcome, there is good reason to deny that one can have duties to oneself. To have a moral duty is to be subject to the constraint of moral reasons. Such a duty is a duty *to* some second party when the duty-bearer is subject to constraint *by* that second party. Now when that second party is someone other than oneself, this constraint consists in the power of rendering the duty-bearer liable to negative morality sanctions by appealing to some moral judge. Even granted that I could render myself liable to sanctions for my failure to stop injuring myself by appealing to third parties, this power could not constrain me in anything like the same way that this same power in the hands of another imposes a moral constraint upon me. This is because I could never exercise this power against my will. Imagine, to return to our legal paradigm, that the second parties of legal duties had the power to bring suit or to prosecute *but* that they could exercise this power only with the consent of the duty-bearer, a consent that, like consent to medical treatment, the duty-bearer could withdraw at any time. This would render the power of initiating the process of imposing legal sanctions innocuous so that it would no longer impose any additional legal constraint upon the duty-bearer and it would become inappropriate to speak of legal duties as duties to those with the power to sue or prosecute. This is precisely the situation of the moral agent subject to moral reasons. Even if one did have the power to render oneself liable to the imposition of morality sanctions, which I doubt, this power would not make a duty regarding oneself into a duty to oneself because by the very nature of the situation one could never exercise this power against one's will.

Are we, then, to dismiss all talk of moral duties to oneself as mere confusion? I think not. Although such assertions cannot be taken literally, they do have a figurative meaning of some significance. To say that one has duties to oneself means that one is constrained by one's own conscience to act in conformity to moral reasons. This phenomenon of being bound by one's own conscience is real enough, and the motivating force of prospective moral scruples and retrospective moral remorse is an important factor in the moral life. But the pains of conscience are not literally sanctions imposed for a failure to do one's duty, for they follow automatically or not at all rather than resulting from a deliberate reaction to misconduct. Nor does one have any moral power of rendering their imposition justified by appealing to one's own conscience. They are justified, where one's conscience is rational, without any such appeal, for feeling guilty for one's own sins is never meddling in another person's business. For these reasons I refuse to follow Mill in holding that the primary sanctions of moral duties are internal rather than external.

Although most legal duties are relative duties, duties to some other individual, corporation or the state, there are also a few absolute legal duties. Are there also absolute moral duties, duties that are not duties to some second party? I believe that there are and, indeed, that such nonrelative duties are more common and probably more important in morals than in the law. There is, however, one significant difference between absolute duties imposed by the law and by morals. Absolute legal duties are the so-called imperfect duties, legally required acts that are not enforced by any liability to legal sanctions. But moral reasons are always reasons for reacting as well as acting and, therefore, every moral duty involves some sort of liability to morality sanctions. The difference between relative and nonrelative moral duties is not the difference between sanctionable and nonsanctionable duties but the difference between sorts of actions where some second party has special moral standing regarding the imposition of morality sanctions and those sorts of actions where there is no determinate second party with the exclusive moral power to render the imposition of morality sanctions justifiable.

In the case of a relative moral duty, any intervention by a third party imposing negative morality sanctions for immoral conduct would be morally wrong without any act of claiming by the second party because it would be meddling in the business of another, specifically of the party to whom the duty is owed. Accordingly, nonrelative duties belong to one or both of two classes. One class of absolute moral duties consists of acts required by moral reasons such that the intervention of third parties imposing sanctions in the event of nonperformance is not meddling in someone else's business, not a wrongful invasion of some zone of privacy. A paradigm case is the moral duty not to treat animals cruelly. The other class of absolute moral duties consists of acts that concern the general public so that any member of the moral community may intervene to impose morality sanctions without failing to mind his or her own business. Acts of public import are the business of every member of the public. If Hobbes and Mill are correct in suggesting that any act of theft or murder threatens the public peace and the security of every member of a society, then the moral duties to refrain from theft and murder are absolute duties rather than duties to the individual victims of each violation.

Although moral duties are essentially noninstitutional, many of them, especially relative moral duties, are parasitic upon institutional duties. For example, the debtor has a legal duty to the creditor to repay the amount due, perhaps with interest, on or before the due date. Given moral reasons to fulfil one's legal obligations, it follows that the debtor also has a moral duty of repayment to the creditor. I call this a "parasitic" moral duty because both the debtor's moral duty of repayment and the creditor's moral power to claim repayment or compensation are derived from and depend for their moral force upon the host legal duty of the debtor to the creditor. Similarly, I have a moral duty to my students to hold regular office hours at convenient times simply because, as a professor at Washington University, I have an academic duty to my students to do so. Again, the answerer's moral duty to the questioner not to answer deceptively is probably parasitic upon the answerer's morality duty to the questioner not to deceive him or her. Indeed so many relative moral duties are parasitic upon prior institutional relative duties that one sometimes wonders whether there really are any independent moral duties to some second party.

I believe, however, that one can find examples of nonparasitic moral duties to a second party. Surely a husband normally has a moral duty to his wife to help feed and change their baby. Yet he has no such legal duty; nor does he have any prior morality duty to do so, for our conventional mores probably still presuppose a more traditional division between male and female responsibilities within the family. Similarly, a wife probably has a moral duty to her househusband to pay him alimony in the event that they separate after he has significantly reduced his job opportunities by giving up his career in order to enable his wife to pursue her own. Finally, a parent has a moral duty to his or her high school child not to eavesdrop on telephone conversations or search his or her room, even though no comparable institutional duty is yet recognized in our society. There seem, then, to be a few independent moral duties to second parties.

But suppose that this appearance is deceptive and that all relative moral duties turn out to be parasitic upon prior institutional duties to some second party. It still would not follow that there are no relative moral duties and that all genuinely moral duties are nonrelative ones. Rather, what would follow is that moral duties to some second party arise only within institutional contexts. The duty-bearer would still be constrained by moral reasons, whatever moral reasons there are to fulfil his or her institutional duty, and the second party would still have a moral power to claim performance or remedy, a moral power derived from the presupposed institutional power. A parasitic moral duty to some second party is still a genuine relative moral duty just as a parasitic organism is really an organism in spite of its dependence upon its host organism.

Moral Claims

A moral claim of X against Y can be correctly defined as a correlative moral duty of Y to X. The language of relative duties looks at this moral relation from the perspective of the duty-bearer and, therefore, makes the moral constraint involved in relative duties central. The language of moral claims views the same moral relation from the perspective of the claimant and, hence, emphasizes the power to claim. Having discussed the nature of moral duties at some length, let me try to complete my account by explaining the notion of claiming more fully and clearly.

A moral claim is one kind of position under morals. To have a specific moral claim against some second party is to be situated so that the body of moral reasons confers on one the moral power to claim the performance of some moral duty by that second party or, in the event of nonperformance, a remedy from that party. Not everyone will have this moral power; the position of the claimant consists in the special moral standing that the second party of a relative duty has under moral norms. To be sure, any bystander can object to a failure to perform a moral duty and demand that the duty-bearer compensate the second party in some way. But only the claimant's act of appealing to some third party effects a change in the moral position of that third party so that an intervention to impose negative morality sanctions that would have been morally wrong becomes morally permissible. An act of censure or punishment by the moral judge that would have been meddling in another person's business becomes morally right, and perhaps even a moral duty, when the second party makes it the business of the bystander by appealing to him or her. Others may complain to bystanders also, but their petitions or demands are not genuine claimings because they lack the moral standing required to confer the moral power to claim.

How does the claimant exercise his or her power to claim? There are not, as far as I know, any morally prescribed procedures or traditional formulas necessary for this sort of performative utterance. One simply complains to some bystander or accuses the duty-bearer before some moral judge. If a number of friends are playing cards, for example, one may turn to the others and say "he cheated me," if she believes that she lost the hand because he used an ace he had up his sleeve. A child may complain to one parent that the other parent's instructions to be in before 10:00 p.m. on a weekend evening are unfair. If someone cuts in front of me while I am standing in line to be waited on, I may turn to others standing in line and object to being mistreated in this manner. Such utterances are usually not mere expressions of moral resentment, although they are that too; they are appeals to third parties to intervene in support of one's moral claim against a wrong-doer.

In appealing to some third party in this manner, one is, as it were, appointing that bystander to the position of moral judge in the confrontation between claimant and duty-bearer. Whereas only certain officials who have been appointed judges of a court with legal jurisdiction in the case at issue have the legal power to hear and decide a case at law, any member of the moral community normally can become a moral judge. This is what Bentham meant when he said that the sanctions of morality are imposed by "any chance member" of the society. This does not imply, however, that claimants typically pick the addresses of the moral claims at random. One normally appeals to some third party whose moral judgment one trusts and whose censure or favors mean a lot to the duty-bearer. Although one sometimes seeks out someone before whom to accuse a wrong-doer, as a member of our Philosophy Department might seek out the Chairperson to complain of immoral treatment at the hands of some other member of the department, one most often petitions someone who is literally a bystander because such a person is on the spot, is most likely to know the facts of the case, and is literally in a position to intervene quickly. Again, although a child may complain to a playmate of parental mistreatment, he or she will usually accuse one parent of injustice only to the other parent. Notice that special standing is involved at both ends of the speech act of claiming. Only the second party of a relative duty has the moral power to claim, and only a bystander to whom this second party appeals thereby acquires the moral standing to impose morality sanctions upon the duty-bearer. The injured party might, of course, petition any and all bystanders to intervene; but without such a widespread petition, only the moral judge invited to impose sanctions is morally permitted to do so.

To have a moral claim is to be in the position of one upon whom the body of moral norms confers a moral power of claiming performance of or remedy for nonperformance of some specific moral duty. This is a moral power because its exercise effects the moral position of the third party to whom the claimant addresses his or her petition. It renders the act of imposing morality sanctions by that party morally permissible. Just how the act of claiming effects this moral consequence cannot be known until one knows the ground of this moral power. But that it does so can be seen by reflecting upon the moral norm that one ought to mind one's own business. Therefore, intervention by third parties is morally wrong unless they are specifically asked to judge some issue by one of the parties to that confrontation.

Although my examples of moral claims have all been claims of one individual against another individual, corporate bodies, either political or private, can also be parties to moral claims. Let me close by giving a few examples. One sovereign state has a moral claim against another that the latter not commit any act of military aggression and that it abide by the provisions of any treaty between the two state parties. Given the fragility of international law, such moral claims of one state against another can be of some importance. A state sometimes claims duties of another state to it in the political forum of the United Nations or by asking some friendly power to intervene to censure or withdraw privileges from the duty-bearing state. Again, a state has some moral claims against a citizen. Thus, the United States probably has a moral claim against me that I not cheat on my income tax by failing to report honoraria that are not reported to the IRS by the payer and against practicing physicians that they not charge excessive fees for services performed on Medicare patients. The state could claim performance of this duty by having some official publicly accuse the citizen of wrongdoing, thereby inviting other members of the public to impose morality sanctions upon the offending citizen. Finally, an individual citizen sometimes has a moral claim against his or her state. Thus, an impoverished member of a society may have a moral claim against the state to be provided with welfare benefits, whether or not he or she is legally eligible for some existing welfare program, and even aliens have a moral claim against a state that it not imprison them arbitrarily. The individual can claim such duties by appealing to the general public or to some influential public official to impose morality sanctions upon any state official whose actions constitute a violation of these moral claims of the individual. No doubt, such acts of claiming are typically unavailing and, therefore, not common. This reflects a significant difference between legal and moral claims. The constraint of legal claims probably resides primarily, although not entirely, in the threat of sanctions by which they are enforced; the constraint of moral claims lies primarily in the applicability of moral reasons as practical reasons, as reasons for the duty-bearer to act in one way rather than another and only secondarily in moral reasons as reasons for third parties to react with the imposition of morality sanctions. There is a genuine analogy between the law and morals. While sanctions are, however, central to legal duties and legal claims, they are peripheral, although still present, to moral duties and claims.

Moral Liberties

Just as a legal liberty consists in the absence of any contrary legal duty, so a moral liberty consists in the absence of any contrary moral duty. Hence, to say that X has a moral liberty to do A is to say that X has no moral duty not to do A. Thus, I have a moral liberty to dress in T-shirt and shorts when I teach my classes if and only if I have no moral duty to refrain from teaching in such informal attire, perhaps grounded in some morally binding standard of decency or some regulation of Washington University.

Many moral liberties will be bilateral. Indeed, I probably do have a moral liberty to dress in T-shirt and shorts when I teach or not to so dress. Of more interest are my bilateral moral liberties of giving or not giving to some worthwhile charitable organization and of reading or not reading some piece of pornographic literature. Such bilateral moral liberties are important because they give the moral agent large areas of moral discretion within which he or she is permitted to choose freely between alternative kinds of action. Moral discretion exists in part because specifically moral reasons are only a limited subset of practical reasons in general. Thus, there will be many choices to which moral reasons will not apply. Also, and more significantly, not all moral reasons are duty-imposing reasons. Accordingly, even in situations where one may be acting contrary to some moral ideal-projecting reason in refusing to give to charity, for example, one may still have a moral liberty so to act if one wishes.

In addition to the unqualified concept of a moral liberty, defined by the absence of any contrary moral duties of any kind, it is useful to introduce the concept of a relative moral liberty. X has a moral liberty in face of Y to do some specific action A if and only if X has no moral duty to Y not to do A. Even though one may not have an absolute moral liberty to do what one has a relative moral liberty to do, this moral relation is not entirely uninteresting or unimportant in moral life. Imagine, for example, that I have promised my wife that I will take our son to a basketball game. When we later discover that a distinguished moral philosopher will be speaking at Washington University that evening, my wife releases me from my promise. Presumably I now have a moral liberty vis-à-vis my wife not to take our son to the basketball game. But if our son has been counting upon seeing that game and will be bitterly disappointed if I do not do as I have promised, then it may be that I do not have an absolute moral liberty not to take him to the game. But if a relative moral liberty does not guarantee the moral permissibility of acting accordingly, why bother with relative moral liberties? Their significance lies in the fact that they indicate when the objections or complaints of another may properly be disregarded in making a moral choice. In the example at hand, my wife is no longer in a position to complain that I have violated a moral duty to her after she has released me from that duty.

A legal liberty functions as a defence against a lawsuit of prosecution alleging that one has acted illegally and serves, thereby, to counter one's liability to legal sanctions. Similarly, a moral liberty functions to counter the charge that one has acted immorally and hence as a defence against one's liability to morality sanctions. Appeal to a moral liberty does not, however, justify one's action in the sense of providing any reason for acting as one did or for concluding that one acted as one ought to act. To say that one has a moral liberty to act in some way is to say simply that there is *no* applicable moral duty-imposing reason *not* to so act. But these two negatives do not amount to a positive; to say that there is no reason not to act in some way is not to say that there is some positive reason so to act. Again, one often has moral liberties that one ought not, everything considered, to exercise. Even when there is no moral duty-imposing reason to refrain from some action there may be a variety of other practical reasons against so acting. Thus, it may be true that I ought to give to some charitable organization because my gift would do much to relieve human suffering, even if I have a moral liberty to refrain from this morally virtuous, but nonobligatory, act.

Moral Powers

While the concept of a moral duty is familiar enough, and the related concepts of a moral liberty and a moral claim hardly unknown, the notion of a moral power is virtually unknown and at first seems out of place in moral theory. Since I introduce this concept as a moral analogue of a legal power, let me begin by reminding the reader of my conclusions concerning legal powers. Any adequate theory must distinguish between a legal ability in the broad sense recognized by Hohfeld and a legal power in a stricter sense he failed to note. X has a legal *ability* to effect some legal consequence C if and only if some specified act of X implies C, given the background facts about X and the circumstances of the act together with the applicable legal norms. X has a legal *power* to effect some legal consequence C if and only if X has a legal ability to do so and this legal ability is contingent upon X's legally imputed intention of effecting some such legal consequence.

I propose that we introduce analogous concepts into moral theory in order to facilitate our understanding of the ways in which human actions can change moral positions. Since the expression "a moral power" is not established in ordinary language, there is no question of discovering the correct lexical definition. Instead, what is required is a stipulative definition that will be useful in moral philosophy, especially in our understanding of moral rights. If there is any applicable analogue of the concept of a legal power, as defined in Chapter 2, presumably it should be defined roughly as follows:

> X has a moral power to effect some moral consequence C if and only if some specific act of X implies C, given the background facts about X and the circumstances of the act together with the applicable moral norms, *and* this implication is contingent upon the morally imputed intention of X of effecting some such moral consequence.

Let us examine the credentials of this definition by discussing briefly the several parallels between morals and the law it presupposes.

(1) Do human actions have moral consequences? Legal norms attach specific legal consequences to certain sorts of actions so that performance of these actions effects these legal results. Thus, one who accepts an offer acquires a legal duty to perform as contracted and when a landowner gives permission to another to enter on his or her land, the latter acquires a legal liberty to enter. Now it seems clear to me, and I firmly believe that it is true, that human actions similarly have moral consequences. However, I can imagine no way to prove that this is so. The best I can do is to remind the reader of a few paradigm cases that will, I trust, make this evident. When Jones makes a promise to Smith, one consequence, at least given normal circumstances, is that Jones brings into existence a moral obligation to do as promised. However, if Smith subsequently releases Jones from the promise, this action has the moral consequence of conferring upon Jones a moral liberty of not doing as originally promised and of extinguishing Smith's moral claim

that Jones do so. A patient's act of giving informed consent to an operation has the moral consequence of transforming what would have been a morally wrong violation of his or her bodily integrity into a morally permissible mode of medical treatment. My act of ordering my teenage son to be home before midnight imposes upon him a moral duty to do so; and my act of engaging a baby-sitter confers upon him or her, among other moral consequences, the moral authority to give morally binding orders to my young children. Finally, if I damage the property of another, my action imposes upon me a moral duty to repair the damage I have done or to compensate the owner for the loss. In cases like these, I honestly do not understand how anyone could doubt that human actions do have moral consequences. Of course, just how this is so requires considerable explanation.

(2) What are moral consequences? First and foremost, moral consequences are specifically moral. Thus, they constitute moral positions or the various ways in which moral norms apply to those subject to them. Since morals includes duty-imposing moral reasons analogous to the duty-imposing norms in the law, these will include moral analogues of Hohfeldian legal positions. Among moral consequences will be moral duties, moral liberties, moral powers, and so forth. But morals also contains a set of ideal-projecting reasons that probably define a set of rather different moral positions, such as being virtuous or wicked. I shall ignore these, however, for they seem to play no role in the constitution of moral rights.

Because moral powers and abilities are defined in terms of moral positions, they are conferred by moral norms. It is this that makes them *moral* powers or abilities in contrast to physical powers or psychological abilities. No doubt I have the physical power to break a child's arm. But this is very different from my moral ability to incur a moral duty to compensate the child, and perhaps its parents, for any injury I might cause were I cruel enough to use my physical strength in this manner. Again, one's psychological ability to resist impulses that conflict with duty is quite different from one's moral power to impose a duty upon oneself by making a promise.

Moral consequences are consequences in the logical sense. This is to say that they are moral positions logically implied by human actions. To say that some specified action effects some moral consequence—for example, that giving consent to medical treatment results in a moral liberty of the doctor to treat the patient—might suggest some obscure sort of causal connection between linguistic act and moral effect. Actually, the connection is logical. That the patient has consented to be treated by this doctor in a certain manner implies that the doctor has, in the absence of other relevant considerations, no duty to refrain from such treatment. Thus, moral consequences are moral positions implied by human actions.

Moral powers and abilities are powers and abilities to effect specific moral consequences by one's action. Hence, they are defined in terms of the logical consequences of human actions. That I am the only person in a position to help the injured victim of a hit and run driver may imply that I have a moral duty to do so; that I hit a pedestrian with my car implies that I have a moral duty to dô what I can to remedy the injury for which I am responsible. Only the latter moral implication indicates a moral ability of mine because only the latter is an implication of my action. Similarly, I can be released from my duty to help a friend move by my friend's saying "you needn't bother to help me move tomorrow" or by the untimely death of my friend. The former illustrates the exercise of a moral power; the latter involves no moral power because it is a biological event rather than a human action that implies that I am no longer morally bound by my promise. Thus, moral consequences are moral positions logically implied by human actions.

(3) How do human actions imply moral consequences? Any complete answer to this question would have to address many profound and controversial epistemological issues. Do ethical sentences have truth-value or anything like truth-value? Are moral standards absolute or relative? How can factual premises imply moral conclusions without committing the naturalistic fallacy? This is not the place to attempt to deal with these issues, relevant and important as they may be. Here I shall simply assume that some account of ethical reasoning can be given and, as far as possible, shall remain neutral as between alternative epistemological theories.

My present purpose is to address a more modest question that amounts to something like this: do human actions imply moral consequences in very much the same way that they imply legal consequences? If they do, then presumably there is a significant moral analogue of a legal power; if they do not, then the conception of a power is out of place in morals. Accordingly, let us see whether the salient features of legal reasoning from human actions to legal consequences are reflected in moral reasoning.

(A) Background facts about the agent. "Jones signed a will" implies the usual legal consequences only if one assumes that Jones is an adult and of sound mind. I do not suggest that this is any adequate characterization of the qualifications necessary to establish legal competence; I insist only that legal powers do presuppose some such qualifications. The same is surely true in morals. "Jones said 'I promise to give you $100' " implies no moral obligation to do so if Jones is insane, senile or even very drunk. Again, signing a medical consent form does not render the act of operating upon the patient morally permissible unless the patient knows the relevant facts and has the capacity to understand them. In this respect, the analogy holds.

(B) Background facts about the circumstances. In this respect also the analogy clearly holds. The act of accepting an offer does not imply the existence of any contractual obligations under the law if the offer has been withdrawn. Similarly, the act of saying "I now pronounce you man and wife" does not result in a legally valid marriage if the speaker has not been legally authorized to perform the marriage ceremony or if the authorized minister is standing in an empty church with no couple present to be married. Similarly, "Jones said 'I promise to give you, Smith, $100' " implies no moral duty to do so if Smith was not present when Jones performed this linguistic act or if Jones said this to Smith in the context of a play or to illustrate a lecture on promising. Again, the act of signing a medical consent form does not render the medical treatment described therein morally permissible if done during a class-room demonstration of hospital procedures or if permission is gained through intimidation. Thus, a human action implies moral conse-quences only if certain background facts about the circumstances are presupposed.

(C) Background institutions. Human actions imply legal consequences only against the background of legal institutions. Hence, the concept of a legal power is an essentially institutional one. Is it equally true that human actions imply moral consequences only against the background of presupposed institutions? In order to answer this question with precision, it is necessary to distinguish two different ways in which legal powers may presuppose legal institutions. Imagine that I give you a book from my library. My act of handing you the book while saying "Here, this is yours," assuming my legal competence to give, yours to accept the gift, and the appropriate circumstances, has the legal consequence that ownership of the book passes from me to you. Now ownership, in the sense in which I am using the term here, is a legal status defined by a complex set of legal norms; it is one specific sort of legally defined institution. Also, my legal power to give you the book is conferred upon me by the institutional norms of our legal system. Thus, my legal power to give you a book from my library presupposes legal institutions in two distinct ways. It presupposes the legal institution of ownership and it presupposes the institutional power-conferring norms applied to own-ership. Thus, some legal powers presuppose both some legal institution to which a power-conferring norm is applied and the legal system within which the power-conferring norm exists.

The former sort of institutional presupposition is not essential to many legal powers. My act of accepting your challenge to a fistfight implies the legal consequence of your legal liberty to batter me with your fists. Here the legal norm conferring upon me this power to consent to what would otherwise constitute a legally wrongful battery is being applied to accepting a challenge and fistfighting, prelegal activities that are not constituted by legal norms in the way in which ownership is. Still, my act of consenting to a fistfight has legal consequences only because the law applies to it. Hence, in cases like this also the institution of the legal system is presupposed by my legal power.

Morals is not institutional in the way that the law is. Moral norms are not instituted by any organization, nor are they the conventional norms of any social group. Moral norms are noninstitutional because they consist of moral reasons, reasons for any agent to whom they apply to act or not act in some specific way and for others to react to any agent who acts contrary to a moral reason by imposing negative morality sanctions. Just as legal powers presuppose the law, so moral powers presuppose morals. But since moral norms are not institutional, moral powers do not presuppose any norm-creating and -applying institution in the way in which my legal power to consent to a fistfight does.

It might still be true, however, that human actions imply moral consequences only when moral norms are applied to preexisting social institutions. My paradigms of the moral power to impose a moral obligation upon oneself by making a promise and the moral power of the promisee to release the promisor from a promise seem to be of this sort. Take away the social institution of the promise, the conventional rules constituting the promising game, and using the expression "I promise to . . ." would imply no moral consequences; indeed, the very words "I promise" are meaningful only against the background of the social institution of promising. The institutional norms that define promising confer upon the person playing the social role of promisor an institutional power to bind himself or herself to perform some action, and they confer upon the person playing the role of promisee the institutional power of releasing the promisor from the resulting obligation to do so. Only because moral norms require one to keep one's promises are there any specifically moral powers to make a morally binding promise or to release a promisor from his or her moral duty to do as promised. Thus, moral powers such as these are parasitic upon presupposed institutional powers. The acts of saying "I promise to . . ." or "I release you from your promise" imply moral consequences only insofar as moral norms are applied to presupposed nonmoral institutions.

Is this always so? Do human actions imply moral consequences only within the context of some presupposed institution, so that all moral powers and abilities are parasitic upon host institutional powers or abilities? I think not. The act of injuring or harming another implies a moral duty to do what one can to remedy the injury or compensate for the harm done quite independently of any background institutions of tort law or positive morality. Similarly, the very act of procreating a child imposes upon the parent a moral duty to care for the child in the event that its needs are not met by others. Although this duty of care is conditional upon the failure of existing social institutions to meet the needs of the child, it is not grounded upon such institutions in any way. It would exist in a state of nature, were it possible to procreate and raise children apart from society, just as much as in society. Thus, there are nonparasitic moral abilities. I believe, although this is less clear, that there are independent moral powers as well. My example of the power to consent to a fistfight illustrates this. Although my act of consenting to a fistfight is an exercise of a legal power, it implies the moral permissibility of your battering me with your fists quite independently of its legal consequences. Even if there were no legal tort of battery or no legally recognized defence of consent to suits alleging battery, there would be a morally significant difference between beating someone up in the course of a fistfight to which the victim had consented and battering someone without his or her consent. That the moral power to consent is not parasitic upon any presupposed legal power of consent can be seen more clearly by an examination of cases to which legal norms do not apply. Although the law of our country does not protect the privacy of a child's telephone conversation from invasion by a parent, usually it is morally wrong for a parent to eavesdrop on any conversation between his or her child and a playmate. If the child consents to the parent's listening in on such a telephone conversation, however, it becomes morally permissible to do so. This seems a clear case of a nonparasitic moral power of the child to confer upon another a moral liberty.

Suppose, however, that I am mistaken and that all moral powers are parasitic, because human actions imply specifically moral consequences only when moral norms are applied to presupposed institutions. It would not follow that there are no moral powers or that the concept of a moral power is out of place in moral theory. What would follow is that moral powers exist and can be exercised only within some presupposed institutional context. Parasitical moral powers are genuine, and often important in both theory and practice, even if they are dependent upon some host institutional powers.

(D) Presupposed norms. Human actions imply legal consequences only if some legal norm is presupposed. This is so simply because there is no logical, conceptual or necessary connection between any specific action *per se* and any legally valid conclusion. Legal consequences are *attached to* actions by the law. They are attached by norms roughly of the general form "if action A, then consequence C." Only if some such legal norm is presupposed does any action imply any legal consequence. Much the same is true of morality consequences such as the rights or duties attached to human actions by the norms of any positive morality. Morals, however, is not institutional in anything like the way that the law and morality are. Thus, if there are moral consequences of human actions, they follow from them by some sort of logical connection, not by virtue of any presupposed organizational or conventional norm.

The very possibility of any such logical connection between human action and moral consequences might, however, be thought to presuppose some moral rule or principle. For example, "Smith promised to do A" might be held to imply "Smith has a moral duty to do A" only if one assumes that one always has a moral duty to keep one's promises. This would be so if moral reasoning were necessarily deductive. But as we saw in the first section of this chapter, this is not so. Since nondeductive reasoning can and often does establish moral conclusions, the inference from an action to the moral position it effects does not logically require any presupposed universal moral norm. I realize that my theory of moral reasoning is not above all doubt. It is worth noting, therefore, that should I be mistaken on this point, my case for the reality of moral powers is strengthened rather than weakened, for moral reasoning would turn out to be even more like legal reasoning than I allege.

Thus, the inference from "Smith promised to do A" to "Smith has a moral duty to do A" does not presuppose any universal moral norm either to attach the moral consequence to the human action or to render the inference deductively valid. At the same time, "Smith promised to do A" does not constitute in and of itself a sufficient reason to justify the conclusion "Smith has a moral duty to do A." This is because human actions are incomplete reasons; only in conjunction with additional considerations does the fact that some action has been done constitute a complete practical reason (Raz, 1975, 22-25). "Smith promised to do A" is a reason for Smith to do A and for others to react to his failure to do so with negative morality sanctions only against a background of facts about the importance of keeping promises in human lives, our frequent temptation to break our promises, the propriety of the promised action, and so forth. These background presuppositions will include ultimate practical reasons, such as facts about human suffering or betrayal of trust. Thus, the inference from human actions to moral consequences does presuppose one or more norms, but these norms are ultimate practical reasons rather than universal moral rules or principles. Arguments from human actions to moral consequences are enthymematic, but in a different way and for a different reason than arguments from actions to legal consequences. Legal reasoning inevitably presupposes some legal norm that attaches the consequence to the action. Moral reasoning, since it appeals to moral reasons that are typically and perhaps always incomplete reasons, presupposes the background that in conjunction with the fact that some action has been done constitutes a complete reason for the moral conclusion. This background will usually contain ultimate practical reasons that are practical, although nonmoral, norms for human conduct.

Do human actions imply moral consequences in very much the same way that they imply legal consequences? Yes, in very much, but not exactly, the same way. Human actions imply moral consequences only if one assumes certain background facts about the agent and the circumstances. The implication from human actions to moral consequences does not presuppose any norm-creating and -applying institution comparable to the legal system, for moral norms are noninstitutional; but sometimes these moral norms imply moral consequences insofar as they are applied to presupposed institutions such as legal ownership or the promising game. Since moral reasoning is typically nondeductive and moral consequences are not attached to human actions by any posited norms, the inference from some action to its moral consequences need not presuppose any general moral norm. Since moral reasons are typically incomplete reasons, however, the inference from human action to moral consequence does presuppose background facts that will include ultimate practical reasons. Still, although incomplete reasons, the fact that some action has been done *is* a moral reason. As such, they do imply, in conjunction with their presupposed background, moral positions. Therefore, human actions do effect moral consequences and there really are moral abilities and powers.

(4) Are moral powers distinguished by intention? Legal powers in the strict sense are distinguished from legal abilities in a broader sense by the fact that their efficacy is contingent upon the legally imputed intention of the exerciser to effect some such legal consequences. Are moral powers similarly marked off from mere moral abilities by some similar morally imputed intention? Well, there does seem to be a distinction between moral powers and moral abilities hinging in some way upon the intention of the exerciser. Thus Jones cannot impose upon himself or herself any moral duty to do as promised without intending to effect some such duty, because promising simply is the act of binding oneself by saying "I promise to . . ." in the appropriate circumstances and knowing what one is doing. The same utterance in similar circumstances would not constitute a promise if uttered by a young child or an elderly drunk who did not understand that the utterance has this performative force. By contrast, Jones can incur an obligation to remedy injury or

compensate for harm done even if Jones inflicted the harmful injury by reckless driving or angry attack and with no intention to incur any such duty at all. Again, the difference between my power to impose upon myself a duty to return your book by borrowing it and my ability to incur a duty to return your book by stealing it is that borrowing is (while stealing is not) *essentially* an act of changing my legal and moral position regarding your book. One can and should, therefore, distinguish between moral powers in a strict sense where the efficacy of the exercise is contingent upon the normative intention of the possessor of the power and moral abilities in a broader sense where the moral efficacy may or may not be so contingent.

But precisely what sort of intention is required for the efficacy of a moral power? At this point, one must distinguish between parasitic and independent moral powers. Since a parasitic moral power is dependent upon and resultant from some prior host power, the requisite intention is that upon which the efficacy of the host power is contingent. Thus, one's moral power to bind oneself morally by entering into a legally binding contract is contingent upon one's legally imputed intention of imposing upon oneself some such legal duties, because this intention is essential to the host legal power to contract. Independent moral powers are a different story. Their efficacy is contingent, not upon some morally imputed intention (whatever that might mean), but upon the exerciser's reasonably imputed intention to effect some such moral consequences. For example, before I left Saint Louis to go on sabbatical leave, I exercised my moral power of conferring upon the secretary of Washington University's philosophy department a moral liberty of opening my mail. Although there is nothing illegal in the secretary's opening, even without my permission, any mail addressed to me arriving at my university address, there is, I believe, a moral duty not to invade my privacy by doing so. But if I give my permission to the secretary to open my mail in order to decide which items are worth forwarding to me while I am on leave, then this moral duty is extinguished and replaced with a moral liberty. I could not, however, give my moral permission to open my mail without saying or doing something that it would be reasonable for an objective observer to take as an act intended to make opening my mail morally permissible.

I conclude that there is a moral analogue of a legal power. The definition proposed near the beginning of this section, you remember, is as follows:

X has a moral power to effect some moral consequence C if and only if some specific act of X implies C, given the background facts about X and the circumstances of the act together with the applicable moral norms, *and* if this moral consequence is contingent upon the morally imputed intention of X of effecting some such moral consequences.

We have discovered two important ways in which this definition must be modified to take account of the fact that morals does not parallel the law in every respect. Because legal consequences are attached to human actions by posited legal norms, a specific act of X implies a legal consequence C only when taken together with applicable legal norms. Since the connection between act and moral consequence is logical rather than institutional, a specific act of X implies a moral consequence C without presupposing any applicable moral norm. How can this be? It is simply because human acts, more precisely the fact that some human action has been done, is a moral reason and thus constitutes a moral norm. To be sure, it is an incomplete practical reason and it will, therefore, presuppose background facts including some more ultimate practical reasons. But these need not be more ultimate specifically moral reasons. Secondly, although the efficacy of a moral power is contingent upon intention, it is never a morally imputed intention. In the case of parasitic moral powers, the required intention is whatever intention is requisite for the efficacy of the host nonmoral power; in the case of independent moral powers, it is the reasonably imputed intention to effect some such moral consequence. Accordingly, I now propose a revised and more accurate analysis of a moral power.

X has a moral power to effect some moral consequence C if and only if some specific act of X implies C, given the background facts about X and the circumstances of the act, *and* this implication is contingent upon either, whatever intention of X is required for the efficacy of the exercise of some host power or the reasonably imputed intention of X to effect some such moral consequence.

Thus revised, the analysis of a moral power defines a genuine and important moral position. Morals, the body of moral norms, does confer such moral powers upon those subject to morals because among the reasons that constitute morals are human actions. Thus, "Jones promised to do act A" is a moral reason for "Jones has a moral duty to do A" and "Smith consented to be operated upon by Wilson" is a moral reason for "Wilson has a moral liberty of operating upon Smith." Actions do make a moral difference. In some cases they effect moral consequences contingent upon some sort of an intention to effect normative consequences; in other cases no such intention is necessary. In the former cases, such moral reasons confer moral powers upon those who might act; in the latter cases, such moral reasons confer mere moral abilities upon those who might so act. I contend that the significance of moral abilities and powers has too long been ignored by moral philosophy.

Moral Immunities

At this point the logic of Hohfeldian conceptions enables us to define a variety of related moral positions. A "power over" has as its logical correlative a "subjection to" and as its logical contradictory an "impotence regarding"; an "ability over" has as its logical correlative a "liability to" and as its logical contradictory a "disability regarding." Thus, for example, X has a moral impotence regarding Y to effect some moral consequence C for Y, if and only if X does not have a moral power over Y to effect C for Y. Similarly, X has a moral disability regarding Y to effect some moral consequence C for Y, if and only if it is not the case that X has a moral ability regarding Y to effect C for Y.

For our purposes, the most important of these logically related concepts is that of a moral immunity. The concept of an immunity, like that of a claim, is an essentially relational one; an immunity is always and necessarily an immunity against one or more second parties. Thus, we can best define the conception of a moral immunity as follows: X has a moral immunity against Y from some specific moral consequence C, if and only if Y has a moral disability to do any action whatsoever that would imply this consequence C for X. For example, a promisee has a moral immunity against the promisor from having the moral duty to keep the promise extinguished by any act of the promisor. Likewise, a daughter has a moral immunity against her father from his rendering sexual intercourse with her morally permissible simply by his giving his consent to a suitor; only if the daughter herself consents to intercourse with the suitor does he acquire any moral liberty of making love to her.

The importance of moral immunities is not far to seek. A moral immunity protects one from some specific change in one's moral position resulting from the action of another. Although this does not necessarily give one control over one's moral duties and liabilities, it does ensure that these are not subject to the control of another. Thus, the possessor of any moral immunity can be assured that in some specific respect his moral position, whether or not it reflects his own will, is not at the mercy of some alien will. This is why it is more appropriate and useful to define a moral immunity as the absence of some second party's moral ability in the broad sense rather than moral power in the narrow sense. In this way, the possession of a specific moral immunity provides the greater degree of protection.

Just as one often has occasion to speak of claims against the world, so it is useful to introduce the analogous conception of a moral immunity against the world. X has a moral immunity against the world from some specific moral consequence C, if and only if every second party Y has a moral disability to do any action whatsoever that would imply this consequence C for X. For example, one has a moral immunity against the world from being morally bound by "promises" made on one's behalf, for only the individual himself or herself, or the individual's authorized agent, can impose a moral duty upon oneself by promising to do something. Again, since only the injured party can waive the moral claim to remedy or compensation, any injured party has a moral immunity against the world from having his or her moral claim to remedy or compensation extinguished by any act purporting to waive it on his or her behalf. Such immunities are important elements in many moral rights.

There are, then, moral positions essentially analogous to the legal positions identified and distinguished by Hohfeld. Morals applies to human agents in a number of distinct ways that parallel the applications of the law to those subject to it. Accordingly, I have distinguished and explained the fundamental moral conceptions of a duty, a claim, a liberty, a power, and an immunity. These are, as I shall argue, the constituents of moral rights.

Chapter 6

MORAL RIGHTS

Just as every citizen is subject to the law, a body of norms embedded in the legal institutions of his or her society, so every moral agent is subject to morals, a set of specifically moral reasons not dependent on any social institutions. It is the different ways in which these moral norms apply to moral agents that will enable us to explain the nature of moral rights.

A Hohfeldian Model

Since there are moral positions analogous to the legal positions identified by Hohfeld, it is certainly possible and presumably illuminating to extend our Hohfeldian model of legal rights to cover noninstitutional moral rights as well. Accordingly, at the core of every moral right stands some specific moral position that identifies the right-holder and defines the essential content of the right. This core element is a moral advantage to the right-holder vis-à-vis one or more second parties in some possible conflict of wills concerning the exercise or enjoyment of the core in that the moral reason or reasons defining the content of the right side with the possessor of the right and against the second party or parties. Around this core element stand a number of associated Hohfeldian moral positions, each of which, if respected, confers some sort of freedom or control concerning the exercise or enjoyment of the core upon the right-holder. Thus, the complex structure of moral positions, taken as a whole and if respected, confers upon the possessor of the core dominion over one or more second parties within the domain defined by that core. Perhaps a couple of examples, one a liberty-right and the other a claim-right, will illustrate how moral rights can helpfully be interpreted in terms of this model.

One theoretically interesting and practically important moral right is, I believe, the right to obtain an abortion. No doubt the existence of any such right is controversial and, even if granted, its precise content debatable. But even if I am mistaken on both of these counts, my analysis of what I take this right to be will serve to show how my model can be applied to moral liberty-rights.

The core of this right, as I conceive it, is the moral liberty of the pregnant woman to obtain an abortion. For the sake of brevity, I shall use the word "woman" somewhat loosely to refer to any woman or girl of child-bearing age. And the morally permitted act of obtaining an abortion is intended to cover both activities of seeking someone willing and able to perform an abortion upon one and of submitting to this medical procedure. It is important to bear in mind that this moral liberty of obtaining an abortion does not logically imply any claim against a physician to perform an abortion or any claim against the state to provide funding for an abortion. Thus, a pregnant woman may in fact be unable to obtain an abortion even though her liberty-right to obtain an abortion is fully respected by all parties. It is also worthy of note that a woman may have a moral right to obtain an abortion even when she ought not to exercise her right. Thus, a woman ought not to seek and submit to an abortion for some frivolous reason, such as looking especially attractive at the annual spring gala at the country club, even though she does not have a moral duty not to obtain an abortion merely for that reason.

The moral right to obtain an abortion is, however, more than this core liberty; it also includes a number of associated elements that, if respected, confer upon the pregnant woman freedom and control over the exercise of this defining core. These seem to include at least the following: (1) The moral duty of others not to use force or the threat of force to prevent a pregnant woman from obtaining an abortion. This is at least a moral duty regarding the right-holder, although it is not clear that it is a duty to her. In any event, it is not a correlative duty, a duty whose content matches that of the defining core of the liberty-right, for it does not render it morally wrong to prevent a woman from obtaining an abortion in ways that do not use or threaten force, for example by persuading her doctor that it would be immoral for him to perform an abortion upon this patient or by withholding the financing needed by the woman in order to pay for the physician's services. (2) The moral liberty of the pregnant woman to resist the use or evade the threat of force intended to prevent her from obtaining an abortion. This associated liberty may render morally permissible violent or deceptive acts by the woman, acts that would be morally wrong in normal circumstances. (3) The moral duty of third parties not to assist any second party in the use or threat of force intended to prevent a pregnant woman from obtaining an abortion; and (4) The moral duty of third parties to assist the pregnant woman to resist the use or evade the threat of force intended to prevent her from obtaining an abortion. The former duty is more unconditional than the latter. Third parties ought morally never to intervene to side with second parties where the right to obtain an abortion is at stake, but they need intervene on the side of the right-holder only if she chooses to exercise her liberty to resist. (5) The moral immunity of the pregnant woman against the termination of her core liberty by any unilateral act of another individual or group or corporate body. Thus, the woman retains her moral liberty of obtaining an abortion even if her husband or the several members of her family object. Although the fact that these persons object is no doubt a practical reason against exercising her right to obtain an abortion, it does not impose upon the pregnant woman any specifically moral duty to refrain from seeking and submitting to an abortion. Again, a law prohibiting seeking and/or submitting to an abortion would not extinguish a pregnant woman's *moral* liberty to do so, although it would obviously rule out any legal liberty of acting in the proscribed manner. This reveals a crucial aspect of moral liberties. Liberty, in general and in the abstract, has no special moral status. It is specific liberties that are to be respected under the norms of morals, and different liberties are protected by moral norms in different ways and in differing degrees. Thus, one typically has a moral liberty, provided one has a valid driver's license, to drive either way on Main Street. But the enactment of an ordinance making Main Street into a one-way street would terminate one's moral liberty of driving in the prohibited direction. The pregnant woman's moral liberty to obtain an abortion is more resistant to legislation, perhaps because any such legislation is deprived of moral force by the way it invades her moral right to privacy.

Interpreted according to my Hohfeldian model of a right, a woman's moral right to obtain an abortion consists of a core moral liberty to seek and submit to an abortion, together with a number of associated moral positions. As a whole, this complex of moral advantages confers upon the pregnant woman dominion over anyone who would will to stop her from obtaining an abortion within the domain defined by her core liberty. This moral liberty holds against such second parties because it makes it impossible for them to constrain a woman who wishes to obtain an abortion by any appeal to moral reasons against so doing or to justify the imposition of morality sanctions upon a woman who has obtained an abortion. In various ways, the associated moral advantages side with the right-holder against any second party in the event of a confrontation between them. To be sure, the moral norms defining this liberty-right may not be respected by all parties; but where they are respected, the will of the pregnant woman to exercise her liberty-right prevails over the will of any opposing second party.

A less-often denied example of a moral right, this one a claim-right, is the right to security of the person. The core of this right is the moral claim of the individual human being against all others, both other individuals and corporate bodies, that they not injure or unduly endanger one's body or mind. This moral claim is, of course, itself complex. It consists of the moral duty of others, both other individuals and corporate bodies, not to injure or unduly endanger one's body or mind, together with the moral power of the individual to claim performance or remedy. I use a formula borrowed from private law in a somewhat extended sense here in this moral context. This power to claim is the moral power to render the imposition of morality sanctions permissible by appealing to one or more third parties and petitioning them to act as moral judges in the event of a violation of the core duty in one's case. But in the event of any such violation, the duty-bearer who has wronged one incurs a remedial moral duty to make good or compensate for any injury or endangerment done. And the right-holder has the moral power to claim this moral duty in turn. Hence, my suggestion that the core claim contains the moral power to claim performance or remedy.

The defining core of this moral right to security of the person is surrounded with a number of associated moral advantages including at least the following: (1) The moral power of the individual right-holder to waive his or her core claim against injury or undue endangerment to body or mind. One exercises this power when one agrees to participate in a boxing match or a contact sport such as football, when one consents to medical treatment by a physician or surgeon, or when one accepts a job that puts one under great emotional stress. Presumably there are limits to this power to waive one's core claim against injury or endangerment to one's body or mind. At least under normal circumstances, consent does not make killing a human morally permissible; and mayhem, unlike manly sports, is also beyond the moral pale, even with the consent of the victim. I do not know, however, precisely where to draw the line here. (2) The individual's moral liberty of exercising or not exercising this power to waive his or her core claim. This liberty extends a considerable distance, for one may volunteer for military service or accept a hazardous position in a police or fire department as well as consent to violent sports or stressful occupations. Special circumstances may, of course, limit this moral liberty, as when obligations to one's dependent children render it morally impermissible to take unnecessary chances with one's physical or mental health. But this susceptibility to curtailment by duties is a feature of any moral liberty. (3) The moral liberty of the individual to resist, even with proportionate force if necessary, others who are injuring or endangering one's body or mind. There are ways of resisting short of force ranging from the use of persuasion, the appeal to others to exert social pressures, or taking legal action. But these may be unavailable, too slow or uncertain, or unavailing. Although the use of force against others is morally impermissible under normal circumstances, one has no moral duty to refrain from forceful resistance to any violation of one's core claim to security of person. The moral limit to such permissible use of force is, however, more constraining then when one is defending one's very life. The moral liberty of self-defense when one's life is at stake permits the use of all necessary force, even maiming or killing another if, but only if, this is genuinely necessary. But one is not morally permitted to kill or even maim another merely to prevent slight bodily injury or modest mental endangerment to oneself. There must be some due proportion between the threat one is resisting and the harm one is threatening to impose upon the attacker when one is defending one's security of person. (4) The moral duty of third parties to prevent serious injury or endangerment of any individual's body or mind unless the victim has waived his or her moral claim to security of person regarding such injury or endangerment. One may not always know whether the victim has waived his or her core claim, although the circumstances are often indicative. Presumably a boxer standing in the ring has and a little old lady being beaten up on a dark sidewalk has not waived the moral claim to personal security. In ambiguous circumstances, one probably has a moral liberty, even if it should later turn out that one did not have a moral duty, to intervene to prevent injury or endangerment, provided it was serious in nature. The qualification "regarding such injury or endangerment" is also important. Suppose that Jones has consented to box with Smith. Third parties have no moral duty, indeed not even any moral liberty, to intervene to prevent Smith from beating up Jones even if it becomes clear that he will require some medical care after their fight. But if Smith begins to kick Jones in the groin or to hit him with a stick, then one does have a duty to intervene. This is because in waiving one's claim to security of person one waives it only against some specific second party or parties and in some limited regard; one does not renounce it entirely. (5) The individual's moral immunity against the termination of his or her core claim to security of person by any act of another, either another individual or any corporate body. It is this associated element that, in the traditional language, makes this moral right of the individual imprescriptible.

I have not proved the existence of the individual's moral claim-right to security of the person, much less defended my detailed description of its constitution. What I do hope to have shown is that it is possible and illuminating to apply a Hohfeldian model of legal rights beyond the sphere of institutional rights. It is possible because there are moral positions analogous to the fundamental legal positions identified by

Hohfeld. Thus, one can legitimately conceive of a moral right as a complex structure of moral advantages that, if respected, confer upon the right-holder dominion concerning the exercise or enjoyment of some core vis-à-vis one or more second parties. Moreover, there are two related uses of this model, each of which is illuminating in its own way.

One use of the model is to guide our thinking about moral rights toward greater theoretical and practical adequacy. The advantages of thinking about moral rights in terms of a Hohfeldian model are several. It forces one to go beyond the usual inarticulate labels and catch phrases, such as "the right to an abortion" or "the right to property," and to a helpful specificity of content. Spelling out the content of each right in specific detail constantly reminds one of the complexity of moral rights, a complexity that is essential to their nature as rights and that one cannot ignore without error. The Hohfeldian model structured in terms of dominion concerning some possible confrontation emphasizes what is distinctive about moral rights, in contrast to moral oughts or moral values in general, and thus underlines the special importance that rights have in moral thinking and decision. Since each Hohfeldian element involves some specific human action, the use of a Hohfeldian model makes the practical relevance of any moral right explicit. Recognizing the diversity of normative elements that constitute any moral right reveals a complexity in the justification of assertions or denials of rights, a complexity too often ignored. Finally, the model suggests fruitful questions for theoretical investigation or moral discussion, for example "What is the place of the concept of a power in moral theory?" or "Does a terminally ill patient have the moral power to waive his or her moral right to life?" I do not intend to suggest that the use of my Hohfeldian model in thinking about moral rights will solve all philosophical problems or lead to inevitable agreement on moral issues hinging upon rights. Indeed, the first effect of adopting this model is to introduce a new complexity and unfamiliar complication into our thinking. In the end, however, it is my conviction that analyzing the ostensibly simple but really complex phenomena into genuine elements will lead to greater accuracy of thinking and a deeper understanding.

The other illuminating use of a Hohfeldian model is as a heuristic device in the interpretation of the language of moral rights. Although references to moral rights abound in the philosophical and juristic literature and in practical moral debate, the meaning of most assertions or denials of rights is far from clear. The interpretive use of this model requires one to translate the usual abstract names of rights into much more concrete terms that lead to greater understanding of precisely what is, or might be, meant. It also reveals the essential imcompleteness of most sentences asserting or denying rights. "Mary has a right to an abortion" is a semantically incomplete sentence in the same way that "Mary is sitting on the right" is. One does not understand what the latter means unless one knows on whose right and from what viewpoint is intended by the speaker. Similarly, one does not understand what the former means until one knows vis-à-vis whom and concerning what sort of possible confrontation the speaker has in mind. The most obvious advantage of the use of this model to clarify the meaning of the language of moral rights is the one Hohfeld emphasized in his discussion of the language of the law. Distinguishing between the very different positions that can constitute the core of a right marks essential distinctions, such as the distinction between a liberty-right and a claim-right. Thus, in interpreting the meaning of "Mary has a moral right to an abortion," it makes a great difference whether one is asserting Mary's liberty-right to seek and submit to an abortion or her claim-right to be provided with an abortion by her physician or the state. Spelling out the content of any moral right in terms of its constituent moral advantages goes a long way toward making the implications of any assertion of that right explicit. This increases our understanding of precisely what is being asserted at the same time that it makes the application of the statement to particular circumstances much easier. Finally, this Hohfeldian model of moral rights in which dominion concerning some possible confrontation is central limits the use of the vocabulary of rights in moral discourse. The recent inflation of rights claims has been often noted and almost as often lamented, but there is no agreement about just where to draw the line between appropriate and inappropriate applications of the language of rights. My Hohfeldian model suggests that assertions or denials of rights can be made significantly and taken literally only in a context in which the will of the right-holder could conceivably conflict with the will of some second party. Thus, the language of rights has a much narrower province in moral discussion than the language of moral obligation or the vocabulary of moral value.

How was I using my Hohfeldian model earlier in this section when I sketched two sample moral rights, the right to obtain an abortion and the right to security of person? Primarily and for the most part to guide our thinking about these moral rights, but secondarily and in part to interpret the language of moral rights. The core of any right defines its essential content; the associated elements go beyond what is definitive. Although there must be some sorts of associated elements that, if respected, confer freedom and control over the exercise or enjoyment of the core upon its possessor, the definition of the right does not by itself determine precisely which ones these may be. Thus, in specifying the cores of these moral rights, I was giving a stipulative definition to the expressions "the right to obtain an abortion" and "the right to security of person." But in specifying the associated elements I was going beyond the language of rights to the substantive, normative content of these two rights. My model guided me in deciding whether some moral position was related to the core in a manner that would make it an associated element were it real, but it was my very fallible moral judgment that decided whether this or that moral advantage actually did, or might plausibly be assumed to, exist. Thus, my interpretations of these sample moral rights went beyond linguistic analysis to substantive moral philosophy.

Even within the bounds of linguistic analysis, it is important to bear in mind that a model is not a definition. This is why I spoke of using the Hohfeldian model as a heuristic device in the interpretation of the language of moral rights. To translate the ordinary language of rights into Hohfeldian terminology is to render more articulate and precise what that ordinary language might mean. Sometimes one will thereby come to understand more clearly what some speaker or reader did mean, for sometimes a Hohfeldian interpretation will be confirmed by the larger context within which some assertion or denial of a moral right occurs. At other times, one will misinterpret the speaker, either because some other Hohfeldian interpretation is more accurate or because any Hohfeldian interpretation would misrepresent the meaning of someone who was not thinking in Hohfeldian terms at all. But if such a failure of communication takes place within an ongoing discussion between speaker and hearer, then by suggesting what the speaker might have meant it may lead to a redefinition of the speaker's language of rights by causing him or her to begin thinking in Hohfeldian terms after all. Thus in a peculiar way, the misunderstanding of the speaker's language may lead to a greater understanding between speaker and hearer in the future and quite possibly to a greater understanding of the moral right about which they are speaking. This is not to suggest that we should replace our ordinary language of moral rights with a more precise vocabulary defined in Hohfeldian terms. It is theoretically illuminating and helpful in practice to think about rights in Hohfeldian terms as far as we can. But our moral insight and judgment are not always as detailed and precise as the Hohfeldian model would require. Our exploratory thinking and much of our speaking about rights must inevitably be formulated in our existing preanalytic language.

I have argued that a model of a right articulated in terms of Hohfeldian fundamental legal conceptions can be extended from legal rights to other species of institutional rights and finally to noninstitutional moral rights. Should we conclude from this that the expression "a right" is unambiguous and can be taken to have a single meaning when used in speaking of legal rights, academic rights, morality rights and moral rights? Given my insistence that a model is not a definition, this conclusion does not follow from what I have said. And I believe that this is not the case. The language of rights is not unequivocal. At the same time, the expression "a right" is not equivocal in the way "a plane" is used in two different senses in geometry and in aviation. It is, to borrow a traditional and unfashionable term, analogical. In the law and in the normative language of other institutions, "a right" has directive meaning, for the legal or institutional positions involved in such rights are defined by institutional directives. When used by social scientists or lawyers to speak about the law or other institutions, "a right" has descriptive meaning. In morals, "a right" has critical meaning, for all moral positions are defined in terms of moral obligations, and the meaning of "ought morally" involves rational criticism (Wellman, 1961, 289-91). Although the language of rights has different kinds of meaning in different uses, these are tied together by a network of analogies that I have tried to capture in my Hohfeldian model.

The Existence of Moral Rights

Moral rights, in contrast to the rights conferred by the norms of positive morality, are noninstitutional. They exist independently of any organizational rules or social conventions. They are, in the traditional language, natural rights. There is, however, a long tradition of scepticism regarding the existence of natural rights. Philosophers quite willing to grant the reality of practical obligations and even noninstitutional moral duties doubt or deny the reality of natural rights. They would dismiss my model of moral rights as a figment of my imagination of no theoretical interest or practical importance, because there are no moral rights for it to model.

I, on the contrary, believe in the existence of moral rights. Indeed, I regard the first seven sections of this chapter as a sustained argument to prove their existence. My argument presupposes my conception of a right in general together with the reality of specifically moral reasons. I have shown that moral reasons do define moral positions analogous to the legal positions Hohfeld distinguishes. Therefore, if one grants that a right is a complex of normative positions that if respected confer dominion and that there really are moral reasons, then it follows that there are noninstitutional moral rights conferred by those moral reasons. But to rest my case here would be unfair to my opponents and unsatisfying to my readers, for I have yet to consider the reasons one might have to remain sceptical of the existence of moral rights.

In order to become clearer on just what is at issue between myself and my opponents, it will be helpful to begin by explaining what I mean by asserting the reality of moral rights. Precisely what does it mean to assert the existence of a moral right such as the right to obtain an abortion or the right to security of the person? Since a right is a complex structure of Hohfeldian positions, it means to assert the existence of a set of moral positions related in the special way revealed by my dominion model of rights. Moral positions are not entities in the world in anything like the sense in which physical objects or even persons are; they are not even entities in whatever sense points in space or positions in space-time are ontological realities. To speak of moral positions is to speak figuratively about the way in which one or more moral norms bear upon the conduct of some moral agent, or set of moral agents in the case of relational positions. If I am correct in my contention that moral norms are moral reasons, rather than moral rules or principles, then to assert the existence of a moral right is merely to assert the existence of a set of moral reasons bearing upon human conduct in that very special way in which rights have practical relevance. But what are moral reasons? They are statements that imply some moral conclusion. Hence, to assert the existence of moral reasons is to assert the truth of certain statements plus their relevance to moral judgments of human actions. Thus, what at first appears to be a dubious ontological commitment to a nonnatural realm of moral entities, because we speak of the "existence" or "reality" of moral rights, turns out to be an epistemological presupposition instead.

This undermines one of the most powerful objections to the existence of moral rights. Traditional natural rights theory developed out of natural law theory. Just as legal rights are conferred by positive law, so moral rights are conferred by a moral law independent of human legislation. But how could there be any such law independent of any and all social institutions? One view is that natural law consists in divine commandments. This commits one to the existence of God and, specifically, the sort of God who is a supernatural legislator and judge. Another view is that the natural law expresses, not the will of God, but human nature. Somehow there are moral norms implicit in human nature, perhaps in tendencies or purposes built into a universal human nature. More recently natural rights theory became less dependent upon natural law and natural rights were thought of as ideal entities, as objectively real but not empirically observable. Although conceptions of the nature of moral rights differed, it was generally thought that they must have some sort of being or some existence in the world in order to serve as objective standards by which to judge human institutions. A Hohfeldian model of rights makes it clear that this sort of ontological commitment is unnecessary. What seem to be assertions of the existence of dubious nonnatural objects are, literally, assertions about moral reasons and their bearing upon human conduct. Thus, there is no need to deny the existence of natural rights on metaphysical grounds.

Epistemological doubts cannot, I fear, be so easily dismissed. Traditional natural rights theory typically presupposed a dubious rationalism. Sometimes it was thought that the existence of a moral right could be established only by direct inspection. One can be directly aware of a natural right, such as the right to life or liberty, by a nonsensuous purely intellectual vision. Thus, rational intuition assures us that moral rights do exist much as our very eyes assure us that physical objects, or at least colors, are objectively real. And one discovers the content of any moral right by direct inspection, by looking at it carefully with the mind's eye. More often it was thought that our knowledge of the existence and content of natural rights comes from our rational intuition of universal rights principles, such as that all men have a moral right to life. The existence of natural rights is assured by such self-evident moral truths. There are, however, many reasons to deny that moral knowledge can arise from rational intuition or, indeed, that we have any such faculty of nonsensuous vision. Fortunately, no such epistemological presupposition is required for my theory of moral rights.

On my analysis of moral rights, moral rights consist in complexes of moral positions defined by moral reasons. Thus, moral rights are known, not by intuition, but by discursive reasoning from specifically moral reasons to their moral implications. Since these reasons are typically facts, such as the fact that Jones promised Smith to mow his lawn, there is usually no special problem about how moral reasons themselves are known. But this reminds us of another source of scepticism about the existence of natural rights. Some traditional natural rights theories also eschewed intuition and appealed to discursive reason instead. Certain facts about human nature—for example, that all human beings naturally seek to prolong life and to shun injury—imply that all humans have a natural right to life and a moral right not to be injured. Thus, the existence of fundamental moral rights can be established by reasoning from the facts of human nature. This sort of reasoning is indeed dubious and might well make one sceptical of the existence of natural rights.

I think it imperative, however, to distinguish two sorts of scepticism that might arise from critical reflection upon traditional arguments of this sort. A dogmatic scepticism would deny the existence of natural rights on the grounds that all reasoning of this sort is in principle invalid. If natural rights theory presupposes that one can reason from the facts of nature to the existence of moral rights, it must be mistaken. Such reasoning is inevitably invalid because it obviously commits the naturalistic fallacy; it cannot be genuine reasoning because all logically valid argument is deductive and one cannot deduce the existence of any right (or anything else, for that matter) from premises that do not explicitly or implicitly contain the conclusion to be derived from them. I emphatically reject this dogmatic scepticism, for it takes for granted an inadequate epistemology. I have argued at length in *Challenge and Response* (Wellman, 1971, 4-31) that not all reasoning is deductive and that factual statements can rationally justify moral conclusions. To be sure, I might be mistaken on these controversial matters. But if I am mistaken, then the objective validity of all moral judgment is undermined and the scepticism involved is not specifically a scepticism about moral rights. This broader issue is too large to be addressed here.

The other sort of scepticism that might arise from critical reflection upon traditional reasoning from the facts of human nature to natural rights is more modest and more tentative, but not therefore to be taken lightly. A provisional scepticism would doubt the existence of natural rights on the grounds that one has yet to find any reasoning of this sort that is undoubtedly valid. I must confess that I am sometimes of this mind myself. In any event, I am not yet prepared to demonstrate that this sort of undogmatic scepticism is mistaken. This challenge can be met, if at all, only by identifying the grounds of moral rights and showing how these grounds do rationally justify conclusions about such rights. That is a task reserved for another occasion. Meanwhile I ask only that the sceptic keep an open mind on the subject. This much I will concede to my opponent, the burden of proof is mine. Unless one can find more persuasive arguments from premises about natural facts to conclusions about moral rights, one ought not to abandon a provisional scepticism about the existence of moral rights.

Although my Hohfeldian model of moral rights shows that one can assert the existence of natural rights without making any dubious ontological commitments or presupposing the epistemology of intuitive reason, it hardly sweeps aside all scepticism about the existence of moral rights. Not only does it suggest a provisional scepticism arising from reflection upon the traditional discursive reasoning from natural facts to moral rights, it also poses a new sceptical challenge of its own. Moral powers and moral immunities (themselves defined in terms of moral abilities) are essential elements in my model of a moral right. One may well doubt, however, that there are any purely moral powers. The very notion of a moral power is one I have defined by analogy with the Hohfeldian concept of a legal power. The fact that this concept, unlike the concepts of a duty or even what is permissible, is unfamiliar in moral theory suggests that it is inapplicable outside a legal or quasi-legal context. This suspicion is confirmed by the observation that paradigm cases of so-called moral powers, such as the power of a moral agent to impose a moral duty upon himself or herself by promising or the power of a promisee to release the promisor from such a duty, seem to be essentially institutional. Thus, if any complex of moral positions that could constitute a genuine right must include one or more powers and immunities and if there are no noninstitutional powers, then there cannot be any real moral rights.

This is a serious challenge, and for the reason just mentioned, one more worrisome for my theory than for other theories in which powers are not central to moral rights. Accordingly, I have tried to meet this challenge in section 5 of the preceding chapter. For one thing, I have tried to give clear cases of *non*institutional moral powers, such as one's moral power of consenting to being attacked in a fistfight or the child's power to make it morally permissible for a parent to listen in on a telephone conversation by giving his or her permission. For another, I have argued that even if all specifically moral powers are parasitic upon some host institutional powers, they are still genuine *moral* powers. Here let me add only one remark. I have found in the literature no convincing reason to conclude that all powers must be institutional. To be sure, it is sometimes alleged that powers must be conferred by social rules or that the exercise of a power necessarily invokes some rule, but it is not explained why this must be so. In any event, this raises a different and more general ground for scepticism concerning moral rights to be discussed shortly.

But first it might be well to pause to consider a special case of scepticism arising from doubts about the existence of noninstitutional powers. It is often held that rights in the strict sense are claims, and Joel Feinberg has suggested that the most illuminating analysis of the nature of a claim can be given in terms of the activity of making a claim. Although his paradigm of claiming is that of legal claiming, he holds that moral rights can be explained in terms of an analogous activity of moral claiming. William Nelson, however, denies that there is any genuine moral power to claim.

> But, in morals, there are no courts or investigative boards which are required to respond when holders of rights make claims. Consequently, the distinction between the power to complain and the power to claim which can be so important in law seems to have no analogue in morals. [Nelson, 1976, 153]

Thus, if rights in the strict sense really do presuppose a power to claim and if there is no such moral power, then there can be no strictly moral rights.

I have tried to show in section 3 of the preceding chapter that there is a moral power to claim analogous to the power of making a claim in the law. I have explained how it is that the second party of a relative moral duty does have the special standing of moral claimant and how it is that there is the informal office of moral judge. If I am correct, then there are moral claim-rights strictly analogous to legal claim-rights. Of course, I may not be correct. My analysis of relative duties and their correlative claims in morals is controversial and will not seem convincing to some readers. But since I reject the claim theory of rights, an incorrect analysis of moral claims would not be fatal to my Hohfeldian model. It would, however, be distinctly awkward, for if there is no analogue of the legal power to claim, then either I must find some alternative conception of a moral claim or admit that there are no moral claim-rights. Since neither alternative is tempting, I shall hold fast to my conception of moral claiming until someone can give me good reasons to reject it. The unfamiliarity, even strangeness, of the view is not, in and of itself, sufficient ground for scepticism.

There is another ground for scepticism about the existence of moral rights that is as easy to recognize as it is hard to articulate. It is often thought that any genuine right must be conferred by social rules so that there could not be any noninstitutional moral rights at all. Although I can find no explicit and fully developed argument for this position in the literature, a plausible argument could be constructed out of materials contained in the influential writing of H. L. A. Hart. The language of rights, like the language of duties, has proved persistently puzzling to philosophers. Hart suggests that these concepts, at least as applied to the law, can be solved by an elucidation of "a right" in terms of the application of a rule to a particular case (1953, 16-17). He has also argued that the related concept of an obligation, moral as well as legal, involves the application of social rules (1958, 100-105). If this is correct, then there could be morality rights, rights conferred by the rules of a positive morality, but not purely moral rights.

Now it is true, I believe, that moral rights and moral duties do belong to a special part of morals quite different from the domain of moral obligation in general and much narrower than that of broadly practical obligation, including action governed by the norms of prudence and technical rationality. Moreover, many of the special features of rights and duties might plausibly be explained in terms of rules. But it is not clear to me why these must be institutional rules defined by social practices as Hart suggests. Indeed, I have argued in section 1 of this chapter that it is a mistake to identify the norms of morals with rules at all. Although it is true that the distinctive features of moral rights and duties do presuppose a very special sort of moral norm, morals consist in the body of moral reasons, not moral rules. It is the double-aspect nature of moral reasons, as reasons for action and for reaction, that best explains the logic of moral rights.

Another ground for scepticism regarding traditional natural rights, and a challenge that would apply equally to my own conception of moral rights, is the conviction that social recognition is essential to the reality of any right. T. H. Green, for example, holds that the so-called natural rights actually presuppose a social recognition grounded in a shared recognition of some common good (1941, 121-125). His reasoning is implicit in his discussion of political authority. Since any right of one party imposes some duty upon some second party, rights necessarily are the basis of demands of the right-holder upon the duty-bearer. But since morality must distinguish between might and right, between sheer force and moral claim, the demand of the right-holder must be one already implicitly recognized by the duty-bearer. Therefore, the rights of each individual holding against the other members of his or her society must presuppose some social recognition.

I agree that the rights of one individual, whether legal or moral, do hold against second parties and that what constitutes the dominion of right-holder over second party cannot consist in mere superiority of brute strength or social power. However, since not all rights are claim-rights, the relation of holding against does not always amount to that of imposing duties upon the second party. Liberty-rights or power-rights, for example, advantage the right-holder vis-à-vis the second party in very different ways. More important, however, is the fact that my conception of moral reasons can explain moral constraint in a way that distinguishes it sharply from mere force. A large part of the constraint of moral reasons, and hence moral rights, consists in the constraint practical reasons impose upon the choice of a rational agent. And the additional constraint of moral reasons derived from the fact that they are also reasons for the imposition of morality sanctions is also different from the mere threat of force because it is the threat of rationally justified imposition of sanctions short of force. What is necessary for the existence of moral rights, therefore, is not the implicit social recognition of the right based upon a prior recognition of some common good but the existence of moral reasons relevant to the choices of the parties to any moral right.

Green's scepticism about the reality of natural rights is taken one step farther by Rex Martin (1980, 392-95). He argues that the very concept of a right includes within it practices of recognition and promotion. He observes that a legal right that is never enforced by the courts or promoted in any way by the legal system is a merely nominal right and that if the law does not even recognize an alleged right in some unenforced statute or ignored judicial precedent, then it does not exist at all, not even as a "paper right." He maintains that much the same is true of any moral right, such as an alleged human right to travel. If the right to travel is not promoted or enforced in any way in some society, then in that society it is infirm *as a right;* and if it is not recognized by any moral agent or moral judge in a society, then in that society the alleged moral right to travel does not even exist. Martin is not alone in believing that without some form of social recognition and protection the concept of a right loses its practical relevance and moral significance.

I disagree. It is true that some individual right written into the constitution but never enforced by the courts or promoted by the legal system is a right in name only and that any alleged right that is not recognized at all in the law of the land has no existence as a legal right in that jurisdiction. Similarly, other sorts of institutional rights are real only as practices of recognition and promotion exist in the society. But this is just because these are institutional rights. They consist in complexes of institutional positions created and defined by the norms existing in the practices of certain social groups. Precisely because moral positions are noninstitutional, moral rights can exist independently of any such social practices of recognition or promotion. To say that a moral right, such as a moral right to travel, exists is simply to assert the truth of some set of moral reasons and to assert also that they are relevant to human conduct in the appropriate sorts of ways. Since neither the truth nor the relevance of moral reasons depends upon social recognition or promotion, moral rights can exist independently of these also. To be sure, if some moral right is in no way reflected in the moral practices of a society, then its practical importance for any right-holder in that society will be greatly reduced. It does not follow, however, that the moral right is infirm as a right, but only that the practices of the society are defective from the moral point of view.

Some may imagine that I cannot brush aside social recognition and promotion quite so lightly. After all, I admit that a legal right that is not promoted in the legal system is a merely nominal right and that without recognition no such right exists at all. Moreover, the essential similarity of moral to legal rights is presupposed by my own Hohfeldian model of moral rights. Thus, I may seem committed to the view that social recognition and promotion are as essential to moral rights as they are to every sort of institutional right. This is not so. Specific social practices are essential to any genuine institutional right in order to provide the objectivity that would enable a right of one party to hold against second parties and involve third parties. Moral rights can be equally objective, although in a fundamentally different way, because moral reasons have an objective truth and moral reasoning an objective validity. While it is true that my Hohfeldian model presupposes that moral positions are essentially similar to legal positions, they need not be similar in every way. Thus noninstitutional moral rights can exist and can still be analogues of legal rights.

One of the traditional criticisms of natural rights theory is that it is too atomistic because it imagines that the isolated individual can possess fundamental moral rights independently of his or her society. It imagines that moral rights exist in a state of nature, a condition in which human beings might live without any political state or organized community, in order to explain how it is that the natural rights of the individual can hold against society. If individuals, however, could live in a state of nature, which is dubious, they could not have any rights because rights are essentially social. In a more contemporary idiom, Martin Golding has argued that one of the significance conditions of rights talk is the existence of a community.

> Robinson Crusoe can consciously engage in purposive activity, has desires and interests, can communicate demands and be receptive to them. But it is idle to speak of his rights when he is yet alone on the island, when no other men know or care about him. Although he can talk, he lacks someone to talk to and someone to talk or think about him. . . . If what I have been maintaining is correct, then we cannot speak of rights existing anterior to or outside of a community. [Golding, 1968, 528-29]

Sceptics sometimes go on to argue that since rights are essentially social, there cannot be any moral rights as I conceive them, rights independent of any and all social institutions.

It is this last step in the argument that is mistaken. I concede, indeed I insist, that rights are essentially social. It makes no sense to speak of the rights of Robinson Crusoe except as one imagines him to belong to some community from which he is only temporarily isolated. Since rights talk makes sense only in the context of some possible conflict of wills between a right-holder and some second party, the existence of any right presupposes the existence of at least two parties and parties that can, or at least could, meet and confront one another. Moreover, since every right also defines the role of third parties, the existence of any right presupposes a community with more than two members. But it does not at all follow that the existence of a moral right logically or semantically presupposes any social institutions. Since the moral positions that constitute a moral right are defined by moral reasons, rather than by institutional norms, the fact that rights are essentially social does not imply that they are necessarily dependent upon social institutions.

The invalidity of the sceptic's argument is obscured, however, by the conceptual connection between the concept of a moral right and the social institution of positive morality. In order to explain the specifically moral character of moral reasons and certain essential features of moral rights, I have defined moral reasons in terms of morality. Duty-imposing moral reasons are essentially similar to the rules of positive morality in being both dual-aspect and nonelective norms. Since moral rights do presuppose the existence of moral reasons and moral reasons are defined in terms of the social institution of conventional morality, it might seem that the existence of moral rights does presuppose the existence of social institutions. But this is not so. Although the concept of a moral reason is derived, logically as well as psychologically, from positive morality, moral reasons can exist independently of any such institution. Why this is so is shown more clearly by reflection upon another concept. *Webster's New International Dictionary* defines "sea horse," in one of its several senses, as "any of a number of small fishes . . . having the head and fore part of the body suggestive of the head and neck of a horse." Now although this concept of a sea horse clearly presupposes the concept of a horse, the existence of fishes so defined does not in any way presuppose the existence of horses. Similarly, there could be moral reasons even in a society which had no positive morality and which, therefore, did not conceive of them as I have defined them. It might be that the members of such a community simply would not recognize such reasons as reasons for action and reaction, or they might so recognize them but conceive of them in other terms, much as the contemporary marine biologist presumably conceives of small fishes of the genus Hippocampus in terms quite independent of horses.

I conclude that there is no compelling reason to deny the existence of noninstitutional moral rights. If one admits that any judgment of what one morally ought to do can be rationally justified, one is implicitly admitting the existence of moral reasons. This implies the reality of moral positions analogous to the legal positions identified by Hohfeld. Thus, a Hohfeldian model of rights is applicable to morals, and one who takes moral duties seriously is equally committed to taking moral rights seriously.

Varieties of Rights

The diversity of moral rights is readily apparent. There are the promisee's right that the promisor do as promised, the injured party's right to a remedy, the patient's right to refuse medical treatment, the human subject's right to withdraw from biomedical experimentation at any time, the employee's right to just remuneration, the employer's right to a full day's work, the child's right not to be abused by the parent, the parent's right to discipline his or her child, the wife's right to pursue her own career, the husband's right to the fidelity of his wife, and many others. As these examples show, most moral rights are possessed by virtue of the possession of some special status. It is *as* a parent that one has a moral right to discipline one's child; it is not morally permissible for others to interfere in one's family life and punish one's child for what they consider to be misconduct. It is *as* a patient that one has a moral right to refuse medical treatment; one's priest cannot make it morally impermissible for the physician to perform an abortion on one by refusing such treatment. Thus, most moral rights are possessed by limited classes of individuals, not by all. Only the employees of Washington University have any right to just remuneration from that private corporation; most human beings have no such moral right. Rights of these sorts may appropriately be called rights of special status.

In contrast, human rights are rights one possesses *as* a human being. One needs no special status, such as being a patient or a virtuous moral agent, in order to have a moral right to life or to liberty; one has such fundamental moral rights simply by virtue of being human. Accordingly, human rights are universal in the sense of being possessed by each and every human being. Presumably they are limited to human beings. If it is true, as some allege, that chickens and cows have a right to life, it is not a human right. Still, human rights differ from those rights possessed by only some persons by virtue of their special status because human rights are possessed by everyone, at least if everyone is human in the relevant sense.

I have already explained how my Hohfeldian model of moral rights can helpfully interpret these two sorts of rights. The right to obtain an abortion is a right of special status; it is *as* a pregnant woman that one has this moral right. On the other hand, the right to security of person is a human right, as Article 3 of the *Universal Declaration of Human Rights* reminds us. Possession of this moral right is not limited to some special class of persons; everyone has this right simply by virtue of being human.

The language of moral rights is frequently ambiguous so that it may be hard to tell whether some asserted right is supposed to be a right of special status or a universal human right. Article 11 of the *Universal Declaration* reads in part: "Everyone charged with a penal offence has the right to be presumed innocent until proved guilty according to law in a public trial at which he has all the guarantees necessary for his defence." How should we parse this sentence? At first glance, it seems to say "Everyone charged with a penal offence, *as* one so charged, has the right. . . ." But if this is what it means, then it is affirming the existence of a right of special status and not a human right at all. Presumably its authors meant to assert "Everyone, as a human being, has, *if* charged with a penal offence, the right. . . ." Only when it is read in this way does it belong in any declaration of universal human rights.

What is the difference between these two readings? It lies in the different interpretations of the grammatical function of the words "charged with a penal offence" in the sentence. On the former reading, these words specify the status one must have in order to possess the right. Since one has the right to be presumed innocent *as* one charged with a penal offence, only those so charged have any such right. On the latter reading, these words specify a necessary condition of the exercise or enjoyment of the right. Although everyone possesses the right to be presumed innocent simply by virtue of being human, one can exercise or enjoy this right only *if* one is charged with a penal offence. Both status and condition must, of course, be distinguished from the content of the right, that to which one has a right; the content is specified by the words "to be presumed to be innocent." What, then, is the difference between the status necessary for the possession of a right and a condition necessary for its exercise or enjoyment? The status is the ground of or an essential part of the ground of the right. The rational justification for the assertion of this right will include essential reference to what it is to be human. A condition is something that must be true in order for the moral reasons that confer the right to be applicable to any given case; when a condition is not fulfilled, the grounds of the moral right lose their relevance.

When the status necessary for the possession of a right is made explicit, it turns out that not all the moral rights affirmed in the *Universal Declaration* are human rights in the strict sense. Article 25 affirms in part: "Everyone has . . . the right to security in the event of unemployment, sickness, disability, widowhood, old age or other lack of livelihood in circumstances beyond his control." Since this fundamental right is attributed to everyone, one presumes that it is a moral right anyone possesses simply by virtue of being human. But against whom does this right hold? Since it is a right to social security, one presumes that it holds against one's society, and this presumption is confirmed by an examination of the extensive literature dealing with the nature and implementation of this right. Reflection upon why it might be that the individual has such a moral claim against his or her own society, rather than another more affluent society or chance individuals in other parts of the world, suggests that the right to social security is grounded in certain aspects of what it is to be a member of a society. Thus, it is not as a human being, but as a member of this or that particular society, that one possesses this right. This is recognized in the words of Article 22 of the *Universal*

Declaration: "Everyone, as a member of society, has the right to social security. . . ."

There is, I believe, a more general lesson one can learn from this illustration. Philosophers have been much exercised by the newfangled economic, social and cultural rights affirmed in various United Nations documents. Many have argued that there are not, indeed could not be, any such rights at all. Their arguments lose much of their force, however, if one recognizes that these rights should not be construed as universal human rights, but as civic rights. By a "civic right," I mean a moral right one has as a citizen, as a member of a society. Just as civil rights are the most fundamental and universal category of legal rights, legal rights every citizen has just by virtue of his or her citizenship or membership in a society, so civic rights constitute a fundamental category of moral rights possessed by every citizen simply by virtue of belonging to this or that particular society. To my mind, this category of moral rights has been unduly neglected by moral, legal and political theory.

Their internal structure and practical import can be best understood in Hohfeldian terms. (See also Wellman, 1982, 115-23 and 150-57.) Let me explain how I would interpret the civic right to social security. Its defining core consists in the moral claim of the individual citizen against his or her state to be provided with a minimal livelihood in the event that he or she lacks the means of sustaining life because of circumstances beyond his or her control. This fundamental right contains also a number of associated elements including the following: (1) The bilateral moral liberty of the right-holder to exercise or refrain from exercising his or her moral power of claiming performance or remedy in the event that the state threatens or fails to fulfill its moral duty to provide a substitute livelihood in the specified circumstances; (2) the moral liberty of the individual citizen to accept and make use of any substitute livelihood provided by the state; (3) the moral power of the possessor to waive his or her moral claim against the state to social security; (4) the bilateral moral liberty of the individual right-holder to exercise or not exercise this moral power of waiving his or her moral claim to social security; (5) the moral immunity of the individual right-holder against having his or her core moral claim to social security extinguished by any act of the state. This is one more illustration of the ability of my Hohfeldian model of moral rights to transform the usual vague and ambiguous language of moral rights into more specific, precise and unambiguous terms whose logical presuppositions and practical implications are more readily ascertainable.

All the examples of moral rights so far considered have been rights possessed by individual human beings, whether *as* humans or *as* having some special status such as that of promisee, patient, or injured party. Just as artificial persons as well as natural persons have legal rights, so corporate bodies as well as individual humans have moral rights. By a corporate body I mean a group of persons organized in such a way that identifiable individuals are authorized to act in specific ways for the entire group so that the acts of these agents constitute acts of the group. Obvious examples are business corporations, private clubs, political states and international bodies such as the International Labor Organization or the United Nations. Such corporate bodies also have moral rights. Thus, the state presumably has a moral right to subject its citizens to legislation, the moral right to tax, to conscript citizens for military service, to punish, to exclude aliens from its territory, to enter into legally and morally binding treaties, to resist armed attack and to declare war.

Let us see how this last right, the moral right of the state to declare war, can be better understood when interpreted according to my Hohfeldian model. Essentially, this is a power-right, for the act of declaring war against some foreign state or internal rebel band changes the legal and moral positions of various parties. Since our present subject is moral rights, let us ignore the right to declare war conferred upon each sovereign state by the norms of international law and focus instead upon the closely related moral right. The defining core of this right is the moral power of a sovereign state *as* a state to make participation in a just war morally permissible, provided one does not engage in any atrocity. Presumably individual soldiers and entire armies of any country have a moral duty not to kill soldiers of another state or destroy its oil fields and factories in time of peace. But if one's country has declared war against another country, one has a moral liberty of acting in these ways vis-à-vis that country, but not others. Thus, the act of declaring war effects moral positions; this is why it is a moral power. This power is limited in content or scope. The declaration of war cannot create any moral liberty to participate in an unjust war, however an unjust war should be defined, or any moral liberty to engage in any moral atrocity in the course of armed combat. Over whom does the state have this moral power? Whose moral position is changed by the declaration of war? Certainly over its own citizens and corporate bodies. Thus, the act of declaring war against an enemy can, given the appropriate circumstances, render it morally permissible for its soldiers and sailors to kill enemy soldiers and sailors and to destory the military supplies of the enemy state. More broadly it can make it morally permissible for its other citizens to contribute to the war effort in various ways and for corporate bodies to provide military supplies knowing full well that these will be used to destroy life, cause immense amounts of human pain, and destroy valuable and sometimes irreplaceable property. Declaring war changes the moral position of other parties as well. It makes it morally permissible for the enemy state to attack and for its citizens and corporate bodies to wage war against the country that thus exercises its moral power to declare war. The act of declaring war may, although this is more controversial, change the moral position of the state that declares war. At least traditionally it was thought immoral to wage war without any formal declaration, perhaps because this constituted a failure to give due notice of attack or because the morally justified rules of war became applicable only after war had been declared. In any event, one can understand the moral right of the state to declare war only if one recognizes that it is essentially a power-right and can define the power involved in some such way as I have suggested.

Any moral right is more than its core element. The state's moral right to declare war also includes a number of associated moral advantages such as these: (1) The moral immunity against others—other states, international bodies, individual citizens or groups of individuals—declaring war on one's behalf. No allied state intent upon getting our country involved in a war on its side can by any act of its own declare war for the United States. Although the American Philosophical Association could be foolish enough to issue a formal declaration that the United States is now at war with some other state that has persistently denied freedom of philosophical inquiry within its borders, this futile and foolish action would not constitute a declaration of war in the moral sense, because the APA lacks the moral power that defines the core of the state's moral right to declare war. It is this immunity of the state that makes the state's core moral power to declare war an exclusive power. (2) The bilateral moral liberty of exercising or not exercising the core power to declare war. The norms of morals give the state considerable, but not unlimited, discretion regarding the declaration of war. There are limits on the liberty of the state to declare war. Presumably it has a duty not to do so if peaceful avenues for settling the current dispute have not been exhausted, or if declaring war would expose its citizens to excessive danger. But the limits on the liberty to declare war must not be confused with the limits on the power to do so. Thus, any act purporting to declare an unjust war—for example, a war of unprovoked aggression aimed at genocide—would not effect the permissibility of armed combat for its citizens. A wrongful declaration of war, perhaps to defend some small island or bit of territory at excessive risk to its citizens, would effect these moral consequences and thus constitute an exercise of the moral power to declare war but would, at the same time, be a violation of the state's duty to protect its citizens. (3) The moral claim of the state against other states that they not try to make the state declare war or refrain from declaring war by the use of force. This moral claim constitutes some minimal moral protection of the state's freedom to exercise its bilateral moral liberty to declare or not declare war as it wishes. (4) The moral immunity of the state against having its moral power to declare war extinguished unilaterally by any other party. Thus, no formal resolution by the United Nations ostensibly cancelling the power of all states to declare war and no action by any organization within a country dedicated to peace would have the effect of terminating the defining core of the moral right of the state to declare war. In some such way, a Hohfeldian model of rights is as readily and helpfully applicable to the moral rights of corporate bodies as to the moral rights of individual persons.

We are now in a position to complete, or at least virtually complete, an overall topology of rights. The reader will recall that one family of rights consists of institutional rights, rights defined and conferred by institutional norms. This family has two genera, organizational rights and conventional rights, the former constituted by the norms of organizations of corporate bodies and the latter constituted by some body of conventional norms generally accepted within some social group. Sample species of organizational rights are legal rights, academic rights or club rights. Species of conventional rights include morality rights, etiquette rights and rights conferred by the informal rules of games such as sandlot baseball. The other family of rights consists of moral rights, rights defined and conferred by moral norms, that is by moral reasons. There are at least two genera of moral rights, individual rights and corporate rights. The former are rights of individual human beings, and the latter are the moral rights of corporate bodies. Species of individual rights are human rights, civic rights, children's rights, patient's rights, and so on. Species of corporate rights are rights a corporate body has as a state, as a business enterprise, as a private club, as a charitable organization, and so forth. Thus each genus of moral rights is defined by the nature of the possessor of the right; each species is defined by the status required for possession. If other kinds of entities, such as nonhuman animals or unorganized groups, also have rights, then additional genera of moral rights must be added to our classification. But since the principles of classification are already specified, the topology of rights is essentially complete. This is not the only way of classifying rights, of course. But this is a way that has the advantages of being both exhaustive and revealing.

Chapter 7

THE IMPORTANCE OF RIGHTS

There has been considerable debate recently about whether rights have any special importance in theory or practice. Professor Hart and others have argued that there is something distinctive about the concept of a right, at least in the strict sense, so that any attempt to reduce rights to some more fundamental conceptual category, such as that of duties or individual interests, will necessarily omit something essential. Thus, any jurisprudence or moral theory that omits an explicit discussion of rights or attempts to define them in more basic terms will necessarily be inadequate, for it will at best be incomplete and will probably misrepresent the law or morals in significant ways. In a parallel fashion, Professors Wasserstrom and Feinberg have argued that there is something distinctive about rights so that any individual who lacked rights would lack a sort of legal or moral commodity that it is especially useful to stand upon and any society that failed to recognize rights would be imperfect or defective in important ways. Hence, the possession of rights by each individual and the respect of one's rights by others are of great practical value. Let us examine some of the ways in which the concept of a right is supposed to be distinctive, in order to discover what light a Hohfeldian model can throw on the special importance of rights.

Strength

It is often said that one of the essential characteristics of rights is their special strength. For example:

> I use this strong sense of right when I say that you have the right to spend your money gambling, if you wish, though you ought to spend it in a more worthwhile way. I mean that it would be wrong for anyone to interfere with you even though you propose to spend your money in a way that I think is wrong. [Dworkin, 1977, 188]

The context clearly indicates that only rights in this strong sense are to be taken seriously.

Dworkin's example of a right in his strong sense, one's right to spend one's money as one wishes, reminds us that (1) a liberty-right is stronger than contrary prima facie obligations. Thus, one may have a moral right to spend one's money gambling even when one ought not to do so. The same point is sometimes expressed by asserting that one sometimes has a right to do what is wrong. In some sense, the right to exercise a liberty-right overcomes the wrongness of exercising one's right in a way one ought not to do. Not, of course, in the sense of outweighing the wrongness so that exercising a liberty-right is always and necessarily right. Quite the contrary. A liberty-right is strong precisely because it can persist in situations in which some ways of exercising the right are not right actions at all. The strength of the liberty-right consists in its resistance to the wrongness of its exercise, in its ability to exist undefeated by the reasons why one ought not to act on it.

This feature of liberty-rights is preserved in my model by the way in which I define a liberty as the absence of a contrary duty. Were one to conceive of a liberty as the absence of any contrary prima facie obligation, then since in most situations there are some reasons why one ought not to do this or that act, liberty-rights would be fragile. Indeed, if one thinks in terms of prima facie obligations, one would almost never have any liberty-right, for in almost every situation of consequence there is some wrongmaking feature imposing a prima facie obligation not to act on any available choice. If one thinks instead in terms of actual obligations grounded on the balance of reasons when everything is considered, then liberty-rights would almost never leave the right-holder with any options, for the relevant obligation-making considerations are almost never exactly balanced. In my model, however, a liberty is defined as the absence of a contrary duty. Since the concept of a duty is an especially strong one of quite limited applicability, my model explains this sort of strength of a liberty-right in a manner that also explains how it is that a right-holder may often choose whether to exercise his or her right rightly or wrongly.

Some philosophers try to explain the strength of liberty-rights in a very different manner. Ronald Dworkin, for example, writes "when I say that you have the right to spend your money gambling, . . . I mean that it would be wrong for anyone to interfere with you." But this is to confuse one's right to spend money as one wishes with the very different, although related, right not to be interfered with in the spending of one's money. The former is a liberty-right; the latter is a claim-right. The former has a liberty to spend at its core; the latter a claim against interference at its core. Just because Hohfeld distinguishes so clearly between liberties and claims, a Hohfeldian model of rights enables one to avoid this lamentably frequent confusion of one sort of right with another. At the same time, the model readily allows for those special cases in which a liberty-right does contain as one of its associated elements a claim against interference. These special cases have, as my Hohfeldian model clearly indicates, two distinct sorts of strength—that of the core liberty of action plus that of the claim against any interference with one's action.

Nozick's assertion that the rights of the individual make certain ways of treating individual right-holders wrong (1974, ix) refers essentially to claim-rights. It reminds us that every individual has specific moral claims not to be mistreated in certain ways by other individuals or groups. And when Nozick goes on to insist that rights are properly conceived of as side-constraints rather than as goals (1974, 28-29), he reminds us that (2) a claim-right is stronger than a good, even a great good. A good, something of value, is an end of rational conduct, something to be chosen and pursued. But just because one may choose to pursue a good, one may also choose not to pursue some good. And the choice not to pursue some good will even be rational if one must weigh one good against another in a situation where one cannot have both. Thus the obligations imposed by goods are typically conditional obligations, prudential or technical imperatives that are, in the language of Kant, hypothetical rather than categorical. Claim-rights, in contrast, impose categorical obligations, constraints that cannot be evaded by one's choice of alternative goals in life. It is this imperativeness or demandingness that Nozick describes by calling rights side-constraints. My model captures this same sort of strength, the requiredness of the actions demanded by rights, by defining a claim in terms of a correlative duty. Duties are a very special sort of obligation: they are practical constraints reinforced in one way or another by the constraint of potential sanctions. It is this second dimension to the constraint imposed by duties upon human choice and action that explains the way in which every claim, and therefore every claim-right, is stronger than any good or goal of conduct.

Although one aspect of the strength of every claim-right is the strength or stringency of the obligation it imposes upon the second party, an obligation consisting in its correlative duty, this is not the whole story. One must immediately go on to add that (3) a claim-right is stronger than any correlative duty it imposes. This is because a claim is more than a duty. A claim of X against Y consists of a duty of Y plus a power of X to claim performance or remedy for nonperformance of the duty. This adds to the constraint that the duty imposes upon the second party by backing it up with a second constraint in the form of a supplementary duty that would be imposed upon him or her in the event that the right-holder exercises this power to claim. Thus, the choice and action of the second party is constrained, not only by the original correlative duty, but also by the threat that the right-holder might initiate a procedure of claiming that would bring into existence a reinforcing secondary duty. Since every claim is stronger than its constituent duty by virtue of containing also a power to claim, every claim-right is stronger in just this way than its correlative duty.

Just as every claim is more than its constituent duty, for it is a complex consisting of that duty plus a power, so every genuine claim-right is more than its core claim, for it consists of a complex including several associated elements. Indeed, this can be generalized beyond claim-rights; any sort of right is more than its core. Hence, (4) every right is stronger than its core element. Just how do these associated elements add to the strength of the right? Given the diversity of these elements, it is obvious that various associated elements contribute strength in various ways. But what makes any element an associated element in a specified right is the way in which, if respected, it contributes some sort of freedom or control to the right-holder vis-à-vis the second party. These are summed up in my notion of a dominion of the former over the latter with respect to the defining core of the right. Thus, the net import of these various elements is brought out and built into my confrontation model of rights. Whether one refers to the dominion the right-holder ought to possess or the fact that the right holds against the second party so as to stand fast against his or her resistance, this overall strength of any right can be readily explained by my model.

There are, however, other sorts of strength often ascribed to rights that are not reflected in my Hohfeldian model. Consider, for example, this passage from Ronald Dworkin:

> Individual rights are political trumps held by individuals. Individuals have rights when, for some reason, a collective goal is not a sufficient justification for denying them what they wish, as individuals, to have or to do, or not a sufficient justification for imposing some loss or injury upon them. [1977, xi]

Dworkin is here writing about the way that assertions of rights function in the rational justification of political actions or policies. Having distinguished two sorts of political reasons, individual rights and collective goals, he asserts that the latter is never a strong enough reason to override the former. He goes on to suggest that this shows that the distinctive features of rights can be preserved only by conceiving of rights as nonutilitarian reasons. In my own very different conceptual scheme, the real lesson is that Dworkin is concerned, not with the intrinsic nature of a right, but with the grounds of political rights. It is no wonder that a model of rights does not reveal this alleged strength of the grounds of rights and, hence, of the strength of rights assertions justified by such grounds. I do not point this out to belittle the importance of Dworkin's thesis. Quite the opposite. I wish to indicate the limits of my model and to remind the reader that it will be unable to illuminate every sort of strength ascribed to rights.

What conclusion can we now draw about the strength of rights and the importance, in theory and practice, of this strength? First and foremost, one should recognize that there is not *a* distinctive feature of rights, their special strength, but that there are a number of very different ways in which rights are especially strong. Some sorts of strength belong to a single sort of right, such as a liberty-right or a claim-right; others belong to every sort of right by virtue of the complex structure shared by every genuine right.

Probably what is most important for theory is to distinguish the different sorts of strength, for these reveal the essential features of a number of concepts highly significant for moral, legal and social theory. These include the concept of a duty in the strict sense, a claim as a duty plus a power, and of the dominion of one party over some second party within some specific domain. What is most important in practice, however, is probably the way in which these various sorts of strength combine or function together to advantage the will of the right-holder vis-à-vis some second party in some potential confrontation. It is this special value of rights to which Joel Feinberg refers when he writes "They are especially sturdy objects to 'stand upon,' a most useful sort of moral furniture" (1970, 252). The practical value to the right-holder of having his or her own way when confronted with some conflicting will is often obvious. It is obviously in the interests of almost any creditor to be advantaged in any confrontation with a reluctant or resistant debtor. To be sure, the possession of a right is not always in the interest of the right-holder, for one may exercise his or her rights imprudently. Still, it is probably in the interest of any reasonable agent to be thus advantaged in conflict situations. Therefore, the way in which the various strengths of rights combine so that, if respected, rights confer dominion upon one party in face of some second party is of great practical importance to the right-holder. Indeed, it is of equal practical importance, although generally not equally valuable, to the disadvantaged second party of any respected right.

Distributiveness

Another characteristic that is often said to be essential to rights is their distributiveness. Thus:

> In fact, neither lawyers nor laymen treat rules of law which impose beneficial duties as always conferring rights. When they do think and speak of laws as conferring rights it is because as well as imposing duties such laws also

provide, in a distinctively distributive way, for the individual who has the right. [Hart, 1962, 314-15]

In what way or ways might rights be correctly said to be essentially distributive?

A Hohfeldian model of rights shows us that the distributiveness of rights has several aspects. One of these is (1) the possession or ownership of rights. Every right is someone's right; there can be no right without a right-holder. One need not be a jurist or moral philosopher to think and speak of rights possessively. My right to be paid at the end of each month is in some sense correlative with Washington University's right to my services. The pregnant woman's right to obtain an abortion is not inconsistent with her doctor's right to refuse to perform an abortion. When one seeks to devise admissions policies for professional schools, it often seems that the right of blacks to equal opportunity conflicts with the right of whites to equal treatment. Since each right has a possessor, rights are distributed among right-holders in much the way that real estate in a community is distributed among a number of owners of the lots in the township or city.

Such talk of ownership, at least if ownership is identified with the possession of a right, is, of course, figurative. Its literal meaning can be provided by interpreting my model of rights properly. The right-holder is the "possessor" of the core element in any right. Since the elements in a right are positions, legal positions in a legal right and moral positions in a moral right, this means that the owner is the party whose position defines the essential content of the right. But to talk of someone's position under the law or under the norms of morals is once more to speak figuratively. A person's position under the law, for example, is literally the way the law bears on someone subject to the law. Obviously, the law cannot bear on anyone if there is no one to whom it applies. Thus, a position can be actual only if there actually exists someone to occupy that position. Accordingly, the literal import of the notion that every right belongs to someone is that every complex of norms that confers a set of Hohfeldian positions of the sort to constitute an actual right necessarily bears on someone subject to those norms.

To be sure, the complex of norms could exist even in the absence of anyone to whom they apply. Accordingly, there is a weaker sense in which a right is sometimes said to exist, and in this sense it is not necessary that there actually be any right-holder. For example, the President of the United States can be said to have the legal right to veto legislation even when there is no one actually holding that office, for example during the period between the assasination of President Kennedy and the time that Lyndon Johnson was sworn into office. But what actually exists in such cases are the norms that define a complex of legal positions that would be actual if there were anyone to occupy those positions. Since a right consists in a set of positions, such rights exist only potentially. And even here the conceptual link between a right and its possessor remains. Since a potential position is simply the way a norm or set of norms would bear on someone if there were anyone in that position, every potential position is necessarily the position of some potential possessor. Accordingly, even in this weaker sense in which rights can be said to exist, a right is conceptually tied to some possessor.

There is another side to this aspect of possession yet to be explained. One typically has a right by virtue of belonging to a certain class. It is as an employee that I have a right to be paid and as a patient that I have the right to refuse medical treatment. Since each right-holder has a right by virtue of some status, there is some sense in which everyone else who shares this same status has the same right. We often speak of "the patient's right to refuse medical treatment," referring indiscriminately to a specific right of any and every patient. But when this talk is interpreted in Hohfeldian terms, it becomes clear—at least if one is faithful to Hohfeld's insights—that this is merely a shorthand way of speaking about a set of similar rights. Hohfeld insisted, and I agree with him on this matter, that strictly speaking each position under some set of norms is the way those norms bear upon some individual. To speak of "the creditor's" claim against "the debtor" is a way of speaking about a very large class of similar positions. Thus, even though an individual patient is subject to legal norms that apply in the same way to a large number of similarly situated patients, each individual patient has his or her own right to refuse medical treatment. So that the act of some patient in the next hospital bed in waiving his or her right to refuse treatment does not in any way deprive me of *my* right to refuse similar treatment. In this way, individual rights are distributed to the individual members of a class, all of whom may possess "the same" right—generically but not numerically the same right. Since the concept of a normative position is essentially distributive, both in the sense that any position must be someone's position and in the sense that each member of a class has his or her (or its) own position, a Hohfeldian model of rights can explain how it is that every right is necessarily possessed by some right-holder.

There is, however, another aspect of the distributiveness of rights that cannot be explained in this way. (2) Every right necessarily holds against some second party. Duties share with rights the distributiveness of possession. Every duty is someone's duty; every duty "belongs" to some duty-bearer. But although some duties are relative duties—duties to some second party—many duties are nonrelative. Every right, however, is a right of one party, the right-holder, vis-à-vis some second party, the one against whom the right holds. The first aspect of distributiveness reflects the way in which the norms that define and constitute rights confer rights on right-holders. The second aspect of distributiveness reflects the way in which the norms that constitute rights serve as standards for the distribution of dominion between first and second parties.

This aspect of distributiveness is brought out in my Hohfeldian model by the way in which the various associated elements belong to a specific right. Each associated element is tied to the defining core of the right by the way in which it confers some sort of freedom or control upon the right-holder rather than the second party. The two parties to any right are identified by the possible confrontation or conflict of wills to which the right would be relevant or that is presupposed in thinking of some complex of norms as constituting a unified right. It is the way in which any right distributes freedom and control *between* the right-holder and the second party that explains how it is that every right necessarily holds *against* some second party. This second aspect of the distributiveness of rights is illuminated by my model because of the way in which an associated element within a right is conceived.

Rights are also distributive in a third way. (3) Every right confers a special standing upon its right-holder, and often upon one acting as representative of that right-holder. This is a *special* standing in that all other parties lack this standing. The paradigm case is probably the standing to take legal action. Feinberg reminds us that only the possessor of a right, or someone acting on his or her behalf, can claim something as of right. This point can readily be generalized. Only a right-holder, or someone acting for the right-holder, has the standing to claim, exercise, insist on, forgo, waive, renounce a right. Thus, any right distributes the standing to act in certain ways upon some parties and at the same time withhold this special standing from all other parties. This special standing conferred by any right is not identical with possession, the first aspect of the distributiveness of rights we discussed, for two reasons. Someone other than the possessor of a right, the right-holder's representative, may on occasion share in this special standing; but the representative does not thereby become the possessor. Also, special standing, as I conceive of it, is limited to the standing to act in certain ways, but possession may also have passive aspects. Thus, duties owed to the right-holder or immunities of the possessor of a right are not included within the special standing distributed by the right.

It is easy to see, therefore, how this third aspect of distributiveness figures in my Hohfeldian model of rights. Since every right must necessarily confer, if respected, freedom and control upon its possessor, every right must necessarily contain some liberties and powers. When these are liberties or powers of the right-holder, they distribute the standing to exercise these liberties and powers. Some of these may include powers to delegate liberties or powers to one's agent; these allow for the special standing a right-holder can confer upon some representative to act on his or her behalf. It is along these lines that we can understand how it is that every right distributes special standing upon some parties while denying it to others.

It should be clear by now that I agree with Hart and others who have asserted that the concept of a right is an essentially distributive one. There are three aspects of the distributiveness of rights. Every right is possessed by some individual right-holder, and each individual right-holder has his or her individual right. Every right concerns the distribution of some specific domain of dominion between the right-holder and one or more second parties. Finally, every right distributes a special standing to act in certain ways upon some, but not all, of those subject to the body of norms that define that right.

Now that we have described the three aspects of the distributiveness of rights, it is time to consider the importance of this essential feature of rights. Every right is possessed by some individual right-holder. This has suggested to some that there is an essential or conceptual connection between rights and a moral or political individualism, in contrast to moral or political statism or corporatism. This notion may underlie Ronald Dworkin's frequent distinction between individual rights and collective goals. No doubt it is true that the primary, although not the exclusive, focus of traditional natural rights theory and of more recent human rights documents has been on fundamental rights of the individual person against his or her society or state. But this may well be a historical accident revealing more about the moral and political concerns of the times in which these theories and declarations arose than about the very concept of a right. Although each individual right is possessed by some individual right-holder, these possessors need not be individual persons, either citizens or natural persons imagined to exist outside any state of society. Corporate bodies, either governmental or private, have legal rights, and presumably moral rights also. Groups other than those organized into corporations also have rights. A simple example is the small group consisting of my wife and myself. Since we hold joint title to our Volvo, *we* have a legal (and moral) right to sell our car, a right that neither of us possesses as a single individual.

Although it is not necessary that the possessor of a right be an individual in the substantive sense defined by the OED as "A single human being, as opposed to society, the family, etc.", it is essential that each right and each right-holder be individual in the adjectival sense defined as "Existing as a separate indivisible entity . . . Single, as distinct from others of the same kind." Thus, the theoretical importance of the concept of the possession of rights is that rights recognize and mark the separateness or distinctness of each right-holder. Nozick is on the right track when he writes: "But why may not one violate persons for the greater social good? . . . To use a person in this way does not sufficiently respect and take account of the fact that he is a separate person, that his is the only life he has" (1974, 32-33). We can and should generalize this insight. Rights take seriously the separateness of right-holders, whether natural persons, corporations, or groups.

What is the practical importance of this feature of rights? Does it, for example, rule out every tradeoff between a recognized right and other morally, legally or politically relevant factors such as obligations or goals? I think not. Since rights can conflict, it may be necessary to violate one right in order to respect one or more conflicting rights. It may even be justifiable to sacrifice someone's right in order to avoid some grave harm. But the recognition of rights does differ from the maximization of utilities in an important respect. In summing up utilities to arrive at the net balance, one need figure in only the amount of the value or disvalue: *whose* value or disvalue it is drops out of the sum total. But in weighing rights one must bear in mind whose right may have to be sacrificed; for when a right has been violated, the right-holder has a secondary right to a remedy. Thus, one cannot ignore the possessor of a right even when one must infringe his or her or its right. In this way, respecting rights requires one to respect the right-holders. And this respect can have very practical consequences including both a reluctance to infringe rights and a willingness to remedy necessary and justified infringements.

Possession is only one aspect of the distributiveness of rights; another is that every right necessarily holds against some second party. This is explained in my Hohfeldian model by the way in which the complex structure of normative elements that constitute the right allocates dominion to the right-holder in face of the second party: by the way in which these elements distribute freedom and control between these two parties to the right. The theoretical importance of this sort of distribution is that it reveals a semantical presupposition of the language of rights. The very concept of a right presupposes some possible confrontation between the possessor of the right and one or more second parties. Thus it is that rights are relevant to confrontations between parties in a way in which obligations and values are not. The concept of what one ought to do or a duty or a right or wrong action presupposes only a single agent choosing between alternative actions. The concept of a value or disvalue presupposes only a single purposive being pursuing goals and seeking to avoid unwanted outcomes. This semantical presupposition of rights helps to explain why it is that rights are peculiarly relevant to conflicts between the will of one party and the contrary will of some other party.

The fact that every right necessarily holds against one or more second parties goes far toward explaining the practical importance of rights also. Rights might well be useless in a perfect Kantian kingdom of ends in which every will is, because perfectly rational, perfectly consistent with every other will. It is only when wills conflict and moral agents wish to pursue incompatible courses of action that rights make a real practical difference. Given a confrontation, a right, *if* respected, advantages the will of the right-holder in face of the will of the second party within the domain of the right. And if the possessor of the right is rational and reasonably well-informed, having his or her way in relation to some second party is usually advantageous to the right-holder in the sense of being in his or her interests. Thus, rights typically are of value for their possessors. Not always, of course, for one's rights may not be respected by others or one may choose to exercise one's rights in ways that are harmful to oneself.

The way in which rights necessarily hold against second parties, and thus favor the will of the possessor vis-à-vis some second party is also of considerable importance to society. Precisely because of their relevance to confrontations, rights are standards for the resolution of conflicts between the members of a society. Conflicts are socially harmful in many ways, and the settlement of disputes correspondingly valuable in a society. Rights help to settle disputes because, at least where generally known and respected, they provide norms determining which of the conflicting wills ought to prevail. Indeed, respect for rights often prevents confrontations from arising because the parties whose wills might well come into conflict voluntarily modify their actions in accordance with the relevant rights of the parties involved. It is sometimes suggested that rights are harmful because insisting upon one's rights can be disruptive by transforming loving and caring relationships into impersonal and antagonistic ones. This is true, and this is one reason why one ought sometimes to refrain from standing on one's rights. But what may be true of insisting upon or demanding one's rights is not at all true of respecting rights, both one's own and those of others. Respecting rights tends to prevent confrontations and tends to settle conflicts when they do arise. In these ways, then, this second aspect of the distributiveness of rights is important in theory and practice.

The third aspect of the distributiveness of rights is the way in which they give their holders special standing. The possessor of a right, and only the possessor or the possessor's agent, can exercise, claim, waive or stand on his or her right. This feature of rights is of theoretical importance because it shows us that some version of the will theory of rights is closer to the truth than any version of the interest theory. Since the special standing distributed by rights to their possessors consists in the authorization to act in certain ways, such as insisting upon or forgoing a right, it involves a special standing of the will of the first party rather than his or her interest. Thus, incorporating rights into a legal system or a moral theory recognizes those who hold rights as agents, as capable of rational choice and of pursuing their purposes by acting on their choices.

Special standing is typically of considerable practical importance to the possessor of a right, both positively and negatively. Positively, it enables the agent to act in certain special ways to pursue his or her ends—whether selfish or unselfish. Burch recognizes this when he writes:

> The unique contribution of the notion of rights to our moral system—the contribution that the notion of rights makes over and above the contributions of the notions of duty, virtue, and the rest of our general moral notions—involves the idea that the possessor of rights is a special agent on his own behalf from the point of view of morality. [Burch, 1977, 54]

This passage implicitly recognizes the negative value as well. Each right-holder is a *special* agent on his own behalf; that is, others lack the authority to claim, waive, forgo, insist on, or exercise one's rights. Thus each right creates a kind of sphere of privacy in the sense of a limited domain within which the agent can do certain things and others cannot intrude into the possessor's domain by pretending to do them on behalf or in place of the possessor. At the same time that a right authorizes its possessor to pursue his or her purposes in certain ways, it withholds the authority thus to intrude from other parties.

The value of any distribution of special standing is not limited to value for the right-holder. For example, in many legal systems only the public prosecutor has the legal standing to indict and prosecute someone charged with a crime. The reason for allocating this special standing to this official, however, is not to benefit this individual but rather to benefit the public. This example illustrates the way in which rights enter into the constitution of the social roles individuals may play. Social roles, and hence the rights that partly define them, are of practical importance both because of the way in which they make organizations, with their specialized offices, possible and the way in which they structure interpersonal relationships such as those of wife and husband or physician and patient. It is clear, I believe, that the distributiveness of rights is of both theoretical and practical importance in each of its aspects.

Freedom

It is widely held that rights are in some distinctive way necessarily connected with freedom. Some philosophers even identify rights with liberties.

> For though they that speak of this subject, use to confound *Jus,* and *Lex, Right* and *Law;* yet they ought to be distinguished; because RIGHT consisteth in liberty to do, or to forbeare; Whereas LAW, determineth, and bindeth to one of them: so that Law, and Right, differ as much, as Obligation, and Liberty; which in one and the same matter are inconsistent. [Hobbes, 1839, 117]

I shall not pause to discuss the nature of freedom, or liberty, for the proper analysis of this unclear but important concept is most problematic. What I do intend to discuss is whether rights are essentially connected with freedom in some distinctive way.

A very tempting, but mistaken, way to explain the essential connection between rights and freedom is to adopt a liberty model of rights. Hobbes, for example, seems to conceive of a right as a bilateral liberty of acting or not acting in some specific manner. He thought of obligations, legal or moral, as obliging or constraining the duty-bearer to act in some required way even against his or her will. Accordingly, he thought of obligations, or perhaps the sanctions that enforce them, as "externall Impediments" that hinder one from doing what one will. Since a liberty is by definition the absence of any contrary duty, every liberty necessarily involves some freedom of action; and a bilateral liberty must also involve some sort of freedom of choice between alternative actions.

But matters are not that simple, as Herbert Hart saw but could not fully explain. Naked liberties of action—that is, liberties unprotected by any duties of noninterference—are not genuine rights because they fail to hold against any second party. Therefore, his own model of rights consists of a central bilateral liberty together with a "protective perimeter" of duties of noninterference. This protected liberty model of rights is a great improvement over the much simpler view of Hobbes, for it recognizes and helps to explain the way in which different sorts of Hohfeldian elements, liberties and duties, can each contribute to the freedom of the right-holder in different ways. Unfortunately, Hart failed to follow out the logical implications of his own insight. Just because elements other than liberties can be essentially connected with freedom, it is not necessary to adopt a liberty model of rights in order to explain the necessary tie between rights and freedom.

Indeed, a liberty model is bound to be inadequate because not all rights are liberty-rights. There are also claim-rights, power-rights, immunity-rights and even liability-rights. Thus, even at best, a liberty model cannot explain how rights as rights are necessarily connected with freedom. Nor will it do to suggest that it is only one species of rights, liberty-rights, that necessarily confer freedom. A claim-right against interference with one's action by its very nature has some connection with the right-holder's freedom of action. And if one decides that poverty or ignorance are to be classified with other hindrances to action, then claim-rights to welfare benefits or education will also be essentially related to freedom. Even granted the importance of liberties in explaining the connection between rights and freedom, these liberties need not constitute the core of the right. Part of what makes a claim-right a genuine right is typically a bilateral liberty of exercising or not exercising one's core power of claiming performance or remedy, a bilateral liberty that is one of the associated elements in that complex right. Finally, Hohfeldian elements other than either liberties or protective duties can contribute to the freedom of the right-holder. Thus, a power can broaden one's liberty of action by enabling one to perform some act-in-the-law or some act-in-morals that one could not carry out without this power. Again, an immunity against the loss of some liberty can protect that liberty just as much, although in a different way, as a duty of noninterference. Clearly, some other model is required to explain adequately the essential connection between rights and freedom.

It may come as no surprise to the reader to discover that that other model is my dominion model of rights. On my model, a right consists of a core Hohfeldian element that defines the essential content of the right together with a number of associated elements that, if respected, confer dominion over this core upon the right-holder in face of one or more second parties. Although some liberty-rights or claim-rights are related to freedom in special, and especially important, ways, the essential connection of every right as a right to freedom arises, not from liberties at its core, but from its associated elements. Each associated element is tied to the defining core of the right in one of two ways, by conferring freedom or conferring control over that core. Since one aspect of dominion is freedom and since every right by its essential nature involves dominion, rights are necessarily connected with freedom. And since associated elements need not be liberties, mere absences of contrary duties, the relation of rights to freedom need not be merely negative. Since claims and immunities can protect freedom and powers can extend it, rights do more than leave the right-holder free; they also serve to secure and sometimes even create freedom of some sort.

One must be careful, however, to make clear the precise connection between rights and freedom. It is not that every right necessarily confers dominion and, therefore, that aspect of dominion consisting in freedom. To talk about the Hohfeldian elements that make up rights is an elliptical way of speaking about the norms that define and confer rights. But while rights are normative in nature, freedom is a de facto absence of hindrance or restraint. Thus, rights confer actual freedom only if they are respected. Fortunately, rights are often enough and widely enough respected so that they very often do in fact contribute to human freedom.

Do rights increase freedom? Would there be, for example, more individual freedom in a society with many legal rights than in a society with a legal code devoid of rights in the strict sense? Or, to hint at the most plausible alternative, does every right take away freedom from the second party equal to the freedom it confers, if respected, upon the possessor of the right? I do not know. Indeed, it is hard to give any clear sense to the notion of the sum total of freedom within a society. What I do know, and what is most significant about the connection of rights to freedom, is that rights articulate freedom. Rights carve up, as it were, an undifferentiated generic freedom into specific freedoms. It is the associated elements within any right that, if respected, confer dominion, and thus freedom, upon the right-holder; but it is the defining core that specifies the domain of that dominion. Thus, rights constitute complex norms governing *who* is to have *which* freedom in face of *whom*. Rights are essentially connected with freedom because of the way in which they govern the allocation of freedoms. This connection is best explained, not by a liberty model of rights, but by a dominion model.

What is the theoretical importance of this essential connection of rights to freedom? Perhaps, although I cannot explore this complex subject thoroughly here, it gives us a theoretical basis for disregarding many of the alleged rights so vociferously claimed these days. If it is of the essence of every genuine right that, if respected, it contribute to the freedom of its possessor, then one can meaningfully ascribe rights only to such beings as can literally be said to be free. On this ground, one can rule out of court the alleged rights of trees or works of art and quite possibly, depending upon more reliable knowledge of animal psychology, the so-called rights of animals. Since only beings capable of rational choice and voluntary action can be said to be literally free, only beings capable of action in this sense are capable of being right-holders.

One way in which the distinctive connection between rights and freedom is of practical importance is suggested by Thomas Scanlon: "But concern with rights is based largely on the warranted supposition that we have significantly differing ideas of the good and that we are interested in the freedom to put our own conceptions into practice" (1978, 107). The special contribution of rights to freedom is of great value to the right-holder because it enables him or her to pursue his or her own goals, goals usually, but not invariably, in the interest of that individual. Notice that Scanlon writes of our "differing" ideas of the good. This suggests that what one individual pursues as good others may regard as worthless or even evil. Hence, the individual pursuing his or her own goals frequently finds opposing wills that seek to hinder or prevent his or her goal-seeking activity. This is precisely where the distinctive connection between rights and freedom, the freedom of the possessor *in face of* the second party, is of special value to the right-holder.

Another aspect of the essential connection between rights and freedom, the way in which rights carve up generic freedom into specific freedoms, is also of great practical importance. Complete freedom, if it even makes sense to speak of a condition where every individual is subject to no hindrances or restraints upon his or her actions, is impossible in practice either within any society or in a state of nature. Brown cannot be free to buy that big house on Elm Street while White is free to refuse to sell to a Negro. I cannot be free to read undisturbed in the tiny park across the street from my house if the neighborhood children are free to play football there while listening to rock and roll on their portable radios. Both the pursuit of individual happiness and the preservation of social peace require selecting from among all possible, but not compossible, freedoms those that are to be permitted and even protected. This is precisely what rights do. The core of any right defines a limited domain over which the associated elements, if respected, confer freedom upon the right-holder. Rights give normative priority to limited freedoms of the possessor at the same time that they deny certain incompatible sorts of freedom to the second party. Thus, they distinguish between desirable and undesirable, legitimate and illegitimate freedoms. In this way they make a very considerable contribution to individual happiness and social welfare.

Control

Experience suggests that the owner of a piece of property or a tangible object usually has and always ought to have control over its use and disposition. This suggests that an essential feature of rights is to give the right-holder some sort of actual or normative control over that to which he or she has a right. This sort of view is not uncommon in the literature. The following is an example: "We may therefore define a 'legal right,' in what we shall hereafter see is the strictest sense of that term, as a capacity residing in one man of controlling, with the assent and assistance of the State, the actions of others" (Holland, 1916, 83). How should we interpret and explain the connection of rights to control?

Just as one is tempted to link rights to freedom exclusively in terms of liberties, so one might try to explain how rights are necessarily connected with control in terms of powers only. But since both attempts fail for similar reasons, one should not rely upon a power model of rights here. In effect, this is precisely the mistake that Holland makes, for his conception of a legal right, and by extension a moral right also, is that of a power conferred by society. Since not all rights are power-rights, no power model can explain how all rights by their very nature are connected with control. Moreover, other sorts of rights sometimes make their contribution to the control of the right-holder. Thus, my claim-right against others that they not use my car without my permission and my liberty-right of resisting a would-be thief add considerably to my control over how my car is to be used. Finally, associated elements other than associated powers contribute in their several ways to the right-holder's control over the core of his or her right. For example, the owner's immunity against divestiture ensures, or helps to ensure, that control of his car remains in his or her hands rather than falling into the hands of another.

Precisely how rights are necessarily connected with control can best be explained, not by a power model of rights, but by a dominion model. Dominion by its very nature involves two inseparable aspects—freedom from restraints imposed by second parties and control over others who might wish to restrain one. Thus, the explanation of the essential relation of rights to control is the obverse of the explanation of the relation of rights to freedom. Given the somewhat extended discussion of the latter in the previous section, this section can be quite brief.

The essential points can be readily summarized. (1) Rights confer control on the right-holder, when they do, not by virtue of core powers as much as by the associated elements that combine with the core to confer dominion over that core. Different kinds of associated elements—for example, powers in contrast to liberties or immunities—contribute to the control of the possessor of the right in characteristically different ways. (2) Each right confers a limited sphere or realm of control. Just as rights "break up" freedom into freedoms, so the defining cores of specific rights distinguish between specific limited domains of control. (3) Just as each political realm has its own set of subjects, so each domain can at best confer control over some limited range of second parties. Any control of the right-holder is necessarily control over others, but the range of others is limited to the second parties identified by the specific right. (4) Rights actually confer control to their possessors only if they are respected. Those in a position to uphold a specific right obviously include those second parties upon whom it imposes disadvantages of various kinds, but others who must uphold a right if it is to give effective control include first parties, who may need to stand on and claim their rights, and third parties, who may be called upon to intervene to side with the right-holder against some recalcitrant second party. In sum, since a right by its very nature confers, if respected, a specific dominion upon its possessor, each right, if respected, gives its holder some specific domain of control vis-à-vis one or more second parties.

What is the theoretical import of this distinctive way in which rights are necessarily connected with control? One crucial insight is that the practical significance of the special standing any right confers upon its possessor lies primarily, although not exclusively, in control. Although the full interpretation of special standing probably involves both aspects of dominion, freedom and control, the fact that the legal standing to sue is the paradigm of special standing suggests that the primary practical importance of special standing lies in the control it gives one. Indeed many of the verbs central to the vocabulary of rights—to claim, waive, renounce or transfer—refer to exercises of control. Reduce or take away this dimension of control, and any right surely becomes diminished or even transformed into something less than a genuine right. As already remarked, this in turn shows that some form of the will theory of rights is more adequate than any version of the interest theory. The centrality of the concept of control in the concept of a right shows us that an essential feature of any right is in this important way to respect and support the will of the right-holder.

Another, and perhaps deeper, insight one can learn from the essential connection between rights and control is that rights are not reducible to or definable entirely in terms of duties. It is at least conceivable that freedom could be explained entirely in terms of duties and their absence—that is liberties. But the way in which rights relate to control requires a richer conceptual apparatus, including at least the notions of a power and an immunity. To be sure, the connection between rights and control cannot be explained exclusively in terms of the powers they contain. But it is equally and more importantly true that the way in which rights, if respected, confer control can be adequately explained only by including powers and other power-defined elements such as immunities and liabilities among the Hohfeldian elements that constitute a genuine right. Thus, a recognition of the connection between rights and control points to a richer model of rights, one that rules out the theoretical possibility of analyzing rights entirely in terms of duties.

What is the practical, in contrast to the theoretical, importance of the contribution of rights to control? Let us remember that rights do not create control where none would exist in their absence. A variety of intersecting pecking orders would no doubt exist independently of any institutional or moral norms. Rights, if respected, divide up control into specific domains of control over determinate second parties. Only when so fragmented can control be distributed among individuals and corporate bodies. The value of this allocation to the individual right-holders is suggested by Thomas Scanlon. "I would agree that, while the importance of rights largely flows from the importance of having control over things that affect one, the function of a system of rights is to distinguish between the various ways that things can affect people and to apportion out particular forms of control" (1976, 13). The value to the individual of having control over the things that seriously affect oneself is partly negative and partly positive. It helps to assure that others will not intervene in one's life in disturbing or harmful ways. One common formulation of the right to privacy, the right to be left alone, might well be taken to state one aspect of each and every right. More positively, the possession of control over things that affect one provides the security necessary for the rational planning and carrying out of long-term projects. Lacking control, one must act warily, as one drives defensively, and must often wait to see what others do and then *re*act to their initiative. Given the relevant rights, however, one has some reasonable assurance of having the control necessary to carry out one's plans to completion. The importance of individual projects, both to the happiness and well-being of the agent and to making the individual a particular and developed self can hardly be exaggerated.

The distribution of specific domains of control to determinate individuals and corporate bodies is also of great importance to society. The distribution of rights in a society, carrying with it by necessity the distribution of control, is a way of giving control to those who are most likely to use it best, best in the sense of maximizing social utility. For example, doctors might be given control over medical decisions on the grounds that their knowledge would enable them to use that control most wisely. Parents might be allocated control over decisions affecting their children on the grounds that they are most likely to care deeply about the welfare of the children and hence use it in their best interests, and indirectly in the best interests of us all. The other side of the coin is that the allocation of control to various right-holders is a way of fixing responsibilities. If one wishes to impose upon the parents the primary duty of caring for their children (of feeding, clothing, and protecting them), then one must give the parents control over those things they will need to carry out this duty. At the same time, one is thereby making it reasonable to hold the parents responsible for fulfilling their duties regarding their children. This is another way of pointing to the great social value of having assigned social roles and the fact that social roles presuppose the allocations of control that rights make possible.

Claiming

Right-holders can, and often do, claim their rights. Since only the possessor of a right, or someone acting on his or her behalf, can claim a right, there seems to be some essential connection between rights and claiming. Such a connection has often been asserted. For example:

> If we concentrate on the whole activity of claiming, which is public, familiar, and open to our observation, rather than on its upshot alone, we may learn more about the generic nature of rights than we could ever hope to learn from a formal definition, even if one were possible. [Feinberg, 1970, 250]

Surely there is some sort of necessary connection between rights and claiming. Our task is to see precisely what that connection may be and how it might be important.

The obvious way to explain the connection between rights and claiming is to adopt a claim theory of rights. Partly for this reason, Hohfeld insists that a legal right in the strict sense consists of a single legal claim of one party against one other party. Feinberg follows Hohfeld in distinguishing between rights in the strict sense and "mere liberties" or powers, but he generalizes the notion of a claim to include moral as well as legal claims. Thus he writes: "To have a right is to have a claim against someone whose recognition as valid is called for by some set of governing rules or moral principles (1970, 257). But this identification of rights with claims will not do, and for two reasons. First, not all rights are claim-rights. Liberty-rights or power-rights, not to mention immunity-rights or liability-rights, are also genuine rights in a sense explicated by my theory. Second, even a claim-right cannot be identified with or completely explained by a claim. To be a genuine claim-right the core claim must be associated with a variety of associated Hohfeldian elements that confer, if respected, dominion over that core upon the right-holder.

Having rejected the claim theory of rights, are we therefore to go on to deny that rights are as such necessarily tied to claiming? I think not. Instead, let us rethink our conception of claiming. We need to distinguish a narrow sense of "claiming," in which only claim-rights can be claimed, and a broader sense in which other species can be claimed as well. There are in the recent literature two paradigms of legal claiming. Hohfeld, and probably most practicing lawyers who reflect upon the matter, take suing in a court of law as their model of claiming. Feinberg, on the other hand, takes claiming a checked umbrella by presenting a chit or demanding payment of a note payable on demand as paradigms. In the first chapter of this book, I have followed Hohfeld and tried to defend my analysis of legal claiming. At the same time, I agree with Feinberg that claiming in even this narrow sense is exemplified more generally than in private law alone. Thus, I have argued that, *pace* Hart, criminal prosecution ought to be regarded as a form of legal claiming. I have even attempted to describe analogues of legal claiming outside the legal sphere, even in morals itself. It is this that makes sense of our talk of moral, as well as legal, claim-rights.

None of this, however, helps very much to relate liberty-rights or power-rights with claiming. There is, however, another passage in

Feinberg that goes far beyond either his or Hohfeld's paradigm of claiming.

> Even if there are conceivable circumstances in which one would admit rights diffidently, there is no doubt that their characteristic use and that for which they are distinctively well suited, is to be claimed, demanded, affirmed, insisted upon. They are especially sturdy objects to "stand upon," a most useful sort of moral furniture. [1970, 252]

This passage, and especially the variety of expressions such as "demanded, affirmed, insisted upon" and again "stand on," suggests a much broader sense of "claiming." One might define this roughly as asserting one's right in the face of an adversary. To do this is not merely to assert that one has this or that specified right but to appeal to this right in a way to advantage one's own will in face of the conflicting will of some second party. That rights, all sorts of rights, are essentially connected with claiming in this broad sense is made clear by my Hohfeldian dominion model of rights. It is also clear why legal claim-rights reveal this aspect of a right most obviously, for they exemplify legal dominion in its most obvious and strong form.

But various kinds of rights can be claimed in this broad sense. A creditor claims his or her claim-right to repayment by suing for repayment. A surgeon appeals to his or her liberty-right to operate in accordance with good medical practice with the patient's consent when defending against a medical malpractice suit. H. L. A. Hart has noted the analogous sorts of claiming with respect to moral rights.

> It is I think the case that this form of words ["I have a right to . . ."] is used in two main types of situations: (A) when the claimant has some special justification for interference with another's freedom which other persons do not have (*"I* have a right to be paid what you promised for my services"); (B) when the claimant is concerned to resist or object to some interference by another person as having no justification (*"I* have a right to say what I think"). [1955, 183]

One can claim a right as when a patient stands on his or her rights by refusing to consent to medical treatment, or when a creditor refuses to waive his or her right to repayment on the due date. Joseph Quinlan claimed his power-right to refuse continuing extraordinary medical treatment on behalf of his daughter by petitioning the court for a declaratory judgment in his favor vis-à-vis physicians who would not recognize his attempts to exercise this core power. Claiming in this broad sense in which any and all species of rights can be claimed is not a single activity but a variety of activities illuminated by my complex Hohfeldian model of a right. The variety of claimings is explained by the variety of elements that can enter into a right; their similarity as claimings is made clear by the way in which rights are peculiarly relevant to some possible confrontation.

It is not just that claiming can and does take a variety of forms; rights can be necessarily connected with claimings in a variety of ways. For example, the legal power to sue or to waive a claim-right *enables* the right-holder to claim a remedy for nonperformance by taking legal action in the courts or to stand on a right by refusing to waive its core claim. A duty of another to the right-holder *grounds* or justifies claiming its performance. A liberty *permits* one to act on and within one's rights. Thus it is that the truth so incompletely suggested by the claim theory of rights, that rights are necessarily connected with claiming, is more richly and fully explained by my more complex model of rights.

What is the theoretical importance of this essential connection between rights and claiming? What one claims, in the narrow sense of "claiming," is typically the performance of a duty or some remedy for the nonperformance of a duty owed to the right-holder. Thus, the central place of claiming in the language of rights both reflects and calls to mind the logical correlativity of claim-rights and relative duties. But once we realize that it is claiming in a much more general sense that is essential to any right of any sort, we come to see that the disadvantages imposed upon the second party of a right cannot be limited to duties. Every right necessarily holds against some second party. This is essential to the very nature of a right. But it may hold against another party, not only by imposing duties upon that party, but equally by imposing disabilities or liabilities or even what Hohfeld calls no-claims (the logical implication of the right-holder's liberty in face of the second party). Claims are by their very nature made against second parties. Thus, the necessary connection between rights and claiming shows us that any adequate theory of rights must recognize and explain the fact that a right necessarily holds against, in a broad sense commensurate with the broad sense of "claiming," one or more second parties.

Claiming a right, at least if that right is respected, makes a difference in some confrontation. Claiming a right is not merely asserting that one has that right, but asserting one's right in a way that advantages one's will vis-à-vis some conflicting will. Feinberg remarks on this in the following passage:

> Legally speaking, *making claim to* can itself make things happen. This sense of "claiming," then, might well be called "the performative sense." The legal power to claim (performatively) one's right or the things to which one has a right seems essential to the very notion of a right. [1970, 251]

Thus, the necessary connection between rights and claiming shows us the theoretical necessity of including powers (and related power-defined elements such as immunities and liabilities) in any adequate model of a right.

These two theoretical insights are related in an interesting and at first glance surprising manner. Those who emphasize the centrality of claiming in the language of rights tend to adopt a claim theory of rights in which claims against are logically correlated with duties to the rightholder. This suggests, and perhaps even implies, that rights are reducible to and can be completely analyzed into duties. Both the fact that claiming must be understood in a broad sense in which holding against cannot be limited to imposing duties and the fact that claiming in the relevant sense is the exercise of a power imply quite the opposite, that rights cannot be reduced to any complex of duties. A richer vocabulary is required for any complete and adequate analysis of the language of rights.

In addition to its theoretical importance, the essential connection between rights and claiming is of considerable practical importance in at least three distinct ways. First, it helps to explain how it is that the possession of rights contributes to the self-respect of the right-holder. Feinberg has sketched such an explanation in this oft-cited passage:

> Having rights enables us to "stand up like men," to look others in the eye, and to feel in some fundamental way the equal of anyone. To think of oneself as the holder of rights is not to be unduly but properly proud, to have that minimal self-respect that is necessary to be worthy of the love and esteem of others. Indeed, respect for persons (this is an intriguing idea) may simply be respect for their rights, so that there cannot be the one without the other; and what is called "human dignity" may simply be the recognizable capacity to assert claims. To respect a person then, or to think of him as possessed of human dignity, simply *is* to think of him as a potential maker of claims. Not all of this can be packed into a definition of "rights;" but these are *facts* about the possession of rights that argue well their supreme moral importance. [1970, 252]

Claiming one's rights in face of some second party is an act of self-assertion. Knowing that one is in a position to claim assures one that one has legal or moral standing at least equal to that of the second party within the domain of one's legal or moral rights. It is this that tends to convince one that one is worthy to "look one's opponent in the eye" and stand up in dignity.

In this respect, claiming is frequently contrasted with begging. When one requests a favor or petitions for mercy, one is humbling oneself before the person in a position to give, or withhold, what one wants. The success or failure of one's petition is entirely up to the good will or whim of the addressee. But claiming is the exercise of a power and as such makes a difference in and of itself. Its efficacy, legal or moral, depends upon the relevant set of norms, norms that have conferred the power to claim upon the right-holder. Even in the broader sense of "claiming," in which one may be exercising a liberty or insisting upon some other Hohfeldian position, the claimant is supported by the relevant norms in face of the second party. The contrast with petitioning or begging for favors has been eloquently described by Richard Wasserstrom.

> To observe what happens to any person who is required to adopt habits of obsequiousness, deferential behavior in order to minimize the likelihood of physical abuse, arbitrary treatment, or economic destitution is to see graphically how important human rights are and what their denial can mean. [1964, 57]

Because the right-holder can engage in claiming, rather than having to stoop to begging for what he or she needs or wants, rights tend to create and sustain self-respect in the individual possessor of rights.

This argument has been challenged by William Nelson. His criticism is briefly stated in this passage:

> Why does Feinberg think that people who do not regard themselves as possessors of rights, but who regard others as having obligations and duties towards them, will be unable to demand that those others perform their duties and discharge their obligations? Why should they not be able to stand up, look each other in the eye and complain just as loudly as anyone else when someone behaves toward them in a way in which he was obligated not to behave? [1976, 150]

Now I must concede that one can certainly complain against mistreatment even when one is not in a position, as right-holder, to claim any better treatment. Why is the ability to complain not sufficient to sustain self-respect? The answer is that claiming does, while complaining does not, presuppose the equal or superior position of the speaker. Contrast petitioning a court for a remedy under tort law and petitioning the governor for reduction of an unusually severe punishment under criminal law. If the claimant has an adequate case, then the court must hear that case and hold for the plaintiff, but criminal law merely gives the governor discretion regarding the reduction of harsh sentences no matter how good a case the convicted criminal may make in his or her complaint. Although begging and complaining are typically done in very different tones of voice, both subordinate the will of the speaker to the will of the addressee. Claiming speaks from a position of equality, and often superiority, and so is much more conducive to the self-respect so important to the individual.

A second way in which claiming is of practical importance is as a means to ascendancy. The language of rights presupposes some possible confrontation between a right-holder and one or more second parties. One claims one's rights in face of some conflicting will. Claiming is not merely asserting that one has this or that specific right; it is asserting one's right in a way to advantage the claimant vis-à-vis the second party. Thus, claiming is striking a blow in a struggle to prevail over one's opposition. If rights are respected, then claiming is a means toward winning. Normally, to gain ascendancy, and thus to have one's way in spite of opposition, is of value to the right-holder. It enables him or her to pursue his or her goals and to fend off threats or injuries. In this way, by leading to the ascendancy of one party over another, claiming is important to both parties and valuable for the claimant.

Of course, claiming does not always lead to such good consequences, even from the limited standpoint of the right-holder. If one is misguided or unwise, it may not be good for one to have one's way. Again, claiming will not result in ascendancy unless one's rights are respected; if they are not, one may lose the contest and be vulnerable to retaliation by the angry second party to boot. Finally, even when claiming does bring ascendancy, this may be a Pyrrhic victory for the right-holder. Claiming one's rights against some second party tends to separate individuals from one another and to harden their confrontations into more antagonistic and irresoluble conflicts. What sort of family would it be in which husband and wife were frequently asserting their legal or moral rights against one another? Surely it would be one in which love and trust have long since broken down and in which every victory of one party over the other will make it that much harder to restore any caring and intimate relationship between the parties. Thus, claiming can be destructive of precious relationships between persons and corrosive of social institutions such as the family, the school, or the hospital.

At this point, claiming might well be contrasted with compromising. When conflicts arise, as is inevitable, one may seek ascendancy over the second party by claiming one's rights in face of one's adversary. But a very different, and often more valuable, approach is to negotiate with the opposing party in order to seek either an ideal consensus or at least the best possible compromise between opposed interests and desires. Even for the right-holder, compromising is often better than claiming; and when the well-being of both parties is taken into account, the ascendancy of the first party may seem of negligible importance. Still, two remarks are in order. For one thing, a right-holder can be too compromising. One may give in to one's opponent excessively so that in the process one compromises one's most important interests or even "compromises oneself" by abandoning self-respect and even due consideration for one's legitimate values. For another thing, compromise is not always possible. When the conflict between interests, or imagined interests, become too complete or when mutual trust and concern have been lost, then the best one can do is to seek ascendancy by claiming one's rights.

A third way in which the essential connection between rights and claiming is of great practical importance lies in the fact that claiming disposes both parties in conflict toward reasonableness. Although it is true that asserting one's rights in order to achieve ascendancy over the second party is often destructive, it is surely much less damaging to personal relationships and social institutions than the resort to brute force. The norms that define a right necessarily advantage, if respected, the first party and correspondingly disadvantage the second party. But at the same time it is in the interests of both parties to minimize the harms to themselves and to the society in which they both live. In this respect, rights-conferring norms are like the conventions of war that replace all-out warfare with a more limited combat in which both parties can fight it out at greatly reduced costs in terms of human lives and suffering. Similarly, claiming one's right is an appeal to one's title or to the grounds of one's right and thus an appeal to reasons rather than to mere force. However difficult the distinction between right and might may be to draw in theory, the practical difference is tremendous.

Here the contrast is not between claiming and begging but between claiming and taking. As Feinberg notes with regard to the Nowheresvillians, the inhabitants of an imaginary society without rights:

> Nowheresvillians, even when they are discriminated against invidiously, or left without the things they need, or otherwise badly treated, do not think to leap to their feet and make righteous demands against one another, though they may not hesitate to resort to force or trickery to get what they want. They have no notion of rights, so they do not have a notion of what is their due; hence, they do not claim before they take. [1970, 249]

Claiming a right presupposes some set of norms under which one alleges that one has the right and making good one's title under those norms. Thus, one claims a right by reasoning, by presenting a case to justify one's claim. This appeal to reason tends to call forth counterarguments and a contrary set of reasons from one's adversary. In this way, claiming typically removes the conflict between the right-holder and the second party from that of armed combat, unarmed combat or the threat of such to the arena of reasoning. And the confrontation is to be resolved by a reasonable judgment rather than an arbitrary victory. To be sure, the norms to which the right-holder appeals may be unjust laws or social conventions arising from superstition. Even then, however, they are norms that are presumably shared by the parties to the confrontation, and each party attempts to gain ascendancy by reasoning from these norms. The reasonableness of claiming, in contrast to the undisguised arbitrariness of taking by force, tends strongly towards less damaging and more moderate settlements of interpersonal conflicts.

Even Feinberg, in the passage just cited, seems to equate claiming with demanding, at least making "righteous demands." This is a common error, but an error nevertheless. Much more accurate is the contrast emphasized by Neil MacCormick.

> But apart even from the point that demanding is perhaps a bit stronger or more forceful than claiming, there is one key difference between imperative claims and demands. Bank robbers, blackmailers, extortionists and kidnappers as well as creditors and tax collectors can and do issue demands for money, even "final demands." As that suggests, demands do not as such presuppose legitimate entitlements. Demands can be founded on might as well as on right. Not so claims. [1982, 351]

Claiming a right is necessarily appealing to the grounds of one's claim and is thus intrinsically an appeal to reason rather than to force or the threat of force. In this respect, claiming differs markedly from either taking or demanding. Therein lies its tendency to encourage reasonableness even within the context of confrontation to which the language of rights is applicable. In various ways, then, the essential connection between rights and claiming is of very real practical importance as well as of theoretical significance.

Protection

One need not look far afield to find philosophers and jurists who assert that there is some essential connection between rights and protection. A familiar passage springs to mind: "When we call anything a person's right, we mean that he has a valid claim on Society to protect him in the possession of it, either by the force of law, or by that of education and opinion" (Mill, 1951, 66). It certainly seems that rights provide, or at least ought to provide, some special protection for their right-holders, and it may even be that protection enters, in one way or another, into the very analysis of the concept of a right. Let us try to define more precisely the connection between rights and protection and explore the importance of this connection in theory and practice.

We can, I believe, best find our way over these imperfectly charted seas by using our model of rights as a guiding beacon. What light does the model throw on this dark subject? (1) It shows that rights presuppose precisely the sort of situation in which protection is needed. Every right by its very nature involves the roles of first party and second party, the roles of right-holder and some other party against whom the right holds. Accordingly, the very language of rights presupposes a context in which the will of the right-holder might well conflict with the will of the second party. Every right presupposes and necessarily applies to some possible confrontation. But it is precisely when the possessor of a right finds his or her will opposed by that of some adversary that the right-holder needs protection from that second party. The OED reminds us of the relational nature of protection when it defines the verb "protect" in part as "To defend or guard from injury or danger; to shield from attack or assault; to support, assist, or afford immunity to, esp. against any inimical agency. . . ." The second party of any right is potentially just such an inimical agency. Thus, our confrontation model of a right presupposes exactly the same sort of situation as the concept of protection does. Accordingly, the concept of protection necessarily fits the context presupposed by the concept of a right. This is one sort of conceptual or necessary connection between rights and protection.

(2) Our model also shows that the essential connection between rights and protection is mediated by the concept of dominion. On H. L. A. Hart's model, every paradigm instance of a right consists of a central bilateral liberty together with a protective perimeter of duties of others not to interfere in specific ways with the exercise of that liberty. Thus, the concept of protection enters into his very definition of a right, and the essential function of a right is necessarily to protect liberty. On my more complex model, Hohfeldian elements other than liberties can serve as the cores of rights and it is the addition of several associated elements sufficient, if respected, to confer upon the right-holder dominion over the core that constitutes a full and genuine right. Thus, it is the concept of dominion, rather than that of protection, that enters into the very definition of "a right." And it follows that the essential function of a right is not in and of itself so much to protect freedom as to allocate some domain of dominion. It is only because dominion in turn performs a protective function that rights are by their nature connected with protection.

It is not merely that rights do protect the freedom or interests of the right-holder; they do so in a distinctive manner. What is the difference between protecting the individual's life by criminal legislation forbidding murder and by tort law conferring upon the individual a legal right to life? What does it matter whether the state protects its citizens from hunger by legislation empowering and obliging some welfare agency to provide food to the needy or by giving the needy a legal right to welfare payments and/or food stamps with which they can purchase food? What is distinctive about the mode of protection afforded by a right is that, if respected, it protects the right-holder by a very special means—the allocation of a specific domain of dominion upon him or her. In this manner, our dominion model of a right illuminates both the fact that the concept of a right is connected with protection via the concept of dominion and the distinctive sort of protection afforded by rights.

(3) Our Hohfeldian model reveals and defines the various ways in which rights can, if respected, protect their possessors. Hart's "protective

perimeter" consists entirely of duties of noninterference, although he does distinguish between absolute and relative duties of this sort. But in our model of a right any sort of Hohfeldian element can serve as an associated element and thus indirectly as a protection. Moreover, various kinds of Hohfeldian elements can serve as defining cores and thus in their various ways provide different sorts of protections to their possessors. For example, Jones' legal liberty of speaking out on controversial issues can help to protect his freedom to speak freely. But at least as important to the protection of his or her freedom of speech is the constitutional immunity against legislation that would abridge it. Again, the creditor's financial interests are protected, in part, by the power to take legal action against a debtor who fails or refuses to repay the amount owed to him or her. A very considerable advantage of our complex Hohfeldian model of a right is its power to illuminate the different sorts of protection afforded by rights.

> "Normative protection" may be understood as involving any or all of the various modes identified by Hohfeld and others. Thus an individual A may in the relevant sense be "protected" in his enjoyment of x
> if (a) some or all other people are under a duty not to interfere with him in relation to x or his enjoyment of x,
> or (b) he is himself not under any duty to abstain from enjoyment of, or avoid or desist from x (being therefore protected from any complaint as to alleged wrongful use, enjoyment, etc. of x),
> or (c) some or all other individuals lack legal power to change the legal situation to the prejudice of A's advantage in respect of x (the case of disability/immunity),
> or (d) A himself is in some respect enabled by law to bring about changes in legal relations concerning x in pursuit of whatever he conceives to be his advantage. [1977, 205]

Unfortunately, MacCormick errs by conceiving of an advantage in terms of an interest rather than in terms of a favorable adversarial position and also by building that interest into his model of a right instead of recognizing that it is something that lies outside of the right that, if respected, protects it. My dominion model of rights avoids these mistakes while at the same time revealing equally clearly the very different ways in which the different kinds of Hohfeldian elements can afford protection to the right-holder.

(4) Our Hohfeldian model also shows that the protection provided by rights is normative protection. Any Hohfeldian element, such as a duty or a power, is a normative position, that is to say a position one has under one or more institutional or moral norms. Thus my model of a right as a complex structure of Hohfeldian elements can and should be interpreted literally as asserting that one possesses a genuine right if and only if a complex set of norms applies to one in a certain way, a way I have

explained in terms of dominion. It clearly follows that having a right affords protection to the right-holder in terms of the protection provided to him or her by the norms that constitute the right. To say that rights afford normative protection simply amounts to recognizing that rights are complexes of norms and thus give the sort of protection norms afford.

What sort of protection do norms afford the right-holder? The short answer is "many kinds." The variety of Hohfeldian elements that make up any specific right reflect the variety of ways in which that set of norms bears on the right-holder. This was the third insight about the connection between rights and protection shown by our model. Moreover, it is not merely by being enforced that norms protect. Although the special bindingness of duties can be understood in terms of the prospect of the imposition of sanctions for their violation, even here this is only a part of the constraint they impose on the choice of the duty-bearer. When one turns to other Hohfeldian elements, such as powers, their efficacy must be understood in rather different ways. For example, Smith's legal power to make a will holds good provided it is recognized by the probate court. More generally, the effectiveness of norms in determining human behavior depends primarily upon their acceptance by those to whom they apply. Thus, norms afford protection if respected primarily, and the threat of enforcement plays a rather minor role in our respect for norms.

At this point it would be well to caution against a misunderstanding. To say that rights protect the right-holder against some second party only if respected does not mean simply that they actually protect *only* if respected by that second party. This is because rights are complex structures involving first-party and third-party roles as well. To be sure, the creditor's right to repayment may well protect his or her interest in receiving a certain sum of money on a specified day because of the debtor's respect for that right and consequent reluctance to violate the norms that confer this right upon the creditor. But a resisting debtor who has little respect for legal or moral rights might repay the debt reluctantly as a result of a decision by a judge who does respect legal rights or pressure from friends who are more moral than he. Accordingly, the degree of protection actually provided by any specific right varies with the extent to which that right is respected by the several parties who play various roles in that right.

Recognizing just how the protection provided by a right depends upon respect for the norms that constitute that right also eliminates another misunderstanding. It is tempting to imagine that legal rights and moral rights are connected with protection in radically different ways. Many believe that while the possession of a legal right implies that one is actually protected in some way, the possession of a moral right implies only that one ought to be protected. This is not so. A legal right, just like a moral right, consists in a complex set of norms. Although legal norms tend to be respected, in part because they are often enforced, this is not invariably true. The police do not invariably respect the rights of those with whom they come in contact; courts do not always recognize the rights of all parties appearing before them, and some right-holders lack the financial resources or the determination to take their cases to court. Unfortunately, the possession of a legal right does not necessarily imply any actual protection. Conversely, moral norms do more than project an unactualized ideal of protection. Moral norms are often respected and, thus, often afford very real protection. This is not to deny that the protection provided by legal rights is typically more effective than that afforded by moral rights. But the difference is one of degree, not a difference in kind. Both institutional and moral rights give normative protection to their possessors.

(5) The third-party roles in our model of rights reveal and articulate the social dimension of the protection afforded by rights. Some of the Hohfeldian elements that enter into any right will be normative positions of third parties. It is paradoxical that Hohfeld should take all the fundamental legal conceptions "as applied in judicial reasoning" to refer to legal relations between the two parties before the court and forget that the judge is also a party to the courtroom proceedings. Rights protect in large measure, although not exclusively, because of the ways in which third parties uphold them.

John Stuart Mill clearly saw this social dimension of rights. Recall his assertion that "When we call anything a person's right, we mean that he has a valid claim on Society to protect him in the possession of it . . ." (1951, 66). While close to the truth, the language is misleading. The single word "Society," especially capitalized, suggests a single agency acting in some uniform manner. Actually, the protection afforded by rights, even the most straightforward instances of legal rights, is much more complex than this. Something of the variety of third party roles in the protection afforded by a legal right is suggested by a passage from one of my earliest papers on rights.

> Third parties (individuals other than the possessor of the right or second parties who act to threaten or violate the right) can uphold my right to personal security if they come to my aid and overpower my attacker, or even if they summon police assistance quickly; the law allows this intervention by third parties, and in some cases it imposes a legal duty upon them to intervene. My right to personal security can be upheld by a policeman who overcomes my attacker, who pursues him into the night or arrests him, or who patiently investigates my case until the criminal is apprehended. . . . The public prosecutor may uphold or fail to uphold my right by pressing charges

or neglecting to do so should the attacker be apprehended and prima facie evidence of guilt produced. The judge, and in some cases the jury, can uphold or fail to uphold my right to personal security by rendering judgment or failing to render judgment against my attacker should the indictment against him be proved in court. [Wellman, 1975, 50]

No doubt this account of the third-party roles in the legal right to personal security is oversimplified, and surely the situation is more untidy and complicated with regard to any interesting moral right. But at least it is clear that our Hohfeldian model of rights shows us both the presence and the complexity of the social dimension in the protection that any right offers its possessor.

What is the theoretical importance of the essential connection between rights and protection? One theoretical lesson we can and should learn from this aspect of the nature of rights is immediately suggested by the previous paragraph. The concept of a right is necessarily social in a way that other normative concepts—such as that of a good, an obligation or even a duty—are not. An isolated individual, a Robinson Crusoe on an island with no man Friday must deliberate about which goods to pursue and which evils to shun most assiduously. A Robinson Crusoe lucky enough to find a man Friday would confront moral choices about how he ought or ought not to treat the only other person on the island. But the way in which rights are necessarily connected with protection drives home the theoretical lesson that every right necessarily involves third-party roles as well as the roles of right-holder and second party. This is not to say that rights presuppose any politically organized society or, as Bentham suggested, that the expression "a natural right" is nonsense. Although rights are essentially social, they are not necessarily conferred by society, either by its legal system or by its conventional norms. Rights are social insofar as their holding against the second party depends in large measure upon the protection offered by norms applying to the conduct of third parties. Thus, the language of rights presupposes that the confrontation to which they might apply opposes adversaries within a larger group of individuals, many of whom may be third parties. Accordingly, any normative theory that lacks the concept of a right must either ignore this social dimension of the normative systems that apply to human conduct or deal with it in fragmentary and incompletely systematic ways.

Another conclusion some theorists draw from the essential connection between rights and protection is, however, mistaken. Judicial decisions often move back and forth indiscriminately between the language of rights and the language of interests, and jurists sometimes identify a legal right with a legally protected interest. Indeed, a paradigm case of an interest theory of rights is presented by Salmond's definition of a right as "an interest recognized and protected by a rule of right" (1920,

237). Such interest theories are typically contrasted with *will* theories of rights, in which having a right consists in having one's will recognized and favored in some way. Hart's respected choice theory of legal rights is a paradigm instance of a will theory of rights. When the theoretical alternatives are formulated in this manner, one might be led to believe that the connection between rights and protection is evidence for an interest theory of rights. Neil MacCormick, who opts for an interest theory, explains the theoretical options in just this manner:

> It is against the background of this clash of theories that we must pursue the question announced as to the general characteristics of those rules that confer rights. Are these to be conceived primarily in terms of giving a special status to the choice of one individual over others in relation to a given subject matter, or primarily in terms of the protection of the interests of individuals against possible forms of intrusion (or the advancement in other ways of individual interests)? [1977, 192]

But the clash defined as MacCormick defines it does not present us with incompatible alternatives. There is no need to choose between a theory in which having a right consists in some special status of the will of the right-holder and a theory according to which rights protect the interests of the right-holder, because we have learned that rights protect some interest or interests of their possessors *by means of* giving dominion to the right-holder in face of some second party whose will might be opposed to the will of the possessor of the right. Recognizing precisely how rights are essentially connected with protection permits one to adopt one version of a will theory of rights, a theory built into my dominion model of rights, without rejecting the traditional insights of interest theories that rights do afford an especially important protection to interests that fall within their domain.

What is the practical importance of the essential connection between rights and protection illuminated by our Hohfeldian model? It is widely held, although sometimes denied, that rights are of great value to their possessors because of the special protection they provide. We are now in a position to explain why this is often, but not invariably, the case. First, rights afford protection to those who stand in need of it. Any genuine right presupposes some potential confrontation between the right-holder and some second party. Thus, the context of significant assertions of rights are precisely those in which the possessor of a right needs protection from some adversary. The protection provided by rights will not be needed in practice, of course, if the potential confrontation never becomes actual. Harsh experience indicates, however, that human wills conflict so often that the protection afforded by rights all too frequently answers to a very real need and, accordingly, has a very real value in human life.

Second, the protection rights give is of special value to the weak.

Although the strong as well as the weak, the affluent as well as the poor, are protected by their rights, it is the weak and the disadvantaged who most often and most urgently appeal to their rights. It is no accident that the recent proliferation of rights assertions has been in connection with blacks or other minority groups, and in connection with women, children, patients, and even fetuses and animals, for the members of all these classes find themselves confronted on many occasions with more powerful adversaries or disadvantaged in competing with inimical agencies. Now as we have seen, rights protect by means of the allocation of some domain of dominion to the right-holder. This special sort of protection, protection via the possession of freedom-control, is especially appropriate to the threat or danger to which the weak are exposed when confronted with a stronger alien will. This explains why the weak are most likely to claim their rights, or to have someone claim them on their behalf, and why the special form of protection rights give is of special value to such right-holders in practice.

Third, the fact that rights protect by means of dominion also shows that this special form of protection is not always the best and may even be entirely pointless. It is important to recognize that protection by means of rights is only one of a variety of forms of protection, and that sometimes other sorts may be of greater practical importance. Most legal systems wish to protect the individual's interest in his or her life. One means of doing this would be to confer upon each individual a legal claim-right not to be killed. But by the time any individual would be in a position to take legal action for the violation of his or her right not to be killed, the right-holder would be dead and therefore unable to take action of any kind. A more effective protection might be simply to impose a criminal duty not to kill any individual. Sometimes any attempt to protect the weak or helpless by conferring a right would be entirely pointless. Since rights protect via dominion, it would not even make any sense to pretend to confer rights upon animals, who lack the capacities required to exercise either freedom or control—the two ingredients of dominion. Even when it may make sense to assert some specific right, the right may not protect in any very effective way. For example, a legal claim-right may offer no real protection to someone too ignorant of the law to insist upon it or too poor to hire a lawyer to enable him or her to sue in the courts. Similarly, it is debatable how effectively the moral right to refuse medical treatment protects a patient who has very little knowledge of medicine and who is highly dependent upon his or her doctor for desperately needed medical care.

This takes us to the bottom line, the most practical question of all. Just how effective is the protection afforded by rights? It is not wise to reply with any sweeping generalization; some rights give considerable security within their domain while others offer little or no reliable protection. The crucial point to bear in mind is that a right provides normative security. Thus, the effectiveness of the protection it affords its possessor depends upon and varies with the extent and degree of respect for the norms—legal, moral or other—that constitute that specific right. Since norms are not always respected, and some norms may be honored most frequently in the breach, rights do not always protect. Nevertheless, many norms, especially institutional norms, are generally recognized and normally accepted, so that most rights do provide some form of real protection in practice.

Moreover, the protection provided by rights is typically more reliable than the normative protection offered by duties or obligations because of the social dimension in any right. Thus, a right may protect its possessor even when it is not respected by the second party because of the ways in which various third parties respect the norms that constitute that right. This explains much of the force and practical value of the appeal to one's rights. When some right-holder claims his or her rights against some adversary, he or she is appealing to society, collectively or individually, to intervene and side with the right-holder vis-à-vis the second party. It is this social dimension of rights, a dimension articulated in the third-party role in our Hohfeldian model, that helps to explain the practical value of the protection they offer. Although they protect only insofar as the norms that constitute them are respected, it is not necessary that everyone share this respect or even that the second party be prepared to respect the right without social intervention.

Finale

The question addressed in this chapter can be expressed quite simply: is there something distinctive about the nature of rights such that the concept of a right has some special theoretical importance and the possession of rights some special practical importance? We have discovered that the answer to this question cannot be expressed so briefly or so simply. There are a number of distinct features essential to any right, each of which has both theoretical and practical importance in one or more ways. Given the complexity of any right, a complexity made explicit in our Hohfeldian model of a right, this is precisely what one would expect. Too often in the past moral philosophers or jurists have selected only one of these features, such as liberty or claiming, and asserted that it is *the* defining feature of a right. We are now in a position to avoid any such oversimplification in our theory of rights.

There are a number of features essentially connected with rights that are of special importance. These include strength, distributiveness, freedom, control, claiming and protection. Other writers have recognized and proclaimed each of these time and time again; but my predecessors have still fallen short of the truth, not only by insisting upon the importance of one feature to the exclusion of the others, but by misinterpreting the feature proclaimed to be definitive and of special value. Thus, H. L. A. Hart, who has long championed the distributive nature of rights, has never made clear the precise nature of their distributiveness; and Joel Feinberg, who has analyzed both legal and moral rights in terms of the process of claiming, never has provided a full and accurate characterization of claiming itself. Our model has enabled us to explain these essential features and their importance more accurately and helpfully.

At the same time, there are surely other features of rights that are not illuminated by our Hohfeldian model. For example, both Herbert Hart and Ronald Dworkin have maintained that rights are essentially *non*utilitarian. I have neither accepted nor rejected this thesis because my model remains entirely silent on this subject. Nor have I discussed at length the issue of what sorts of beings are capable of possessing rights—infants, the irreversibly comatose, animals, future generations. Nor have I even attempted to distinguish between those alleged rights that are genuine and those that are unreal. All of these matters, and many more, require that one go beyond any model of a right. It is clear that even a general theory of rights, a theory applicable to every species of rights, is not thereby a complete theory of rights.

What, then, can I plausibly claim to have accomplished in this book? I have explained and defended an original model of rights. These pages have been devoted to the analysis of the concept of a right and to the subsidiary concepts needed in this analysis. But I have proceeded, not by offering some definition of the expression "a right," but by articulating a way of interpreting the language of rights in terms of Hohfeldian fundamental normative concepts. Moreover, I have tried to convince you, my patient reader, that my conceptual framework is both a more accurate and a more useful way to think about rights than the alternatives presented in the literature of philosophy and jurisprudence. In the end, of course, my arguments settle very little. The true test of the philosophical adequacy of my model will come when you and I go beyond the limited subject matter of these few chapters and begin to use my model in thinking through theoretical problems and practical issues concerning rights. It is to this application of my model that I intend to turn next, and I invite you to join me in this important endeavor.

BIBLIOGRAPHY

American Law Institute. 1932. *Restatement of the Law of Contracts*. American Law Institute Publishers, Saint Paul. Vol. I.

Anonymous v. *Anonymous*. 1971. 325 N.Y.S. 2d 499.

Baker v. *Nelson*. 1971. 191 N.W. 2d 185.

Bentham, Jeremy. 1970. *Introduction to the Principles of Morals and Legislation*. Edited by J. H. Burns and H. L. A. Hart. London: The Athlone Press.

Burch, Robert W. 1977. "Animals, Rights, and Claims." *Southwestern Journal of Philosophy* 8:53–59.

Corbin, Arthur L. 1919. "Legal Analysis and Terminology." *Yale Law Journal* 29:163–73.

Dworkin, Ronald. 1977. *Taking Rights Seriously*. Cambridge, Mass.: Harvard University Press.

Feinberg, Joel. 1966. "Duties, Rights, and Claims." *American Philosophical Quarterly*, 3:137–144.

———. 1970. "The Nature and Value of Rights." *Journal of Value Inquiry* 4:243–57.

———. 1973. *Social Philosophy*. Englewood Cliffs, N.J.: Prentice-Hall.

———. 1978. "Voluntary Euthanasia and the Inalienable Right to Life." *Philosophy and Public Affairs* 7:93–123.

Feiner v. *New York*. 1951. 340 U.S. 315.

Golding, M. P. 1968. "Towards a Theory of Human Rights." *The Monist* 52:521–49.

Green, Thomas Hill. 1941. *Lectures on the Principles of Political Obligation*. London: Longmans Green & Co.

Grosjean v. *American Press Co.* 1936. 297 U.S. 233.

Hart, H. L. A. 1953. *Definition and Theory in Jurisprudence*. Oxford: The Clarendon Press.

———. 1955. "Are There Any Natural Rights?" *Philosophical Review* 64: 175–91.

———. 1958. "Legal and Moral Obligation." In *Essays in Moral Philosophy*, edited by A. I. Melden. Seattle: University of Washington Press. Pp. 82–107.

———. 1961. *The Concept of Law*. Oxford: The Clarendon Press.

———. 1962. "Bentham, Lecture on a Master Mind." *Proceedings of the British Academy* 48:297–320.

———. 1973. "Bentham on Legal Rights." *Oxford Essays in Jurisprudence*, 2d series, edited by A. W. B. Simpson, pp. 171–201. Oxford: The Clarendon Press.

Henningsen v. *Bloomfield Motors, Inc.* 1960. 161 A. 2d 69.

Hobbes, Thomas. 1839. *The English Works of Thomas Hobbes*, vol. 3. Edited by William Molesworth. London: John Bohn.

Hohfeld, Wesley Newcomb. 1919. *Fundamental Legal Conceptions*. New Haven: Yale University Press.

Holland, T. E. 1916. *Jurisprudence*. 12th ed. Oxford: The Clarendon Press.

Jones v. *Hallahan*. 1973. 501 S.W. 2d 588.

Loving v. *Virginia*. 1967. 388 U.S. 1.

Lyons, David. 1970. "The Correlativity of Rights and Duties." *Nous*, 4:45–55.

———. 1982. "Benevolence and Justice in Mill." *The Limits of Utilitarianism*, edited by Harlan B. Miller and William H. Williams, pp. 42–70. Minneapolis: University of Minnesota Press.

MacCormick, D. N. 1977. "Rights in Legislation." In *Law, Morality and Society,* edited by P. M. S. Hacker and J. Raz, pp. 189–209. Oxford: The Clarendon Press.
———. 1981. *H. L. A. Hart.* Stanford, Calif.: Stanford University Press.
———. 1982. "Rights, Claims and Remedies." *Law and Philosophy* 1:337–57.
Martin, Rex. 1980. "Human Rights and Civil Rights." *Philosophical Studies* 37:391–403.
Mill, John Stuart. 1951. *Utilitarianism, Liberty, and Representative Government.* New York: E. P. Dutton and Company, Inc.
Minneapolis Railway Co. v. *Beckwith.* 1889. 129 U.S. 26.
Nelson, William. 1976. "On the Alleged Importance of Moral Rights." *Ratio* 18:145–55.
North Carolina. 1983. *General Statutes of North Carolina, 1983.* Cumulative Supplement, vol. 2A. Charlottesville, Va.: The Michie Company.
Nozick, Robert. 1974. *Anarchy, State and Utopia.* New York: Basic Books Inc.
Prosser, William L. 1971. *Handbook of the Law of Torts.* St. Paul, Minn.: West Publishing Co.
Raz, Joseph. 1972. "Voluntary Obligations and Normative Powers." *Aristotelian Society,* Supplementary vol. 46:79–102.
———. 1975. *Practical Reason and Norms.* London: Hutchinson & Co. Ltd.
Salmond, Sir John. 1920. *Jurisprudence.* 6th ed. London: Sweet and Maxwell.
Scanlon, Thomas. 1976. "Nozick on Rights, Liberty, and Property." *Philosophy & Public Affairs* 6:3–25.
———. 1978. "Rights, Goals, and Fairness." In *Public and Private Morality,* edited by S. Hampshire, pp. 93–111. Cambridge: Cambridge University Press.
Terry, Henry T. 1884. *Some Leading Principles of Anglo-American Law.* Philadelphia: T. & J. W. Johnson & Co.
United Nations. 1971. *Universal Declaration of Human Rights. Basic Documents on Human Rights,* edited by Ian Brownlie. Oxford: The Clarendon Press.
Warnock, G. J. 1971. *The Object of Morality.* London: Methuen.
Wasserstrom, Richard. 1964. "Rights, Human Rights, and Racial Discrimination." *Journal of Philosophy* 61:628–41.
Wellman, Carl. 1961. *The Language of Ethics.* Cambridge, Mass: Harvard University Press.
———. 1971. *Challenge and Response: Justification in Ethics.* Carbondale: Southern Illinois University Press.
———. 1975. "Upholding Legal Rights." *Ethics* 86:49–60.
———. 1982. *Welfare Rights.* Totowa, N.J.: Rowman & Littlefield.
West Virginia State Board of Education v. *Barnette.* 1943. 319 U.S. 624.
Williams, Glanville. 1956. "The Concept of Legal Liberty." *Columbia Law Review* 56:1129–50.

INDEX